Automotive Chassis
and
Accessory Circuits

Library of Congress Cataloging in Publication Data

BREJCHA, MATHIAS F.
  Automotive chassis and accessory circuits.

  Includes index.
    1. Automobiles—Electric equipment—Maintenance
and repair.   2. Automobiles—Electric wiring—Maintenance and repair.   I. Samuels, Clifford L.,
joint author.   II. Title.
TL272.B623   629.2'54   76-14835
ISBN 0-13-055475-8

© 1977 by Prentice-Hall, Inc.
Englewood Cliffs, New Jersey 07632

10 9 8 7 6 5 4 3 2

Printed in the United States of America

PRENTICE-HALL INTERNATIONAL, INC., *London*
PRENTICE-HALL OF AUSTRALIA PTY. LIMITED, *Sydney*
PRENTICE-HALL OF CANADA, LTD., *Toronto*
PRENTICE-HALL OF INDIA PRIVATE LIMITED, *New Delhi*
PRENTICE-HALL OF JAPAN, INC., *Tokyo*
PRENTICE-HALL OF SOUTHEAST ASIA PTE. LTD., *Singapore*
WHITEHALL BOOKS LIMITED, *Wellington, New Zealand*

Automotive Chassis and Accessory Circuits

MATHIAS F. BREJCHA

Associate Professor
Automotive Department, Ferris State College
Big Rapids, Michigan

CLIFFORD L. SAMUELS

Assistant Professor
Automotive Department, Ferris State College
Big Rapids, Michigan

PRENTICE-HALL, INC., *Englewood Cliffs, New Jersey 07632*

Contents

771574

Preface

Each year there are more cars on the road displaying new technology and requiring a more knowledgeable auto mechanic to service these cars. Without any doubt the many changes in automotive electrical circuitry have created a need for qualified service personnel.

Automotive Chassis and Accessory Circuits is totally devoted to the subject matter of vehicle lighting, dash instrumentation, and accessory electricity. It supplements current wiring-diagram manuals and automobile manufacturer's service manuals. For the reader with a limited background in electricity, this book provides the basic fundamentals necessary for understanding how electrical circuits work, including sections on electrical terminology, Ohm's law, magnetism, and small motors.

It is a thoroughly comprehensive book that has brought together under one cover the many hard-to-find facts of how automotive chassis and accessory circuits work. Some interesting features include new details on battery and wire service, how to read the new wiring diagrams, the easy-to-use technique of common-point diagnosis for locating difficult-to-find opens and shorts, and the simple use of various test instruments in locating circuit problems. Other topics include circuit protection and power distribution, horns and buzzers, power seats and windows, and windshield wipers.

It is our intent to focus on those lighting, instrumentation, and accessory systems predominantly used in mass-production vehicles. Although solid-state controls have been introduced in some of these systems, mostly as options, their applications are still considered limited in production and coverage is minimal. The technical material is written for automotive students, technicians, and journeymen who wish to broaden their background and expand their job income potential in an area where expertise is a must.

In conclusion we would like to give recognition to those who helped us put it all together:

> BATTERY MAN
> BELDEN CORPORATION
> CHAMPION SPARK PLUG COMPANY
> CHRYSLER MOTORS CORPORATION
> FERRIS STATE COLLEGE
> FORD MOTOR COMPANY
> GENERAL MOTORS CORPORATION
> AMERICAN MOTORS COMPANY.

Big Rapids, Michigan   MATHIAS BREJCHA
                                                         CLIFFORD SAMUELS

Automotive Chassis
and
Accessory Circuits

1

Electrical Fundamentals

This book is intended to provide both the theory of automotive electricity and a series of practical procedures illustrating this theory. A good understanding of electrical principles makes automotive work easier, quicker, and more productive. The problems in this chapter are designed to reinforce your understanding of electrical principles in an interesting and practical way.

Electricity is the biggest helpmate to both the power plant and the drive train of most modern vehicles. Electricity ignites the fuel and air mixture that operates the gasoline engine. It also starts the engine, provides the light, and operates gauges and accessories. Electricity makes the operation of a vehicle easy and convenient.

The applications of electricity are virtually endless. We take for granted that the kitchen lights will come on at the flip of the switch, and that the family car will start each time the ignition key is turned. But what is this invisible force we call electricity? Where does it come from? What is it made of?

ELECTRONS & ELECTRICITY

Electricity consists of the movements of *electrons* in a conductor. In order to understand what an electron is and how it behaves, we will have to look at the composition of matter.

Matter is anything that has mass and occupies space. Matter can

1

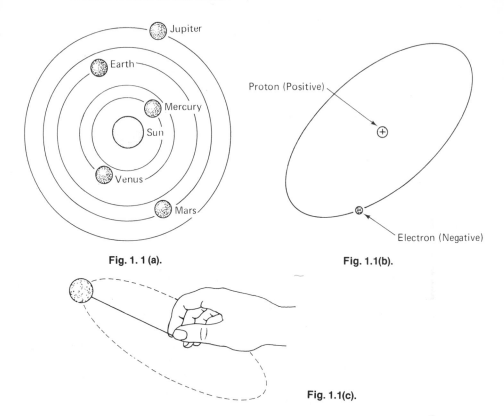

Fig. 1. 1 (a).   **Fig. 1.1(b).**

Fig. 1.1(c).

be a solid, a liquid, or a gas. All matter is composed of chemical build-
ing blocks called *elements*. Nature has provided over 100 elements,
which, alone or in numerous combinations, form all the different kinds
of matter found on earth.

The smallest particle into which an element can be reduced and
still be classified as an element is the *atom*. Many billions of atoms
exist in a single drop of water. Atoms contain particles of positive and
negative electrical charge. The structure of the atom is similar to that
of our solar system, in which the sun is the center and the planets whirl
in orbit about it (Fig. 1-1a). In the atom, the center or *nucleus* is composed of particles called *protons*, which have a positive electrical
charge. The *electrons* that whirl around the center have a negative
charge. Another particle called a *neutron*, having no charge, is found
in the center of all atoms except that of hydrogen.

The simplest element known is hydrogen (Fig. 1-1b). The hydrogen atom consists of one proton, around which whirls one electron.
The electron keeps whirling in its circular path around the proton by a
combination of forces. One force is the attraction that the two
oppositely charged particles have for each other. Opposing electric

charges always attract. Thus, the negatively charged electron is pulled toward the positively charged proton.

Opposing the attraction between the two particles is another force called centrifugal force. This force, acting on the electron, is the result of its own circular motion around the proton, and prevents the electron from moving in toward the proton. This action is similar to the balancing of forces you get when you swing a ball attached to a rubber band, Fig. 1-1c.

Electrons repel electrons, and protons repel protons, except when neutrons are present. Neutrons do not have any electrical charge, but they have the ability to cancel out the repelling forces between protons in an atomic nucleus, thereby holding the nucleus together.

It is important to observe that all the electrons do not occupy the same path around the core. Instead, there are a number of paths, or rings, which are located at different distances from the core. The hydrogen atom has one ring, the copper atom four rings, and the uranium atom seven rings. The number of electrons in the outermost ring is of significance to us, because these electrons determine the electrical characteristics of an element. Henceforth we shall concern ourselves only with the outermost ring, which is often referred to as the valence ring.

If the number of electrons in the valence ring is less than four, the electrons are held to the core rather loosely and can be made to move from one atom to another. Copper is such an element, and it has only one electron in its valence ring. All materials having less than four electrons in the valence ring are called conductors. The movement of electrons from atom to atom constitutes electric current. If the number of electrons in the valence ring is greater than four, the electrons are held to the core rather tightly, and normally cannot be made to leave the atoms. Such an element or material is called an insulator. In any element, the number of electrons in the valence ring is never greater than eight.

An interesting situation arises when the valence ring contains just four electrons. Certain elements of this type are of special interest because they are neither good conductors nor good insulators. Two elements having four valence ring electrons which are widely used in semiconductors are silicon and germanium. When certain materials are added to the silicon crystal, the resultant mixture is said to be "doped." This new material now has an extra electron (free electron) which can be made to move through the material very easily. Any material having an extra electron is called negative.

There are two methods of describing current flow, the conventional theory and the electron theory.

Conventional theory:

In this theory the direction of current flow was arbitrarily chosen to be from the positive terminal of the voltage source, through the external circuit, and then back to the negative terminal of the source. The conventional theory is used in automotive electricity.

Electron theory:

This theory states that current flows from the negative terminal, through the external circuit, and then back to the positive terminal of the source.

CIRCUITS*

In order for electrons to flow, they must have a path to travel in. For simplicity, think of the path as a circle (circuit) from the source (positive battery terminal), around and back to the source (negative batttery terminal). Electrons move through some substances more easily than through others. Some substances, such as copper, iron, and aluminum, form good paths through which electrons can move, and are therefore called conductors. Other substances, such as rubber or glass, strongly oppose electron movement. These substances are called non-conductors or insulators.

An insulator is made up of a substance that does not have many free electrons. Without free electrons, a flow of electrons cannot be set up, for the flow depends upon repelling free electrons along the circuit. If an insulator blocks the circuit, free electrons cannot push through. Insulators are used to cover and protect wires and other metal parts of electrical devices. The insulators keep the free electrons (or current) from going off in the wrong direction and taking a short cut to ground. If an insulator fails, the result can be what is called a "short circuit."

The first step in the study of electricity is to become familiar with electric circuits and how they are used. When voltage forces current through a load, work is done. For instance, in starting an engine the starting motor is the load and the turning of the engine is the work done. When a battery is connected to a headlamp, the headlamp is the load and the production of light is the work done.

Many different types of loads can be connected to a battery. However, all loads have one thing in common: they all convert electrical energy from the battery into some usable form of energy. The headlamps change electric energy to light. The starting motor changes electric energy to motion.

*See Electrical Terms—pages 14, 15, 16.

One side of the load must be connected to the positive terminal and the other side to the negative terminal of the battery. The connection of a load to a battery can be shown in a drawing by using symbols instead of pictures. A drawing using symbols to represent actual parts is called a schematic. Each load is designed to operate with a certain amount of current through it. If the current rating is exceeded for a period of time, the load will be damaged. For example, excessive current through a lamp filament will heat the filament to such an extent that it will burn out. This opens the current path and the lamp cannot light. To avoid this, loads are rated to operate from a source of specified voltage. Automobile headlamps are rated at either 6 or 12 volts. A 6-volt headlamp connected across a 6-volt battery will operate properly with normal light output. If a 6-volt headlamp were connected across a 12-volt battery, the headlamp would burn out from the excessive current. If a 12-volt headlamp were connected across a 6-volt battery, the headlamp would glow dimly because the lower voltage would not force enough current through the headlamp to light it brightly. In some cases a load is designed to work at a lower voltage than that provided by the source. Usually in this case current through the load must be controlled by using a resistor. Resistors are simply a fixed opposition to current. By putting a resistor in series with a load, the current through the load is decreased.

THE CIRCUIT:

A *circuit* means a circle. Electricity must return to its source. A basic circuit should have a switch to turn it on or off, a protection device such as a fuse, and an electrical load, Fig. 1-2.

A simple automotive electrical circuit is made up of four parts:

1. Battery (power source).
2. Wires (conductors to carry the electricity).
3. Load (lights, motors, radio, etc.).
4. Ground (return back to the battery).

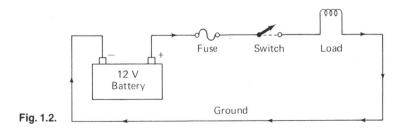

Fig. 1.2.

The battery is the heart of the electrical system and must be kept in a fully charged condition for the other electrical components to operate properly.

The wires carry the electrical current to the load and back to the battery. The wire going to the load is called the hot circuit, and the wire carrying the current back to the battery is called the ground circuit.

The load can be any electrical device that uses electricity—a motor, radio, cigar lighter, light bulb, etc. All electrical circuits must have a load to use the electricity.

The ground returns the electricity back to the battery, since one pole of the battery is customarily grounded. All electrical circuits must have a ground. The electrical symbol for ground is ⏚ .

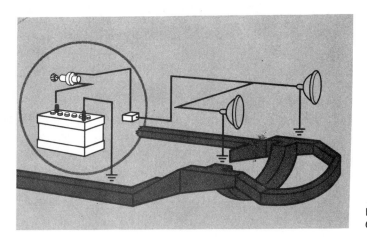

Fig. 1.3(a). *(Courtesy of Ford Customer Service Division.)*

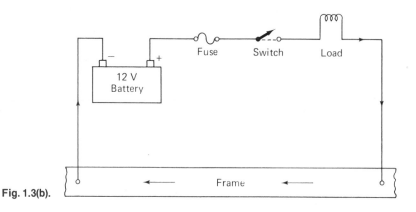

Fig. 1.3(b).

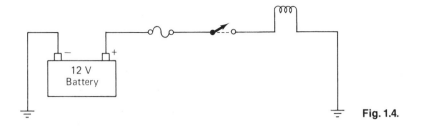

Fig. 1.4.

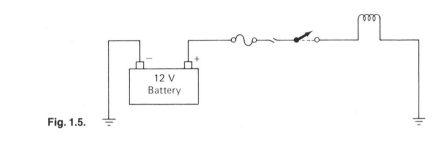

Fig. 1.5.

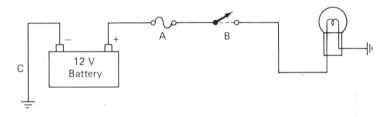

Fig. 1.6.

Most of the circuits in this book are single-wire circuits, as shown in Fig. 1-3. The metal part of the car is used as a ground, to carry the electricity back to the battery.

We identify circuits in three ways: series, parallel, and series-parallel.

In a series circuit (Fig. 1-4), current flows in one path only. Any break in a series circuit stops the current (Fig. 1-5).

The load in the circuit may be grounded by a wire from the load to a metal part of the car. The ground wire need not be insulated (Fig. 1-6), since the common ground is not insulated. The load also may be self-grounded. Many bulbs, for instance, are grounded by the contact of the bulb socket with the car sheet metal.

OHM'S LAW

Ohm's law defines the relationship between current, voltage, and resistance. It is the basic law of electricity, and indicates the amount of current that will flow in a circuit. It is used in designing circuits that will operate efficiently for a maximum amount of time. The service technician must understand Ohm's law (1) to understand the operation of automotive electrical circuits and (2) to diagnose electrical circuit problems.

Series Circuit

A series circuit has three characteristics:

1. The current flow is the same throughout all parts of the circuit.
2. The total circuit resistance is the sum of the individual circuit resistances added together.
3. The source voltage divides itself among the individual circuit resistances. The sum of the individual voltage drops is equal to the source voltage.

Ohm's law states that if one volt is applied to one ohm of resistance one ampere of current will flow. This is determined by the Ohm's law formula:

$$I = \frac{E}{R} \qquad E = I \times R \qquad R = \frac{E}{I}$$

where E = Volts (electromotive force or pressure)
R = Ohms or resistance (electrical symbol Ω)
I = Amps or current

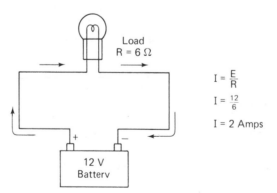

Load
$R = 6\,\Omega$

$I = \frac{E}{R}$

$I = \frac{12}{6}$

$I = 2$ Amps

12 V
Battery

Fig. 1.7.

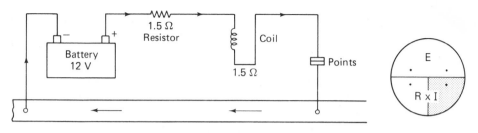

Fig. 1.8.   Fig. 1.9.

Let's take an example and see how Ohm's law can be applied to a simple 12-volt circuit with a miniature light bulb design load resistance of 6 ohms (Fig. 1-7).

Figure 1-8 shows a simplified version of a typical ignition circuit, with a battery, a resistor, a coil, and points. The resistor and the coil are designed to have 1.5 ohms each to control current flow. If we have two known values, we can always find the unknown value, by using the formula circle adapted to Ohm's law, Fig. 1-9.

If you cover the unknown value, you can write Ohm's law in three ways:

$$I = \frac{E}{R} \qquad E = I \times R \qquad R = \frac{E}{I}$$

In this case the unknown value is amps (I). When you cover I, the formula looks like this:

$$I = \frac{E}{R} = \frac{\text{Volts}}{\text{Resistance}} = \frac{12\,\text{volts}}{3\,\text{ohms}} = 4\,\text{amps}$$

Don't forget that in a series circuit the resistances are added together:

$$R_T = 1.5 \quad + 1.5 \quad = 3\,\Omega$$

Parallel Circuit

The parallel circuit has three characteristics:

1. The applied voltage is the same for all the parallel branches.
2. The main circuit current flow divides itself among the parallel branches according to resistance values. The sum of the separate currents equals the total circuit current.

3. The total effective resistance is always less than the parallel branch offering the smallest resistance.

In a parallel circuit current flows in two or more paths or branch circuits. A parallel circuit always starts with a *common point,* where the hot wire splits or branches to supply power to more than one circuit. It could be a terminal, a splice, or a connector.

In Fig. 1-10, the common point provides current to load A and load B. If load A switch is open and load B switch is closed, load B will operate and vice versa, so the common point supplies current to more than one circuit. If the fuse blows open, neither A nor B will operate.

A study of a parallel circuit, Fig. 1-11, shows how Ohm's law relates to the circuit. In a parallel circuit, to find the total current flow in the circuit, we must first find the total effective resistance.

To find total effective resistance we must use a special formula.

$$\text{Total Resistance} = \frac{\text{Resistance of leg \#1} \times \text{Resistance of leg \#2}}{\text{Resistance of leg \#1} + \text{Resistance of leg \#2}}$$

$$R_t = \frac{R_1 \times R_2}{R_1 + R_2}$$

$$= \frac{2 \times 4}{2 + 4} = \frac{8}{6} = \frac{4}{3} = 1.33\,\Omega$$

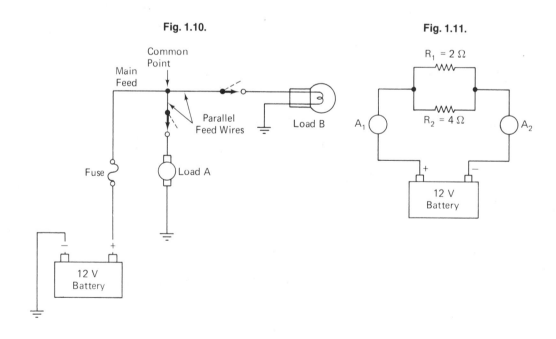

Fig. 1.10.

Fig. 1.11.

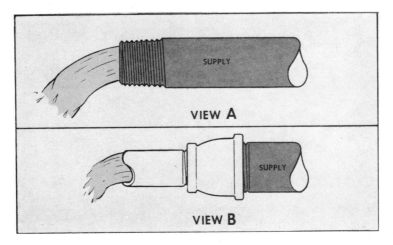

Fig. 1.12.

To find the total current flow reading in ammeter 1 and ammeter 2:

$$I = \frac{E}{R_1} = \frac{12 \text{ volts}}{1.33 \text{ ohms}} = 9 \text{ amps}$$

Ammeter$_1$ reads 9 amps.
Ammeter$_2$ reads 9 amps.

The current flow in R_1 is:

$$I = \frac{E}{R} = \frac{12 \text{ volts}}{2 \text{ ohms}} = 6 \text{ amps}$$

The current flow in R_2 is:

$$I = \frac{E}{R} = \frac{12 \text{ volts}}{4 \text{ ohms}} = 3 \text{ amps}$$

The main circuit current is equal to the current in R_1 and R_2:

Main circuit current = 6 amps + 3 amps = 9 amps

Figure 1-12 will help you to better visualize why the total circuit resistance (equivalent resistance) in a parallel circuit system is even less than the resistance value of the individual parallel circuit with the lowest resistance value.

Let us assume that we have a supply pipe through which water is flowing (Fig. 1-12, view A). In view B, we have taken the original supply pipe and added a reducer and a smaller diameter pipe.

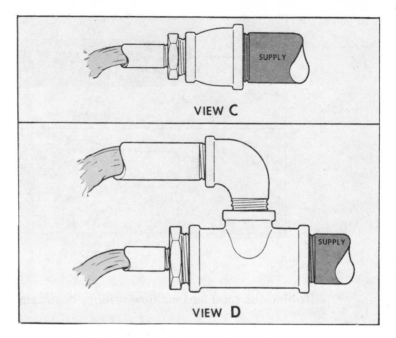

Fig. 1.12. (Continued). *Courtesy General Motors Corp.*

Obviously the resistance to the flow is now greater because of the smaller pipe. Then in view C, we've taken the original supply pipe again and changed to an even smaller reducer and pipe than those used in view B. The resistance to the flow is now even greater.

In view D we've started over with the original supply pipe and changed the plumbing to allow us to incorporate in *parallel* both of the smaller pipes that were used in views B and C. Therefore, the total resistance (equivalent resistance of the two parallel pipes) in view D is obviously less than the resistance of either of the individual pipes (views B and C), because there is now a greater total cross-sectional area of unrestricted flow. Thus it can be seen that when circuits are in parallel, they present less total resistance than the resistance value of either of the individual circuits.

Series-Parallel Circuit

Series-parallel circuit characteristics are a combination of those related to a pure series circuit and a pure parallel circuit. The series-parallel circuit in Fig. 1-13 illustrates how Ohm's law relates to the combined characteristics.

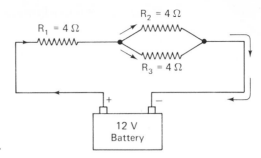

Fig. 1.13.

The total effective circuit resistance is:

$$R_T = R_1 + \frac{(R_2 \times R_3)}{(R_2 + R_3)}$$

$$4 + \frac{(4 \times 4)}{(4 + 4)} = 4 + \frac{16}{8} = 4 + 2 = 6 \text{ ohms}$$

The main circuit current flow is:

$$I = \frac{E}{R} = \frac{12 \text{ volts}}{6 \text{ ohms}} = 2 \text{ amps}$$

The voltage drop across R_1 is:

$$E = I \times R = 2 \text{ amps} \times 4 \text{ ohms} = 8 \text{ volts}$$

The applied voltage to parallel branches is equal to the battery voltage *minus* the R_1 voltage drop:

$$\text{applied voltage} = 12 \text{ volts} - 8 \text{ volts} = 4 \text{ volts}$$

To determine the current flow through R_2 and R_3, we can say that since the resistances are equal, the main current splits equally, and one amp flows through each parallel branch; or we can calculate the current in each resistance:

$$\text{Current } (I) \text{ in } R_2 = \frac{E}{R_2} = \frac{4 \text{ volts}}{4 \text{ ohms}} = 1 \text{ amp}$$

$$\text{Current } (I) \text{ in } R_3 = \frac{E}{R_3} = \frac{4 \text{ volts}}{4 \text{ ohms}} = 1 \text{ amp}$$

The voltage drop across R_2 and R_3 is:

$$E = I \times R_2 = 1 \times 4 = 4 \text{ volts}$$

$$E = I \times R_3 = 1 \times 4 = 4 \text{ volts}$$

13

Table 1-1
OHM'S LAW RELATIONSHIP TABLE

Voltage	Resistance	Amperage
up	down	up
up	same	up
up	up	same
same	down	up
same	same	same
same	up	down
down	down	same
down	up	down
down	same	down

Although the above table reflects the typical relationship between voltage, resistance, and amperage, there are a couple of variables to be considered. For example, line three indicates that if voltage is "up," and resistance is also "up," the amperage will stay the same. It is obvious that in this example the voltage would have to be increased proportionately to offset the increased resistance in order for the amperage to remain the same. Similarly, the example on line seven—in order to be exact, as stated—would require the voltage to be decreased proportionately with the decrease of resistance if the amperage were to stay the same.

Examples three and five, then, are shown only as the probable situation that would exist in those instances. One can better see the relationship of these particular two examples if the table is used from right to left. That is, if the amperage is the same, and the resistance or voltage is "up," the third factor (resistance or voltage) must be up. It follows then that if the voltage is the same and the resistance or voltage is "down," the remaining factor must also be down.

The following list of electrical terms are used throughout the book.

ELECTRICAL TERMS

VOLTAGE: Electrical pressure measured in volts. This is the force that causes current to flow in an electrical circuit. The electrical symbol is E.

CURRENT: Flow of electricity measured in amperes. Current can be compared to the flow of water in a pipe. The rate of flow (amount of current) is measured in amperes (abbreviated as amps). The electrical symbol is I.

RESISTANCE:

Electrical friction (opposition to current flow) measured in ohms (abbreviated as Ω —the Greek letter omega). Everything has some degree of resistance. The resistance in wiring can be compared to the friction in a pipe. Wiring resistance increases as the length increases, and decreases as the cross-sectional size increases. The smaller the size number of the wire, the larger the cross-section of the wire. For example, No. 6 wire is larger in cross-section than No. 14 wire and has less resistance per foot. The electrical symbol for resistance is R.

VOLTAGE DROP:

The loss of voltage caused by a flow of current through a resistance. It increases as current flow or resistance increases. Voltage drop, sometimes called *voltage loss* or *line loss*, can be measured with a voltmeter connected from one point to the other with current flowing in the circuit. The total voltage drop in a circuit is equal to the voltage of the source.

APPLIED VOLTAGE:

The actual voltage read at a given point in a circuit.

AVAILABLE VOLTAGE:

The voltage delivered by the power supply.

CIRCUIT:

A complete path for the flow of electricity. If there is a difference in pressure (voltage) between the ends of the circuit, current will flow. The amount of current that will flow is determined by the voltage applied and the total resistance of the circuit.

SHORT CIRCUIT: A connection in a circuit that results in lower resistance and usually results in higher than normal current flow.

GROUNDED CIRCUIT: A grounded circuit is similar to a "short circuit" in that the current by-passes part of the normal circuit. In this instance, by going directly to ground. This may be caused by a wire touching ground, or part of the circuit within a unit coming in contact with the frame or housing of the unit.

OPEN CIRCUIT: A break in a wire or connection that prevents any current flow through that wire or connection.

EXCESSIVE RESISTANCE: A bad connection due to corrosion, loose connections, or any other connection that would add unwanted resistance in the circuit.

Review questions

1. Name four parts of a simple circuit.
2. What does the word "load" mean in an electrical circuit?
3. What is a single-wire circuit?
4. Circuits are identified in three ways. Name them.
5. Define the following terms.

A. Series Circuit
B. Parallel Circuit
C. Voltage
D. Ampere
E. Resistance

F. Open Circuit
G. Voltage Drop
H. Applied Voltage
I. Available Voltage
J. Short Circuit

6. How do you determine the total circuit resistance in a series circuit? _____.
7. In a 12-volt series circuit with a 2-ohm resistor and a 2-ohm coil, how many amps will flow?
8. In a parallel circuit the applied voltage to each branch is _____.

9. What is the total circuit resistance in a parallel circuit if each branch has a 2-ohm resistor? The circuit has only two branches.

10. What is the total circuit resistance in a parallel circuit if one branch has a 3-ohm resistor and the other branch has a 6-ohm resistor?

11. How many amps will flow in a series circuit with a 12-volt battery and an 8-ohm resistor?

12. How many amps will flow in a 6-volt circuit with a 1.5-ohm coil?

Ohm's law problems

What's your Ohm's law IQ? Test yourself on the following problems, and make a drawing for each problem.

13. In a series circuit consisting of 6-ohm resistor, a 4-ohm resistor, and a 12-volt battery, what is the voltage drop across each resistor?

14. In a parallel circuit consisting of a 4-ohm resistor, a 6-ohm resistor, and a 12-volt battery, what is the total circuit current supplied by the battery?

15. In a series-parallel circuit consisting of a 6-ohm resistor in series, a 10-ohm resistor in parallel, a 15-ohm resistor in parallel, and a 12-volt battery, how much current (amps) flows through the 10-ohm and the 15-ohm resistor.

2

Wiring and Wire Service

A modern passenger car can require more than 1,600 feet or nearly one-third of a mile of wire and cable, divided into as many as 50 individual wiring harnesses with more than 50 connectors and 500 terminals (Fig. 2-1). The fact that these wires must be scientifically selected and put together to meet the needs of the vehicle operation should leave no doubt as to the monumental task performed by the wiring engineer. Passenger car wiring systems are designed to be strong and secure, but they are not indestructible. Deterioration sets in as the vehicle ages from such factors as exposure to heat, vibration, moisture, road salts, etc. Fire and collision damage can often involve extensive rewiring. For the technician, replacement of wiring becomes an important service task.

Selecting the proper wire, proper installation of terminal ends, and the routing and securing of wire are important considerations for quality work. A replacement terminal connection that has not been properly secured will lose its wire end shortly after the vehicle is back on the road; too small a replacement wire size for the electrical load will cause an excessive drop in the battery voltage. A 10 per cent drop in the battery voltage to the lamps will result in a 30 per cent loss in candlepower. This same 10 per cent voltage loss applied to accessories such as power windows and windshield wipers will greatly reduce their motor operation.

The following information provides a guideline to the mechanic for quality wire service.

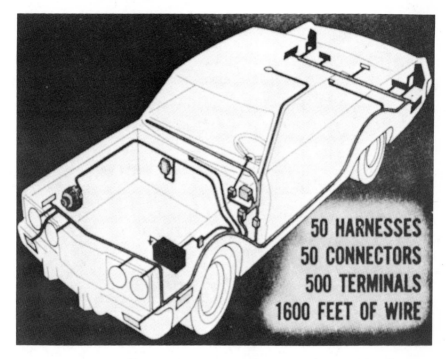

50 HARNESSES
50 CONNECTORS
500 TERMINALS
1600 FEET OF WIRE

Fig. 2.1. *Courtesy of Chrysler Corporation.*

WIRE SIZE

Automotive wires or cables are made of copper wire strands usually covered with a colored plastic used for insulation and circuit wire identification. The wire or cable size is expressed in terms of standard gauge numbers. "Size" refers to the measure of the cross-sectional diameter of all the separate strands (Fig. 2-2).

In Fig. 2-3, note that as the wire gets larger the gauge number gets smaller. Automotive 12-volt electrical wiring generally uses gauge numbers 10, 12, 14, 16, and 18. The 10 and 12 gauge are used for the power distribution between the battery and alternator, ignition switch, fuse panel, headlight switch, and some of the power-hungry accessories. Most generally, interior and exterior car lighting uses 16- and 18-gauge wiring. In this same category are the horn, cigar lighter, radio, etc. The battery cables for passenger car 12-volt systems are usually 4 or 6 gauge.

An experienced automotive technician can usually recognize many of the various wiring sizes by sight and by touch. Should the size be in question, a quick visual check can be made against a known wire of the same gauge number.

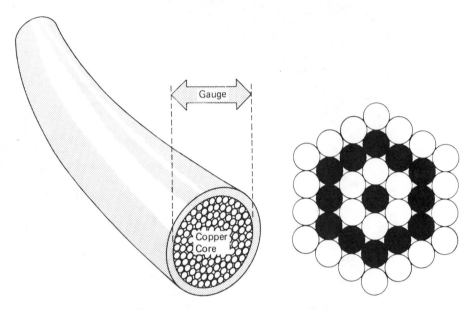

Fig. 2.2. *Courtesy of AC-Delco—General Motors Corp.*

Fig. 2.3.

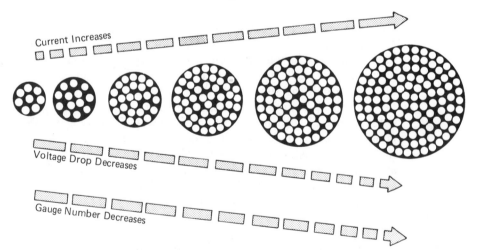

Fig. 2.4.

For service replacement or for the addition of wiring, automotive wiring comes bulk-wound on spools and is cut in lengths as needed (Fig. 2-4).

WIRE SELECTION

Low-voltage wiring systems as used in passenger cars are very sensitive to any form of electrical resistance. A wire too small for the circuit causes high electrical resistance (voltage loss) and a proportional loss in amperage and candlepower, as in the case of lighting circuits. Figure 2-3 illustrates the effect of wire size on the circuit voltage and current. Another factor affecting circuit resistance is the wire length. The longer the wire, the more the resistance; doubling the wire length doubles the resistance (Fig. 2-5).

Fig. 2.5. Longer wire must have a larger gauge core than a short wire to carry the same current without excessive voltage drop.

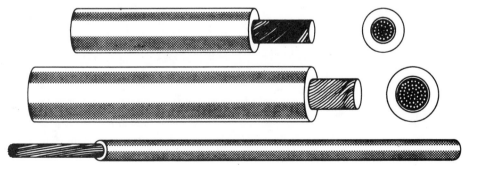

Chart 2.1

Recommended Cable Sizes for Replacement or Additional Electrical Unit Installations

6-VOLT SYSTEM		12-VOLT SYSTEM		Total Length of Cable in Circuit from Battery to most Distant Electrical Unit*			
Amperes (Approx.)	Candle Power	Amperes (Approx.)	Candle Power	10 Feet	20 Feet	30 Feet	40 Feet
				Gauge	Gauge	Gauge	Gauge
0.5	3	1.0	6	18	18	18	18
0.75	5	1.5	10	18	18	18	18
1.0	8	2	16	18	18	18	18
1.5	12	3	24	18	18	18	18
2.0	15	4	30	18	18	18	16
2.5	20	5	40	18	18	18	16
3.0	25	6	50	18	18	16	16
3.5	30	7	60	18	18	16	14
4.0	35	8	70	18	16	16	14
5.0	40	10	80	18	16	14	12
5.5	45	11	90	18	16	14	12
6.0	50	12	100	18	16	14	12
7.5	60	15	120	18	14	14	12
9.0	70	18	140	16	14	12	12
10	80	20	160	16	12	12	10
11	90	22	180	16	12	10	10
12	100	24	200	16	12	10	10
18	—	36	—	14	10	8	8
25	—	50	—	12	10	8	6
50	—	100	—	10	6	4	4
75	—	150	—	8	4	2	2
100	—	200	—	6	4	2	1

Original equipment cable sizes on some vehicles may vary slightly from recommendations due to special electrical system design. See note below.

This chart applies to grounded return systems. For two-wire circuits, use total length of both cables, or the double length to most distant electrical unit.

Some 12-volt systems are designed with No. 20 gauge cable in certain circuits. (Vehicle manufacturers' service manuals generally show the size of cable used for original equipment in each circuit.)

The selection of the proper wire gauge is usually a matter of following the car manufacturer's recommendation as provided in the service manual. This information is found in the wiring diagram section.

When additional lighting or accessories are added to the vehicle, Chart 2-1 can be used to determine the proper wire or cable size. The proper selection is based on two factors:

1. The amperage the circuit will carry, or the candlepower to be handled in the circuit.

2. The length of the circuit, including the return if it is a two-wire system. Where a ground frame is used for a return, only the length of the wire to the electrical load need be considered.

EXAMPLE: A frame-ground boat trailer 12 feet long is designed with two tail lights and two stop lights. Each tail light draws 0.75 amps, and the combined effect is of a 1.5 amp load (2 x 0.75). Find 1.5 amps on the chart and read across to the correct foot length column. The 10-foot length column determines that an 18-gauge wire will handle the job. A stop light draws 2.25 amps. The total circuit current calculation (4.5 amps), and reference to the chart will show that an 18-gauge wire is also adequate.

When the amperage and wire length do not exactly fit the chart always select the chart references closest to your calculations. For example, treat 5.5 amps as 6 amps and 22 feet as 20 feet.

ADD-ON ACCESSORIES

The addition of accessories to a car is an exact science involving:

1. Proper wire gauge selection.
2. Pick-up of the power source.
3. The ability of the battery and the charging system to handle the additional load.

In many cases the battery and the charging system are designed to meet only the electrical system's original load demands. There is no electrical reserve to handle add-on accessories. Typically, the addition of a pair of driving lights to a marginal battery or charging system will result in a continuous discharged-battery condition.

To determine the adequacy of the charging system to handle the extra accessory load, the following procedure can be used:

1. Use a fully charged battery.
2. Insert an ammeter in series with the battery positive post and cable.
3. Turn on all existing lights and accessories.
4. Read the ammeter and add five amps to allow for the ignition system load.

EXAMPLE: 25 amps + 5 amps = 30 amps.

5. Add the new accessory load factor (in amps) to step 4.

EXAMPLE: 30 amps + 10 amps = 40 amps.

6. Run an alternator output test to determine the maximum available output.

If the addition of the new accessory causes a continuous load above factory specifications for the alternator, it should not be added.

When you select the place to attach a new accessory to a source of power, you must carefully consider the wiring plan of the car. Most automotive electrical circuit protection guards more than one circuit, and therefore taping a new accessory into a hot line can easily result in an overload for a circuit fuse or breaker. Also of serious consequence, the power tap can cause an overload on the branch circuit wiring. In some cases the fuse box will provide for an additional power tap.

Any add-on accessory must have circuit protection. In-line fuse protection is a popular method to use if it is not possible to use existing circuit fuses or breakers (Fig. 2-6).

Battery capacity must also be considered, since the battery at times temporarily furnishes all the power or supplements the alternator power during curb idle or heavy city traffic. As a guideline, a battery that is fully charged should not have a terminal voltage of less than 11.6 volts when all the car lighting and electrical accessories

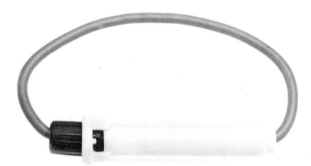

Fig. 2.6. Inline fuse; wire loop is cut and spliced into circuit.

are in operation, including the add-on (engine not running). A reading of less than 11.6 volts warrants consideration of replacing the battery with one of higher capacity.

Keep in mind that add-on accessories can overburden both the alternator and the battery. You must then consider upgrading the original-equipment charging system components with higher capacity units.

PRIMARY WIRE SERVICE

The low-voltage wiring of the vehicle is referred to as the *primary wiring*. The plastic insulation used with this wire is relatively thin and permits using cable of a smaller total diameter that is more economical and easier to work with because of its flexibility. The plastic compound is resistant to the deteriorating effect of oils, fuels, and chemicals. With the exception of the ignition secondary high-tension circuit, primary wire is used throughout the vehicle—for example, in the lighting and accessory circuits, charging system, and ignition primary circuit.

Although automotive wiring systems are carefully planned and given the best possible protection, they do get exposed to heat, chemicals, the weather, mechanical vibrations, and scuffing. The most common wear points occur at the terminals where corrosion has set in from weather exposure or electrical arcing, or when mechanical vibration has induced a flexing action that causes a break in the wire at the terminal itself. Old age, heat, and chemical exposure

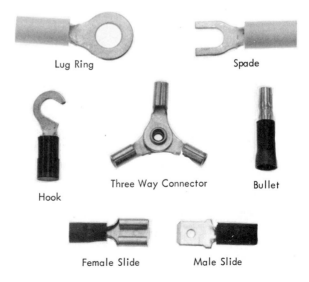

Fig. 2.7. Common types of primary wire terminals.

deteriorate the wire insulation, and breaks occur occasionally in the middle of a wire. Wiring repair or replacement, therefore, is an important service item.

Whether one is repairing original wire defects or adding wire for a new circuit, the techniques for attaching terminals to wire ends and joining these wires together require some understanding and skill. In Fig. 2-7, a variety of automotive wire terminal shapes are illustrated.

The wiring on late-model vehicles makes popular use of "slide-on" or "snap-on" type terminals. Most terminals are made of corrosion-resistant tin-plated copper and are usually attached to wires by two methods, *crimping* and *soldering*.

CRIMPING TERMINALS

Crimping is fast, it provides a firm connection, and it is usually the preferred technique on wire sizes from 22 gauge to 10 gauge. A crimp terminal design with a vinyl plastic insulation sleeve is shown in Fig. 2-8. Crimp terminals are also referred to as solderless terminals.

To make a reliable crimp connection, a crimping tool must be used. Substituting a pair of pliers to crimp a wire will only weaken the terminal barrel and leave a poor connection, although it might appear to be solid. Figure 2-9 shows a plier-type crimping tool which is also

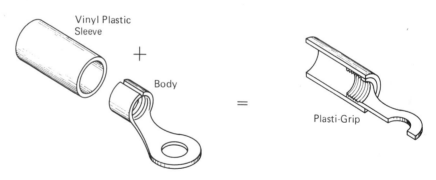

Vinyl Plastic Sleeve

Body

Plasti-Grip

Typical Crimp Terminal Design

Fig. 2.8.

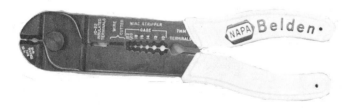

NAPA Belden•

Fig. 2.9.

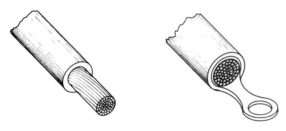

Strip End of Wire to Fit
Terminal Barrel Length   **Fig. 2.10.**

Fig. 2.11.

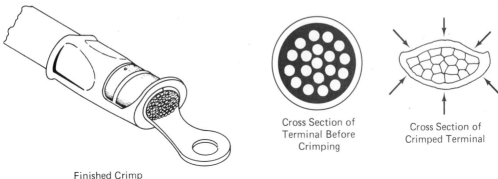

Finished Crimp

Cross Section of
Terminal Before
Crimping

Cross Section of
Crimped Terminal

Fig. 2.12.

designed for cable stripping and cutting. To crimp a wire to a
terminal, strip back the wire insulation from the conductor end until
just enough conductor is exposed to fit into the terminal barrel (Fig.
2-10). *The terminal barrel size and wire size should be matched.* It is
now a simple matter of applying the crimping pliers to form a solid
crimp connection between the wire and terminal barrel (Figs. 2-11 and
2-12).

Crimping tools usually have simple directions printed on the tool

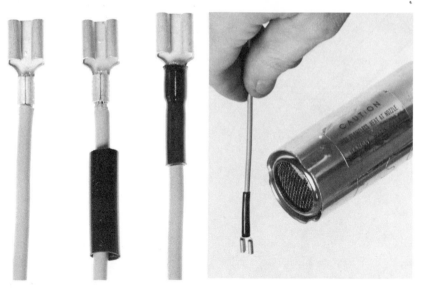

Fig. 2.13. Vinyl heat shrink tube used
for terminal insulation.

Fig. 2.14.

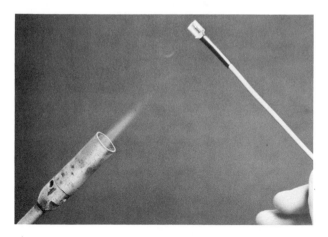

Fig. 2.15.

itself, indicating the correct crimp die to be used with the wire gauge.

Note: Crimp connections will be electrically sound only if *the terminal barrel size is matched to the wire size and the proper crimping die is used.*

Note: Use vinyl heat-shrinkable tubing or slip tubing overall uninsulated terminal connections (Fig. 2-13). It is readily available at automotive parts jobber outlets or at radio-TV repair shops. The tubing seals the terminal connection and makes it air tight. The connection will then have maximum protection against corrosion.

A heat gun, Fig. 2-14, or a propane torch flame, Fig. 2-15, is ideal to use on heat-shrink tubing. A match flame can be used as a substitute. *Do not use any flame near the battery or where gas fumes may pose a safety hazard.*

Note: When stripping wire insulation, it is important that the wire is not nicked by the improper use of the stripper tool. This type of damage will weaken the wire and eventually cause a fatigue fracture. This may seem to be a minor consideration, yet it is one of the leading causes of wire breaks.

SOLDERING TERMINALS

Where terminal connectors are exposed to vibration and extra strength is needed, such as at the alternator, a crimp connector should be reenforced with solder. In Fig. 2-16 a sample of a soldered crimped lug terminal is shown. Note the insulation tang used for added terminal strength.

A terminal soldering operation on a slip terminal is illustrated in Fig. 2-17. The soldering gun tip is held in place just long enough for one drop of solder to flow freely into the wire and crimp barrel. Prolonged application of heat will damage the wire insulation. After soldering, complete the job by installing a terminal insulator (Fig. 2-18).

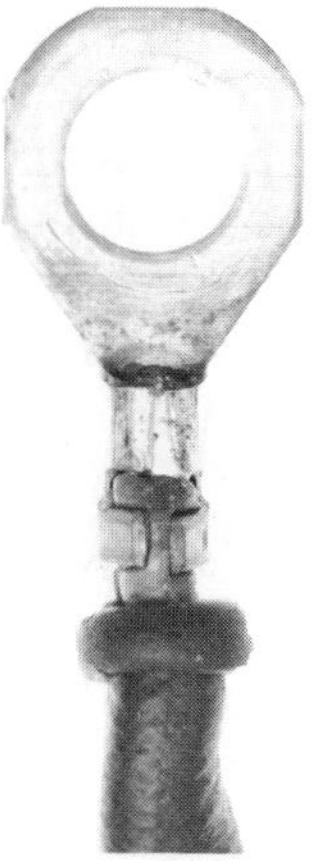

Fig. 2.16.

Fig. 2.17.

Fig. 2.18.

Note: Always use rosin-core solder for an electrical connection. The use of acid-core solder when working with electrical wiring causes a corrosive action and unwanted circuit resistance.

ALUMINUM WIRING REPAIR *

Early 1975 General Motors cars have either aluminum or copper wire in the main body harness. The copper wiring harness has a black plastic conduit covering and the aluminum wiring harness a brown plastic conduit covering. Complete use of aluminum wire in the main body harness was phased into the entire car production as the stock of copper harnesses was depleted.

The aluminum wire harness is made of solid 14- and 16-gauge insulated wires; wires are two sizes larger than the corresponding copper wires to maintain the same current-carrying capacity.

The aluminum harness is used in a location where it is not subject to flexing. The harness is routed in the usual manner beneath the left side of the instrument panel, down to the floor pan and along the left rocker, and then to the top of the left wheelhouse panel where it connects to the regular copper wiring harness to the rear lighting.

The aluminum harness requires special repair procedures that are outlined in the Fisher Body Manual. A repair kit, Part 1684873 (or equivalent), is available for repairing the aluminum harness; it consists of the following parts and materials:

1. Twenty wires six inches long with terminals attached to one end. Both 14- and 16-gauge wires are supplied.
2. Twenty splice clips.
3. One tube of corrosion-preventive compound (petroleum jelly).
4. One sheet of instructions.

Terminals and Splice Clips

To assure minimum resistance through a circuit, a new terminal and splice clip must be used when you repair the aluminum body harness.

The terminal and splice clip have serrations (ribs) in the crimp area to penetrate through any aluminum oxide (coating that forms on the surface of the wire) and to control overdisplacement (crushing) of the wire when the terminals or splice clips are being attached to the wire. These parts are also tin plated to reduce the possibility of

*©Courtesy of Fisher Body—General Motors.

galvanic corrosion occurring between the terminal and wire or splice clips and wire. To further inhibit corrosion, a corrosion preventive compound (petroleum jelly) is also applied at the terminal and/or splice clip locations when repairs are made to the harness.

Terminal Replacement Procedure

1. Cut off approximately six inches of wire connected to defective terminal.
2. Using proper gauge wire strippers, strip off approximately one-quarter inch of insulation from the end of wire to be repaired and from the wire (from kit) with terminal attached.

Caution: Care should be exercised when stripping insulation from wire. If proper gauge strippers are not used, damage to wire may occur and weaken the harness assembly at this point.

3. Place end of one wire in either end of splice clip and crimp firmly to wire. Repeat with remaining wire.

Caution: To prevent possible damage to wire, do not over-crimp near ends of splice clip.

4. When splice is completed, apply a coat of corrosion preventive compound (petroleum jelly) to splice area and terminal.
5. Apply tape to spliced area to insulate.
6. Insert terminal into proper connector cavity making sure it is firmly seated.

To install splice clip only, strip off approximately one-quarter inch of insulation from ends of each wire to be joined together, then complete steps 3, 4, and 5 of the terminal replacement procedure.

Caution: Do not twist ends of the aluminum conductor to make a splice. The clip must be used for proper contact.

BATTERY CABLES AND TERMINALS

For dependable starter cranking and proper operation of the electrical and accessory circuits, especially under extreme weather and climate conditions, it is important that the correct battery cables be solidly connected. If the battery cables are too small or if the cable terminals are corroded or not securely connected, then even a good battery will fail to deliver an adequate current supply.

Battery cables and terminals deteriorate with use and age. The cable terminals, especially on the battery posts, need to be periodically removed and cleaned. Eventually, the cable and terminals need to be repaired or replaced. The standard service practice is to replace the battery cable rather than make a repair. In Fig. 2-19, a variety of battery cable replacements are shown. Note the second wire on one of the cables. It is used on many of today's positive post cables as a power feed for the entire automobile except for the starter motor. The battery is also charged by the alternator through this second wire. In some applications the second wire serves as a fusible link. Also, it is not uncommon to find that some negative battery cables have a second wire to insure a positive ground between the car body sheet metal and the battery. This attachment is necessary for proper operation of the lighting and accessory circuits.

On occasion an odd-length cable cannot be found or, in isolated service areas, it may not be possible to get a replacement. It then becomes necessary to make up an entire cable or salvage the old cable and install new terminal ends as the job dictates. Figure 2-20 shows typical battery cable replacement terminals.

Battery cable terminals can be secured by crimping (use a special crimping plier), clamping, or soldering. The preferred connection in field service is the solder type as it resists corrosion, and gives a connection with the least amount of resistance, and is airtight. Observe the operations in the terminal-to-cable soldering as illustrated in Fig. 2-21 a, b, c, and d. In sequence, use the following procedure:

1. Strip the insulation from the cable end to a length that will fit the terminal barrel. Corroded cable ends should be trimmed back into the fresh wire.

2. Install the cable terminal in a vise with the open barrel facing up and apply heat to the outside using a torch flame. Using a rosin-core solder, apply a solder flow in the terminal barrel until it becomes full.

3. Back the torch flame away from the terminal and keep just enough heat applied to keep the solder in a molten state. Gradually dip the cable end into the barrel and continue to hold the flame for a few seconds to allow the cable strands to heat up. Remove the heat and keep the cable steady until the solder takes a set. The soldered joint must be air tight; therefore, any visible pore holes cannot be tolerated after cooling takes place. Reheat the solder to eliminate the pore holes.

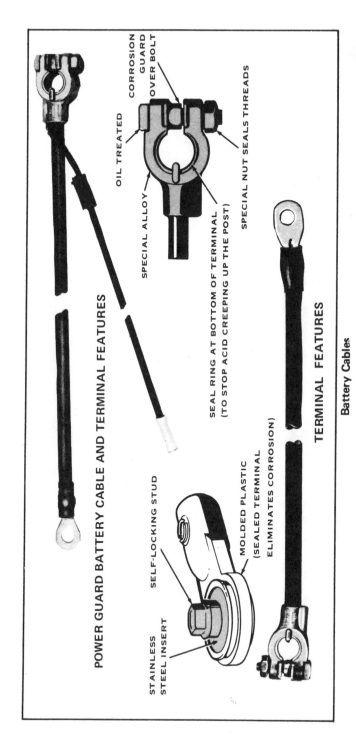

POWER GUARD BATTERY CABLE AND TERMINAL FEATURES

CORROSION GUARD OVER BOLT

OIL TREATED

SPECIAL ALLOY

SPECIAL NUT SEALS THREADS

SEAL RING AT BOTTOM OF TERMINAL
(TO STOP ACID CREEPING UP THE POST)

STAINLESS STEEL INSERT

SELF-LOCKING STUD

MOLDED PLASTIC
(SEALED TERMINAL
ELIMINATES CORROSION)

TERMINAL FEATURES

Battery Cables

Fig. 2.19. *Courtesy of AC-Delco—General Motors Corp.*

33

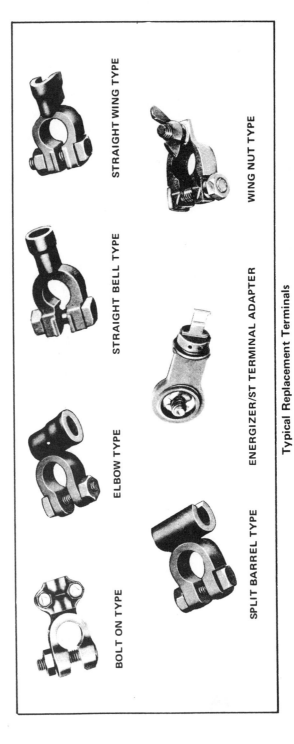

Typical Replacement Terminals

Fig. 2.20. *Courtesy of AC-Delco—General Motors Corp.*

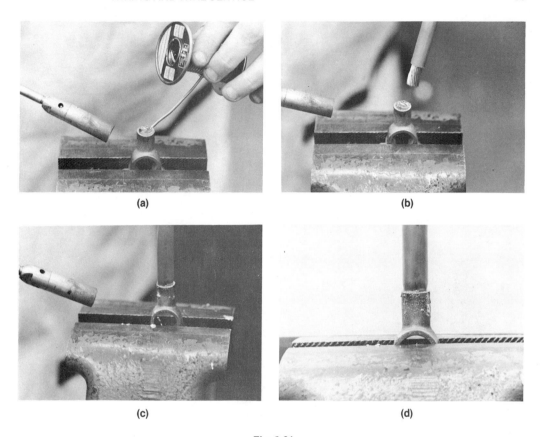

(a)   (b)

(c)   (d)

Fig. 2.21.

4. Allow the terminal to cool at room temperature and then use vinyl heat-shrinkable tubing over the joint for an air-tight connection, Fig. 2-22.

Note: For safety, if the soldered battery terminal is replaced with the cable in place under the hood, remove the battery from the car.

Installation of the clamp-type terminal to a battery cable is illustrated in Fig. 2-23. Although this design has popular use, it should only be considered as a temporary or emergency repair. The terminal connection is not air tight and corrodes easily.

When replacing a standard battery with a side-terminal battery, a cable terminal adapter is necessary (Fig. 2-24). To install the adapter, cut the old clamp off the cable as close to the clamp as

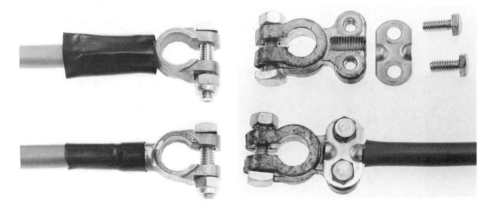

Fig. 2.22.   Fig. 2.23.

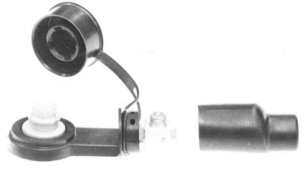

Fig. 2.24.

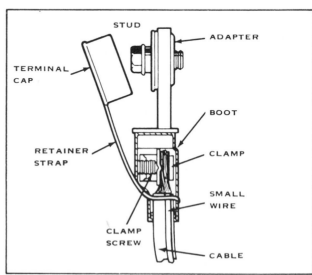

Fig. 2.25. *Courtesy of AC-Delco—General Motors Corp.*

Energizer S/T Adapter

Fig. 2.26.   **Fig. 2.27.**

possible. Strip one inch of the insulation from the end of the cable and any other wire. Place the boot and retainer strap of the terminal cap over the end of the cable wire. Then insert the exposed ends of the cable and wire into the clamp and tighten the clamp screw tightly. The completed installation is shown in Fig. 2-25.

If desired, a side-terminal battery can be made to accommodate standard cable terminals simply by using screw-on battery post adapters (Fig. 2-26).

SOLDERING FUSIBLE LINKS

When a fusible link burns out, it sometimes can be removed quickly at its connector ends and a new section snapped into place (Fig. 2-27). With some fusible link replacements, however, you will have to cut out the burned-out section and splice a new link into place with a crimped and soldering connection.

Figure 2-28 shows the before-and-after appearance of a fusible link when a short circuit occurs; Fig. 2-29 shows the installation procedure for a new fusible link. Note the crimp and soldered

Fig. 2.28.
Courtesy of Oldsmobile Division of General Motors Corp.

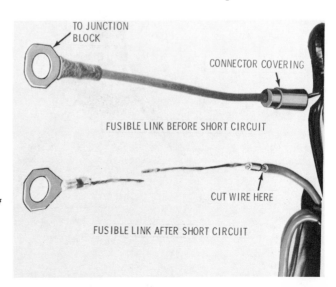

TO JUNCTION BLOCK

CONNECTOR COVERING

FUSIBLE LINK BEFORE SHORT CIRCUIT

CUT WIRE HERE

FUSIBLE LINK AFTER SHORT CIRCUIT

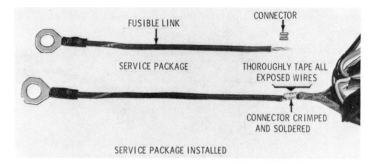

Fig. 2.29. *Courtesy of Oldsmobile Division of General Motors Corp.*

connection that must be made to join the wire ends. This connection should be covered with a double layer of electrical tape, or an insulated connector sleeve.

WIRE SPLICING

A *splice* is the joining of single wire ends or the joining of two or more conductor wires at a single point by soldering, crimping, spot welding, etc. Splices are used in applications where wires are going to be joined permanently.

Figures 2-30, 2-31, 2-32, 2-33, and 2-34 show the stripping and joining of wire ends by soldering as it would be done in shop practice. Other methods of joining wire ends quickly in the shop involve the crimp butt connector and lock connector. These are shown in Figs.

Fig. 2.30. Wire stripper.   Fig. 2.31. Wire stripper head.

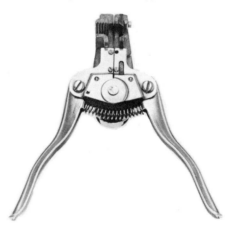

2-35 and 2-36. Figure 2-37 illustrates the wire installation operations for a lock connector.

Where a wire needs to be connected to the electrical power of an existing main wire, a tap splice can be used effectively. Examples of these splices are illustrated in Figs. 2-38 and 2-39.

Figures 2-40 and 2-41 illustrate how production splices are made to join wires within the wiring harness assembly of the vehicle.

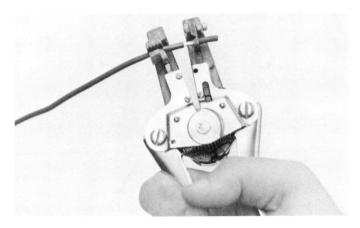

Fig. 2.32. Wire stripping.

Fig. 2.33. Wiring splicing.

Fig. 2.34. Insulating wire splice with heat shrink tubing.

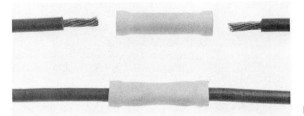

Fig. 2.35. Crimp butt connector.

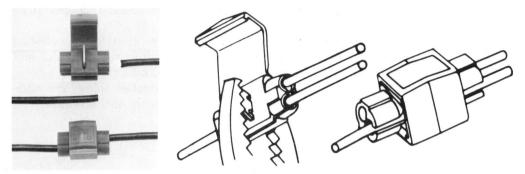

Fig. 2.36. Lock connector.
Courtesy of 3M Corp.

Fig. 2.37. *Courtesy of 3M Corp.*

Fig. 2.38. *Courtesy of Belden Corp.*

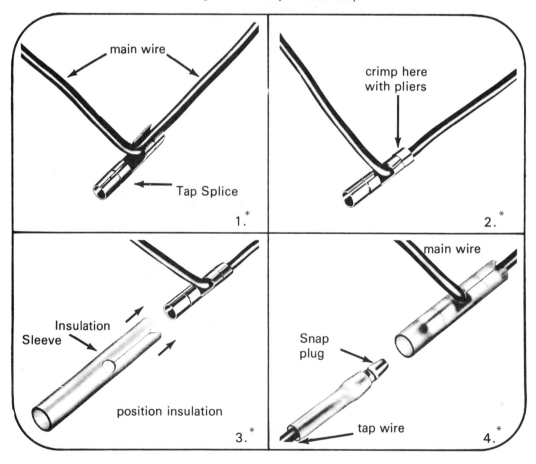

main wire

Tap Splice

1.*

crimp here
with pliers

2.*

Insulation
Sleeve

position insulation

3.*

main wire

Snap
plug

tap wire

4.*

Fig. 2.39.   Fig. 2.40. Production splice.

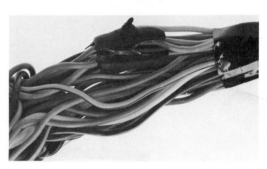

Fig. 2.41. Production splice cutaway.

WIRE CONNECTORS

Wire connectors are used in joining wire ends where the wires need to be logically joined in sections on a continuous circuit run—e.g., from the instrument panel to car body to rear lighting. Wire connectors are also used to attach accessories, light assemblies, and switches to the car wiring. A connector has the feature of offering a wire joint that can be connected or disconnected quickly—a definite advantage for production assembly and field service.

The slide, pin, and "bullet" snap connectors are popular types used in automotive wiring and are pictured in Figs. 2-42, 2-43, 2-44, and 2-45. The male and female connector terminals fit into the connector body halves which are then plugged together.

Connectors that join two or more pairs of wires are referred to as *multiple connector plugs* and are designed to fit together in one way only so that the wire pairs are correctly matched. A retaining or lock tab is used to hold the connector halves together as dictated by the connector design (Figs. 2-46, 2-47, and 2-48). Figure 2-49 shows a multiple connector attached to a headlight switch.

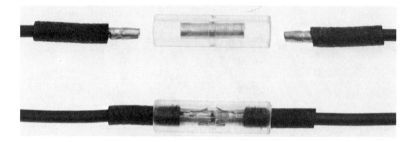

Fig. 2.42. Bullet connector.

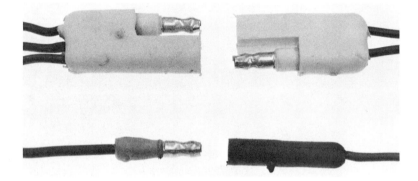

Fig. 2.43. Bullet connectors.

Fig. 2.44. Slide connectors.

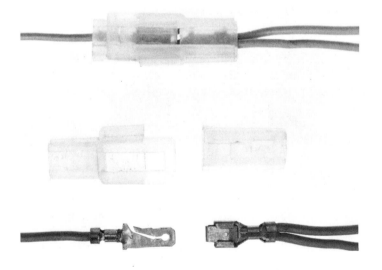

Fig. 2.45. Pin connector.

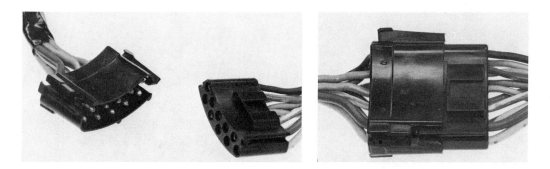

Fig. 2.46. Pin connector.

Fig. 2.47.

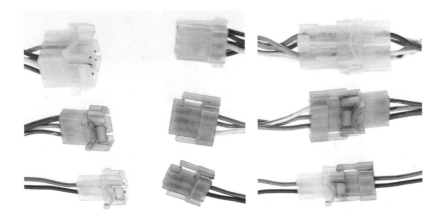

Fig. 2.48.

Fig. 2.49.

Fig. 2.50.

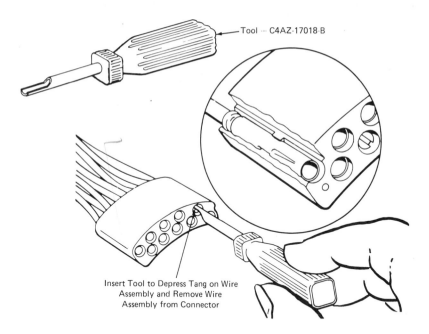

Tool — C4AZ-17018-B

Insert Tool to Depress Tang on Wire
Assembly and Remove Wire
Assembly from Connector

Fig. 2.51. Wire terminal removal. *Courtesy of Ford Customer Service Division.*

Fig. 2.52. *Courtesy of Ford Customer Service Division.*

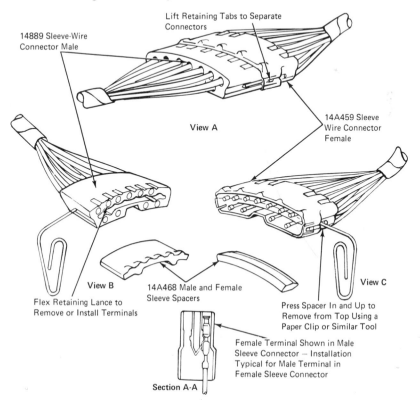

Lift Retaining Tabs to Separate
Connectors

14889 Sleeve-Wire
Connector Male

View A

14A459 Sleeve
Wire Connector
Female

View B

Flex Retaining Lance to
Remove or Install Terminals

14A468 Male and Female
Sleeve Spacers

View C

Press Spacer In and Up to
Remove from Top Using a
Paper Clip or Similar Tool

Female Terminal Shown in Male
Sleeve Connector — Installation
Typical for Male Terminal in
Female Sleeve Connector

Section A-A

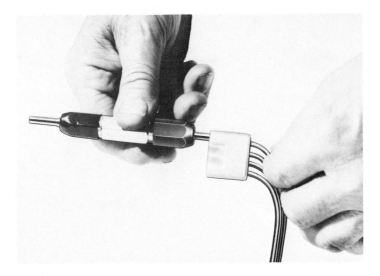

Fig. 2.53. *Courtesy of Chrysler Corporation.*

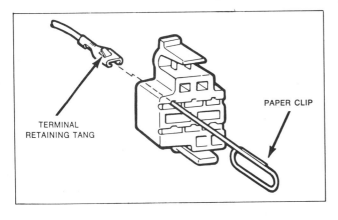

TERMINAL
RETAINING TANG

PAPER CLIP

Fig. 2.54. *Courtesy of Oldsmobile Division of General Motors Corp.*

It is not uncommon to have a wire tap occur at a connector terminal. This is referred to as an external splice at the connector. Examples are shown in Fig. 2-50.

Should it become necessary to remove a wire and its terminal from a connector, use a heavy paper clip, a miniature screwdriver, or a special tool. Some of these procedures are seen in Figs. 2-51, 2-52, 2-53, and 2-54. Most car manufacturer's service manuals have an illustrated description of connector terminal removal for their product. The main objective is to flex the terminal retaining tang from its lock position before removal.

WIRING HARNESS

The routing of wires in a passenger car is an art; the wiring must avoid obstructions and it must distribute the source of power to the chassis lighting and accessory loads. The route must be safe and it must be as short as possible, through existing channels and access holes in the body structure, and in the engine compartment where the main concern is to avoid damage by hot manifolds. Whenever wiring is installed, attention must be given toward insuring that it is not pinched, stretched, or positioned so that it makes contact with movable parts.

For maximum protection and to avoid a maze of loose wiring that would complicate production assembly and field service, automotive wiring is bundled in separate harness assemblies that are joined together by matching multiple connector plugs. Figures 2-55 and 2-56 are typical examples of how wiring harness assemblies are joined together and routed in a passenger car and light truck.

The main wire harness assembly is located under the dash panel and is made up of several groups of branch wiring harnesses which are usually referred to as follows:

1. Dash to Instrument Panel
2. Dash to Headlight Junction
3. Dash to Engine Wiring
4. Dash to Front-End Wiring
5. Dash to Car-Body Wiring
6. Dash to Steering-Column Wiring (Fig. 2-57)
7. Dash to Fuses and Breakers

Sections of the main harness may contain over forty wires. The complexity of the main wiring harness assembly is shown in Fig. 2-58.

The engine compartment and front-end wiring must travel through the fire wall to hook up with the matching wires of the main wiring harness inside the car. This wiring is divided into several wiring harness assemblies that couple to what is known as a *bulkhead disconnect* (Fig. 2-59 A&B).

PRINTED CIRCUITS

Printed circuits are now employed in the instrument and control wiring on automotive dash panels; their use helps to eliminate wiring errors and simplifies the maintenance of the various permanent connections to the panel.

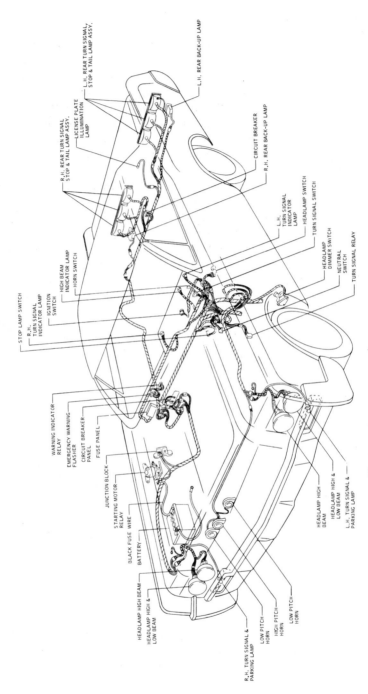

L.H. REAR TURN SIGNAL, STOP & TAIL LAMP ASSY.

L.H. REAR BACK-UP LAMP

R.H. REAR TURN SIGNAL, STOP & TAIL LAMP ASSY.

LICENSE PLATE ILLUMINATION LAMP

CIRCUIT BREAKER

R.H. REAR BACK-UP LAMP

HEADLAMP SWITCH

L.H. TURN SIGNAL INDICATOR LAMP

TURN SIGNAL SWITCH

HEADLAMP DIMMER SWITCH

HIGH BEAM INDICATOR LAMP

NEUTRAL SWITCH

HORN SWITCH

TURN SIGNAL RELAY

STOP LAMP SWITCH

R.H. TURN SIGNAL INDICATOR LAMP

IGNITION SWITCH

WARNING INDICATOR RELAY

EMERGENCY WARNING FLASHER

CIRCUIT BREAKER PANEL

FUSE PANEL

JUNCTION BLOCK

STARTING MOTOR RELAY

BLACK FUSE WIRE

BATTERY

HEADLAMP HIGH BEAM

HEADLAMP HIGH & LOW BEAM

R.H. TURN SIGNAL & PARKING LAMP

LOW PITCH HORN

HIGH PITCH HORN

LOW PITCH HORN

HEADLAMP HIGH BEAM

HEADLAMP HIGH & LOW BEAM

L.H. TURN SIGNAL & PARKING LAMP

Fig. 2.55. *Courtesy Ford Customer Service Division.*

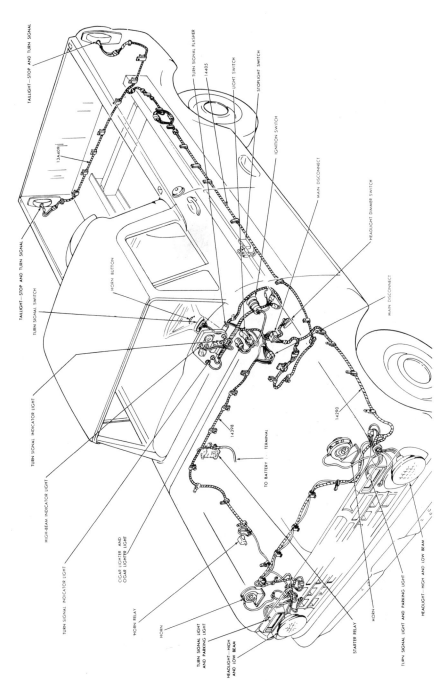

TAILLIGHT—STOP AND TURN SIGNAL

TAILLIGHT—STOP AND TURN SIGNAL

13A409

TURN SIGNAL FLASHER

14405

LIGHT SWITCH

STOPLIGHT SWITCH

IGNITION SWITCH

MAIN DISCONNECT

HEADLIGHT DIMMER SWITCH

MAIN DISCONNECT

HORN BUTTON

TURN SIGNAL SWITCH

TURN SIGNAL INDICATOR LIGHT

HIGH-BEAM INDICATOR LIGHT

14398

14290

TO BATTERY (+) TERMINAL

TURN SIGNAL INDICATOR LIGHT

CIGAR LIGHTER AND CIGAR LIGHTER LIGHT

HORN RELAY

HORN

TURN SIGNAL LIGHT AND PARKING LIGHT

HEADLIGHT—HIGH AND LOW BEAM

STARTER RELAY

HORN

TURN SIGNAL LIGHT AND PARKING LIGHT

HEADLIGHT—HIGH AND LOW BEAM

Fig. 2.56 *Courtesy Ford Customer Service Division.*

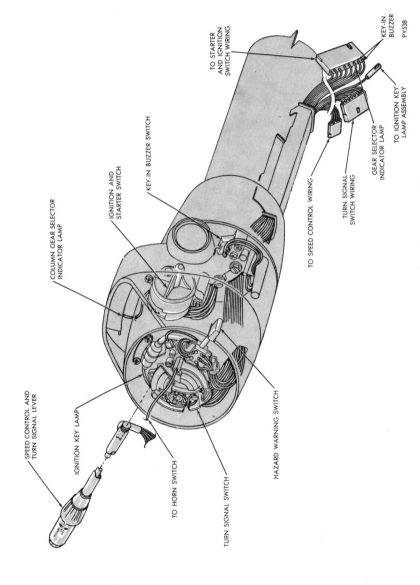

SPEED CONTROL AND
TURN SIGNAL LEVER

IGNITION KEY LAMP

TO HORN SWITCH

TURN SIGNAL SWITCH

HAZARD WARNING SWITCH

COLUMN GEAR SELECTOR
INDICATOR LAMP

IGNITION AND
STARTER SWITCH

KEY-IN BUZZER SWITCH

TO STARTER
AND IGNITION
SWITCH WIRING

KEY-IN
BUZZER

PY538

TO SPEED CONTROL WIRING

TURN SIGNAL
SWITCH WIRING

GEAR SELECTOR
INDICATOR LAMP

TO IGNITION KEY
LAMP ASSEMBLY

Fig. 2.57. *Courtesy of Chrysler Corporation.*

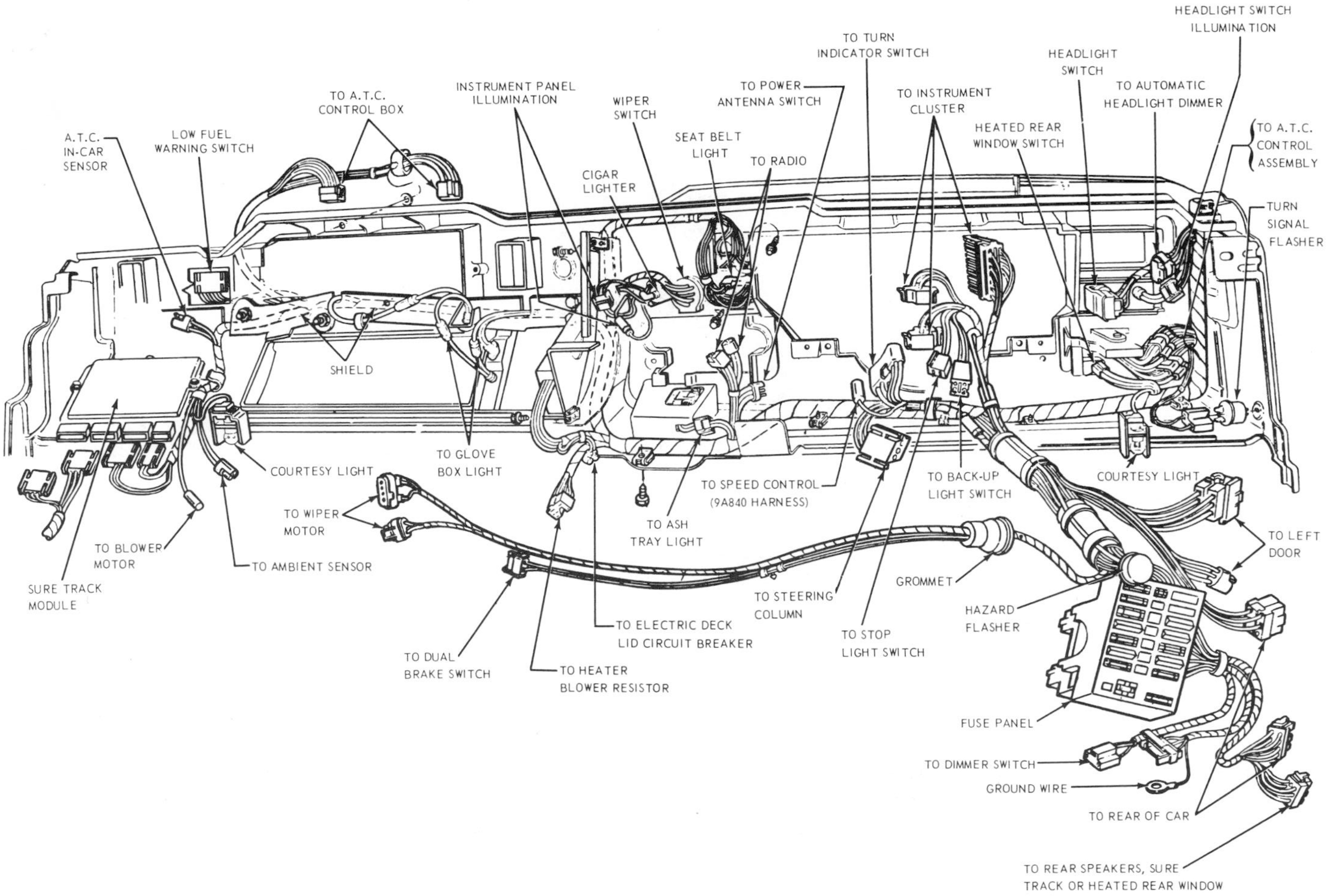

Fig. 2.58. *Courtesy of Ford Customer Service Division.*

The printed circuit features a matrix of copper foil strips that take the place of wires. The foil strips are printed on either flat insulated sheet panels, Figs. 2.60 and 2.61, or are permanently bonded between two flexible films of insulating plastic. The flexible plastic permits the circuit to be bent or shaped to conform with the instrument and control panel design (Fig. 2-63).

Fig. 2.59A.

Fig. 2.59B.

Figs. 2.60 and 2.61. Printed panel circuit for fuel gauge and indicator lights.
(Courtesy of Oldsmobile Division of General Motors Corp.)

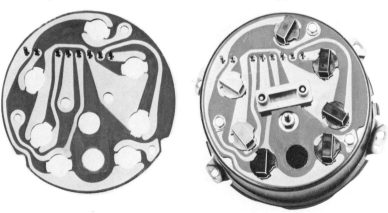

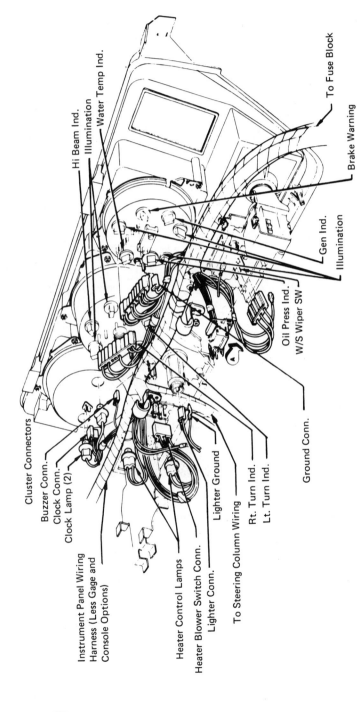

Cluster Connectors

Buzzer Conn.

Clock Conn.

Clock Lamp (2)

Instrument Panel Wiring Harness (Less Gage and Console Options)

Heater Control Lamps

Heater Blower Switch Conn.

Lighter Conn.

Lighter Ground

To Steering Column Wiring

Rt. Turn Ind.

Lt. Turn Ind.

Ground Conn.

Hi Beam Ind.

Illumination

Water Temp Ind.

To Fuse Block

Brake Warning

Gen Ind.

Illumination

Oil Press Ind.

W/S Wiper SW

Fig. 2.62. Instrument panel wiring. Notice multiple connector plug-ins for printed circuit panels. *(Courtesy of Oldsmobile Division of General Motors Corp.)*

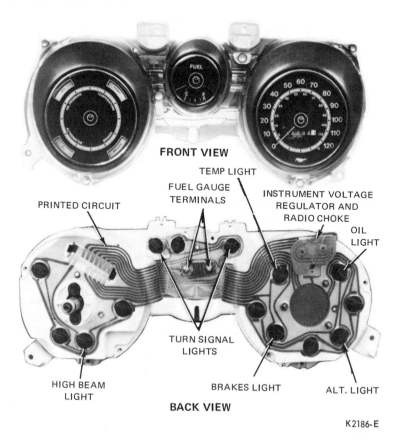

FRONT VIEW

TEMP LIGHT

FUEL GAUGE
TERMINALS

INSTRUMENT VOLTAGE
REGULATOR AND
RADIO CHOKE

PRINTED CIRCUIT

OIL
LIGHT

TURN SIGNAL
LIGHTS

HIGH BEAM
LIGHT

BRAKES LIGHT

ALT. LIGHT

BACK VIEW

K2186-E

Fig. 2.63. Flexible printed circuit. *(Courtesy of Ford Customer Service Division.)*

Review questions

1. What is meant by wire gauge *size?*
2. Which has a larger size (cross-section), 16-gauge wire or 18-gauge wire?
3. What effect does wire size (cross-section) have on circuit voltage and current?
4. What effect does wire length have on circuit voltage and current?
5. What two factors determine the proper selection of wire size?
6. What three factors must be considered when installing an add-on accessory?
7. Define primary wiring. Where is it used on the car?
8. Where do most of the primary wiring problem defects occur?

9. What two methods are used in attaching wire terminals to wire ends?

10. What two important factors must be considered when you make an electrically sound crimp terminal connection? What is another name for a crimp terminal?

11. What is the main advantage of heat-shrink tubing?

12. What feature provides added strength where terminal connections are exposed to vibration areas?

13. What type of solder should be used for electrical connections?

14. What is the importance of the second wire found on the negative battery cable?

15. What are the three methods used in field service for installing new battery cable terminals?

16. What type of terminal insulator is best to use on a crimped or soldered battery terminal replacement?

17. What are the limitations of a clamp-type battery terminal?

18. Why is it important to cut away the corroded part of the battery cable before installing a new battery terminal?

19. When a fuse link replacement requires a splice, what type of connection is used?

20. What is a wire splice? Where are splice applications used?

21. What are three methods used in field practice to permanently join wire ends?

22. What is a wire connector? Where are wire connector applications used? What is the advantage of using a wire connector?

23. Name three popular types of wire connectors.

24. What is a multiple connector?

25. What are two important design features built into a multiple connector?

26. What is meant by "an external splice at the connector"?

27. What is the purpose of a wiring harness?

28. How are wiring harness assemblies matched and joined together?

29. What is a bulkhead connector?

30. What is a printed wiring circuit?

31. Give a classic example of where printed wiring circuits are used on the automobile.

32. In what section of the car wiring is aluminum wiring utilized in G.M. vehicles?

33. What procedure is used for replacing terminal ends on aluminum wiring?

34. What is the procedure for repairing a break in aluminum wiring?

35. How are aluminum wire splices and connectors protected from corrosion?

36. When stripping the insulation from aluminum or copper wire, why is it important that the wire does not get nicked by the stripping tool?

3

The Automotive Battery

The lead-acid storage battery is an electrochemical device for converting chemical energy into electrical energy. It is not a storage tank for electricity as is often thought but, instead, stores electrical energy in chemical form.

Active materials within the battery react chemically to produce a flow of direct current whenever lights, radio, cranking motor, or other current-consuming devices are connected to the battery terminal posts. This current is produced by chemical reaction between the active material of the plates and the sulfuric acid of the electrolyte.

The battery performs three functions in the automobile:

1. It supplies electrical energy for the cranking motor and for the ignition system as the engine is started.
2. It intermittently supplies current for the lights, heater motor, radio, and other accessories when the electrical demands of these devices exceed the output of the generator.
3. It acts as a voltage stabilizer in the electrical system.

BATTERY CONSTRUCTION

The battery is constructed with a number of cells, or individual compartments. In these cells are two dissimilar materials, *lead peroxide* and *sponge lead*. Lead peroxide is the positive plate material and sponge lead is the negative plate material. These materials cannot become active until they are covered by a water solution of sulfuric acid, called an *electrolyte*.

Many positive and negative plates are put into one cell. The plates must not touch each other; they are kept apart with the use of separators, thin sheets of rubber, wood, or plastic between the positive and negative plates.

The difference in voltage between the positive plate (lead peroxide) and the negative plate (sponge lead) is 2.13 volts when a sulfuric acid solution of 1.265 specific gravity is added, and the temperature is 80 °F.

No matter how many plates are put into a cell of this type, its voltage will remain at 2.1 volts. *The type of plate material used determines the voltage. The number of plates per cell determines amperage.* The more plates per cell, the longer the battery will be able to produce electricity.

Lead peroxide and sponge lead are used in the automotive battery today because no other materials have a greater voltage difference. Other materials have been used and compared with the following results:

Lead peroxide and sponge lead	2.13 volts
Silver–zinc	1.4 volts
Nickel–cadmium	1.2 volts

Within the battery, the cells are connected in series. That is, the positive plates of one cell are connected to the negative plates of the next cell. Three cells connected in series form a 6.3-volt battery; six cells connected in series form a 12.6-volt battery.

The electrolyte of a fully charged battery usually contains about 36% sulfuric acid by weight or about 25% by volume. This corresponds to a specific gravity of 1.265 at 80 °F.

Batteries can be fully charged and yet have different values of specific gravity. The following table gives the specific gravity values for typical batteries.

Fully Charged	1.260-1.280
75% Charged	1.215-1.230
50% Charged	1.170-1.180
25% Charged	1.120-1.130
Discharged	1.070-1.080

Some types of batteries are constructed with an extra large space for water above the plates, where over three times the usual water reserve is provided. As a result of the extra water used, the specific gravity of the electrolyte at full level with the cells fully charged is 1.250.

Specific Gravity

Any discussion of the electrolyte of a storage battery automatically leads into a discussion of specific gravity. The specific gravity of the electrolyte is a measure of its sulfuric acid content. If we were to put exactly one pint of water on one side of a simple balance scale, and exactly one pint of electrolyte on the other side, the scale would go down on the electrolyte side, indicating that the electrolyte is heavier. Water has arbitrarily been assigned a value of 1.000; therefore, all other liquids are heavier or lighter than water. Pure sulfuric acid has a specific gravity of 1.835 (spoken as eighteen thirty-five). Commercial electrolyte prepared by the industry for resale in servicing batteries usually has a specific gravity of 1.400 (fourteen hundred). This must be diluted with water that is free from mineral content in order to get a specific gravity of 1.265 (twelve sixty-five), which is the recommended specific gravity for many 12-volt batteries used in today's vehicles. This simply means that the electrolyte is 1.26 times as heavy as the water.

Most manufacturers have reduced the specific gravity of the electrolyte required in their batteries of standard construction from 1.280 to 1.260 to somewhat increase the life of the battery. This has the effect of reducing the initial capacity of the battery, since the capacity of the battery depends upon the amount of acid in the electrolyte.

Diluting pure sulfuric acid (specific gravity 1.835) is not recommended. *Correct electrolyte mix is available at an automotive parts store.* However, in an emergency, *always pour the acid into the water slowly.* The following chart will give you the approximate parts of water to which must be added one part of 1.835 acid.

Specific Gravity	Parts of Water by Volume
1.100	9.8
1.200	4.3
1.250	3.3
1.300	2.5
1.400	1.6

Warning: Concentrated acid of 1.835 specific gravity must be handled with great care. It is advisable to wear goggles, rubber gloves, and a protective apron. If acid is spattered into eyes, wash it out at once with plenty of clean water, and seek medical aid if discomfort continues.

BATTERY CAPACITY RATINGS

Battery capacity is determined by four factors:

1. Weight of positive material.
2. Weight of negative material.
3. Weight of sulfuric acid in the electrolyte.
4. Area of the plate.

Ampere-Hour Rating

This rating indicates the electrical size or reverse capacity of the battery, and basically gives an indication of the amount of lead in a battery. The ampere-hour rating is determined by a very low discharge rate over a long period of time and is a carry-over from days when the only electrical load on a vehicle consisted of lights. The fully charged battery is brought to a temperature of 80 °F and is discharged at a rate equal to one-twentieth of the published 20-hour capacity in ampere hours. For example, a 12-volt battery rated by a manufacturer at 50 A.H. capacity would be discharged at 1/20 of 50 or 2.5 amps until the terminal voltage falls to 10.50 volts. The number of hours required for the discharge, multiplied by the ampere rate of discharge, is the ampere hour capacity.

Watt Rating

Some battery manufacturers rate their batteries in watts. Most people are familiar with the term *watt*, even though they may not know exactly what it means. They have seen and heard it used in relation to light bulbs, toasters, motors, heaters, and other electrical appliances. They also know that watts means power. The higher the wattage rating the more light, heat, etc.

The term *watt* is the unit of measurement of electrical power and is the electrical equivalent of horsepower.

$$watt = volts \times amps$$
$$746 \ watts = 1 \ horsepower$$

The cranking motor converts the electrical power (watts)

supplied by the battery to mechanical power (horsepower) to crank the engine. Under extremely cold or hot conditions, the power required to crank an engine is much higher than at room temperature. Cranking a 6-cylinder engine at 80°F requires approximately 1,500 watts, while cranking a big V-8 requires approximately 2,300 watts. Cranking the same engines under extreme cold or hot conditions may require anywhere from 1,900 watts on the small engine to 2,500 watts or more on the large engine. The more watts available, the better the cranking will be.

Trying to determine the watt rating of a battery in the field is not practical. The wattage a battery is capable of delivering varies with temperature, load, and battery state of charge; it decreases as the temperature drops. This is the reason the battery is rated at 0°F.

Reserve Capacity Rating

Another and more recent method of rating batteries has been accepted by the Society of Automotive Engineers (S.A.E.) and the Battery Council International (B.C.I.). The new rating system clearly defines a battery's ability to provide a given amount of usable cranking power.

The ampere-hour rating is now being replaced by the *reserve-capacity rating*. The reserve-capacity rating is the amount of time that a battery can deliver 25 amperes and maintain a terminal voltage of 10.2 volts at 80°F. The purpose of this rating is to define for the user the length of time the vehicle may be driven after the charging system fails. The *cold cranking rating* is the current a battery can deliver for 30 seconds at 0°F and maintain a terminal voltage of no less than 7.2 volts. The rating is given in amperes at 0°F.

The following chart may be helpful in converting ampere hours to reserve capacity rating.

Ampere Hours	Reserve Capacity
40-41-43	59 min.
70	116 min.
78	130 min.
90-91	160 min.
95-96	180 min.
155	290 min.
172	360 min.
204	430 min.

BATTERY TESTING

There are a number of ways to test a battery and no one test is conclusive. A battery should always be tested at least two ways to give a good indication of the condition of the battery. The two most widely used tests are the specific gravity test and the high-rate discharge test.

Specific Gravity Test

This test is made using a hydrometer, Fig. 3-1, and it measures the state of charge of the battery. A fully charged battery will have a specific gravity reading of 1.260 to 1.280. When the battery is fully charged the float of the hydrometer will float high because most of the acid is in the water and the solution is dense (Fig. 3-2). When the battery is discharged, the float will hardly float, because most of the acid is in the plates and the solution is less dense (Fig. 3-3). All the cells in the battery should have the same specific gravity measurement. If the specific gravity reading in one cell differs by 50 points from the reading in any other cell, the battery is defective and should be replaced. Some manuals still mention 25 points difference between cells, but this test is only 65 per cent effective. Some batteries with 25 points difference between cells have been found to

Fig. 3.1.

Fig. 3.2.

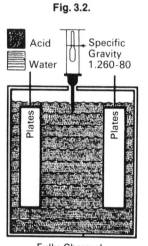

Acid
Water
Specific Gravity 1.260-80

Fully Charged
Acid in Water Gives Electrolyte Specific Gravity of 1.270.

Fig. 3.3.

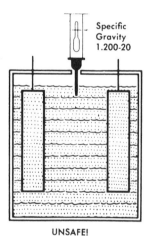

Specific Gravity 1.200-20

UNSAFE!
Battery half discharged. More acid in plates, less in electrolyte. Starting failure in sight if battery is allowed to remain in car.

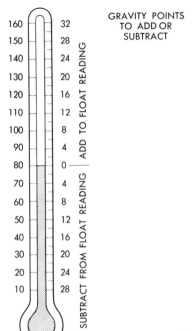

TEMPERATURE °F.

GRAVITY POINTS
TO ADD OR
SUBTRACT

Fig. 3.4. *Courtesy of the Chrysler Corporation.*

be in good operating condition; batteries with 50 points difference between cells are found to be of little use.

Temperature conditions are important in determining the actual specific gravity reading. Let us compare electrolyte with engine oil. Engine oil is thick when cold and thin when hot; the same thing happens to electrolyte. The colder the electrolyte, the thicker the solution and the higher the bulb in the hydrometer will float, to give a false reading. The standard temperature used is 80°F. At 80°F nothing is added or subtracted from the reading. Every 10°F below 80°F, subtract 4 points from your reading. Every 10°F above 80°F, add 4 points to the reading; see Fig. 3-4.

A battery with a low specific gravity reading should be tested to find out why the battery is low. These questions should be answered:

1. Does it pass the specific gravity tests? Not over 50 points difference between cells?
2. What is the state of charge?
3. Is the battery clean?
4. Is there a drain on the battery?
5. Is the electrolyte at the correct level?
6. Does it pass the high-rate discharge test?

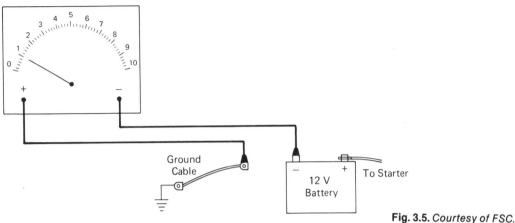

Fig. 3.5. *Courtesy of FSC.*

7. Does it pass the three-minute sulfation test?

8. Does it pass the cadmium-tip test?

A battery with a low specific gravity reading should be checked to see if there is a drain on the battery (Fig. 3-5).

Testing for Battery Drain*

The best way to check for battery leakage current is to connect an ammeter capable of reading in tenths of an ampere (0.1 ampere) in series with the negative battery cable.

If a low-reading ammeter is not available, disconnect the positive cable from the battery. Connect a 12-volt test light with a one candle-power or smaller bulb. The ash tray bulb #1445 can be used between the cable and the battery terminal. If the lamp does not light, there is not enough current drain to be concerned with. If the lamp lights, make certain that the clock is wound by tapping the cable against the battery terminal. If the lamp is still lit, the cause of the drain should be located and corrected.

This method of checking has replaced the old system of connecting a voltmeter in series with the negative battery cable. Late-model cars equipped with diodes and transistors in generators, seat belt warning systems, and pulse wipers have made that check ineffective. It is not unusual for a voltmeter connected in that manner to read over 6, or even 12 volts, without a defect in the system.

In using the proper check for battery leakage, keep in mind that a discharge of one ampere would require 63 hours to discharge a 63

* AC-Delco Marketing News, June 1975, Page 23.

ampere-hour battery. A discharge current of 0.1 ampere would require 630 hours or 27 days to completely discharge. A reading of less than 0.5 ampere is considered negligible.

Battery Capacity Test or High-Rate Discharge Test

The capacity of a battery is the battery's ability to furnish current and maintain a minimum necessary voltage.

> *Caution:* If the specific gravity reading is less than 1.220, the battery capacity test should not be made. The battery state of charge is too low for accurate testing.

This test requires a test instrument, called a Battery Starter Tester, that will measure up to 300-500 amps (Fig. 3-6). The heavy ammeter leads are connected across the battery, positive to positive and negative to negative. A voltmeter is connected in the same manner.

1. Turn the control knob clockwise until the ammeter reading is exactly three times the ampere-hour rating—e.g., 180 amperes for a 60 A.H. battery.

Fig. 3.6.

Fig. 3.7.

2. Maintain the load for 15 seconds, note the voltage reading, and then turn the control knob back to off position.

3. If the voltmeter reading was 9.6 volts or higher, the battery has good output capacity.

Another way to make the high-rate discharge test is to connect a voltmeter across the battery, positive to positive and negative to negative (Fig. 3-7). Disable the ignition so that the engine will not start. Crank the engine for 15 seconds while watching the voltmeter. The voltmeter should maintain a reading of 9.6 volts or higher.

Caution: Tight engines or bad starters can reduce the voltage to less than 9.6 volts.

If the tests indicate that the battery is good and if it is fully charged, but it fails to maintain 9.6 volts while cranking the engine, then the battery probably is undersize for the job it has to do.

Three-Minute Charge Test

The three-minute charge test is a good way to determine if the battery is sulfated. A sulfated battery will not accept a charge due to the hard sulfation covering the battery plates, and the battery capacity will be limited.

To perform the three-minute charge test:

1. Charge a 12-volt battery at no more than 40 amps for three minutes.
2. Connect a voltmeter across the battery, positive to positive and negative to negative.
3. If the voltmeter climbs to above 15.5 volts by the end of the three-minute period, the battery is not accepting the charge and should be replaced.

Warning: If the battery has passed the high-rate discharge test and the specific gravity test, this test should not be made.

If a battery is fully charged and a three-minute charge test is made, the voltage will climb above 15.5 volts because the battery is already charged. This voltage reading may lead to a faulty diagnosis of a good battery.

Remember that:

1. A sulfated battery will resist a charge.
2. A fully charged battery will resist a charge.

Cadmium Probe Test

This test is designed for individual cell voltage checks for both hard-top and soft-top batteries.

1. Connect fast battery charger to battery and adjust charging rate as close as possible to 40 amps.
2. Set voltmeter to 0–4 volt range.
3. Connect cadmium probes to voltmeter leads.
4. Place positive prod on positive terminal post and negative probe in cell #1. Record the exact reading. This cell may read higher or lower than the other cells.
5. Place positive probe in cell #1 and negative probe in cell #2. Record exact reading.
6. Repeat this procedure in the rest of the cells.
7. Place the positive probe in cell #6 and the negative prod on the negative terminal post.
   (a) If the voltmeter reads above zero, add this reading to cell #1 to obtain the correct voltage for cell #1.

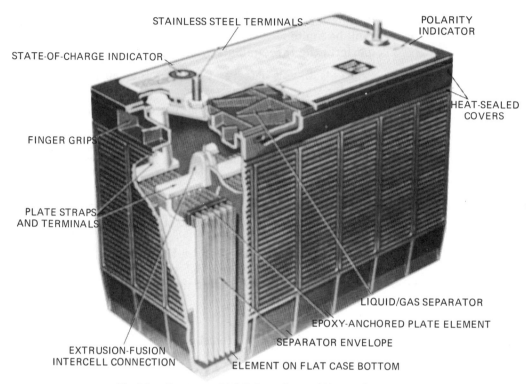

STAINLESS STEEL TERMINALS

POLARITY INDICATOR

STATE-OF-CHARGE INDICATOR

HEAT-SEALED COVERS

FINGER GRIPS

PLATE STRAPS AND TERMINALS

LIQUID/GAS SEPARATOR

EPOXY-ANCHORED PLATE ELEMENT

SEPARATOR ENVELOPE

EXTRUSION-FUSION INTERCELL CONNECTION

ELEMENT ON FLAT CASE BOTTOM

Fig. 3.8.   *Courtesy of AC-Delco—General Motors Corp.*

(b) If the voltmeter reads below zero, reverse the probes and repeat this step. Then subtract the reading from step 1 to obtain the correct voltage for cell #1.

If there is a variance of more than 0.1 volt between individual cell voltages, the battery should be replaced.

SEALED BATTERY

The Delco Remy 1200 sealed battery never requires additional water and it prevents acid corrosion of terminals and cables (Fig. 3-8). By eliminating antimony from the plates, the Delco 1200 reduces overcharge and gassing, both of which cause water and a small amount of acid to be lost from the battery. As a result, the battery can be sealed against water or foreign material entry. The small pressure-relief vent in the case relieves internal pressure build-up. A built-in "state-of-charge" indicator and threaded stainless steel terminals help prolong battery life. Freedom from servicing allows the battery to be mounted in out-of-the-way locations.

TESTING THE MAINTENANCE-FREE BATTERY

Step 1 *Visual Inspection* Check for obvious damage, such as a cracked or broken case or cover that could permit loss of electrolyte. If obvious physical damage is noted, replace battery. Determine cause of damage and correct as needed.

Step 2 *Charge Indicator*
a. Green dot visible (Fig. 3)

If the charge indicator is dark and has a green dot in the center, the battery is sufficiently charged for testing. Proceed to Step 3.

b. Dark—green dot not visible (Fig. 4)

If the charge indicator is dark and the green dot is not visible, charge battery until green dot appears, but not more than 60 ampere-hours—(for example—15 amperes for four hours). Proceed to Step 3. NOTE: Some chargers are constant current chargers, but if a constant voltage charger is used, to get the green dot to appear after prolonged charging may require tipping the battery slightly from side to side a few times.

NOTE: A battery that required charging for testing may indicate a need for checking the charging system of the vehicle.

c. Light (Fig. 5)

If the charge indicator is light and a cranking complaint has been experienced, replace battery. (DO NOT attempt charging or testing when indicator is light.)

NOTE: A battery that failed prematurely, and exhibited a light indicator condition may indicate a need for checking the charging system of the vehicle.

Step 3 *Remove Surface Charge* Connect 300 ampere load across terminals for 15 seconds to remove surface charge from battery.

Step 4 *Load Test*
a). Connect voltmeter and 230 ampere load across terminals.
b). Read voltage after 15 seconds with load connected, then disconnect load.
c). If minimum voltage is 9.6* or more, battery is good.

d). If minimum voltage is less than 9.6*, replace battery. *This voltage is to be used for battery ambient temperatures of 70°F and above. For temperatures below 70°F, use the following:

	70°F & Above	60°F	50°F	40°F	30°F	20°F	10°F	0°F
Minimum Voltage	9.6	9.5	9.4	9.3	9.1	8.9	8.7	8.5

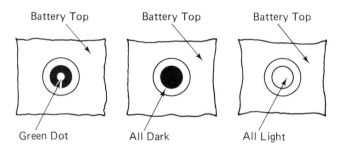

Battery Top   Battery Top   Battery Top

Green Dot   All Dark   All Light

JUMP STARTING IN CASE OF EMERGENCY WITH AUXILIARY (BOOSTER) BATTERY

Both booster and discharged battery should be treated carefully when using jumper cables. Follow exactly the procedure outlined below, being careful not to cause sparks.

1. Set parking brake and place automatic transmission in "PARK" (neutral for manual transmission). Turn off lights, heater and other electrical loads. Observe charge indicator. If indicator is light, replace battery. DO NOT attempt jump starting when indicator is light. If charge indicator is dark and has a green dot in the center, failure to start is not due to a discharged battery and the cranking system should be checked. If charge indicator is dark but green dot does not appear in center, proceed as follows:

Negative ground only

2. Attach one end of one jumper cable to the positive terminal of the booster battery and the other end of same cable to positive terminal of discharged battery. DO NOT PERMIT vehicles to touch each other as this could establish a ground connection and counteract the benefits of this procedure.

3. Attach one end of the remaining negative cable to the negative terminal of the booster battery, and the other end to a ground at least 12 inches from the battery of the vehicle being started. (DO NOT CONNECT DIRECTLY TO THE NEGATIVE POST OF THE DEAD BATTERY.)

Positive Ground Only

4. Attach one end of one jumper cable to the negative terminal of the booster battery and the other end of the same cable to negative terminal of discharged battery. DO NOT PERMIT vehicles to touch each other, as this could establish a ground connection and counteract the benefits of this procedure.

5. Attach one end of the remaining positive cable to the positive terminal of the booster battery and the other end to a ground at least 12 inches from the battery of the vehicle being started. (DO NOT CONNECT DIRECTLY TO THE POSITIVE POST OF THE DEAD BATTERY.)

Negative Ground and Positive Ground

6. Take care that the clamps from one cable do not inadvertently touch the clamps on the other cable. Do not lean over the battery when making connections. The ground connection must provide good electrical conductivity and current carrying capacity. Avoid moving, hot or electrical hazards such as fans, manifolds and spark plug terminals.

7. Reverse this sequence exactly when removing the jumper cables.

CAUTION: Any procedure other than the above could result in: 1) personal injury caused by electrolyte squirting out the battery vent, 2) personal injury or property damage due to battery explosion, 3) damage to the charging system of the booster vehicle or of the immobilized vehicle.

HEAT SHIELD

The under-hood temperatures of modern automobiles are so high that a heat shield is required (Fig. 3-9). An insulated plastic heat-reduction shield will prolong the life of the battery. The heat shield can reduce temperature rise up to 37 per cent with the engine idling. Openings at top permit attachment and service access.

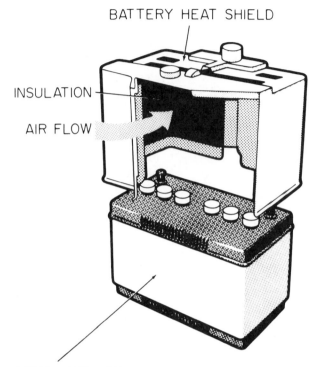

BATTERY HEAT SHIELD

INSULATION

AIR FLOW

Fig. 3.9.   LONG LIFE LOW MAINTENANCE BATTERY

SERVICING THE BATTERY IN THE CAR

Good battery servicing should include the following:

1. Provide protective fender cover for car finish.
2. Clean battery top. Wipe with a cloth wetted with ammonia or baking soda in water.
3. Inspect cables—replace if unserviceable.
4. Inspect the terminal parts to see if they are deformed or broken.
5. Clean the battery terminal post and the inside surface of the terminal clamps.
6. Inspect cable and adjust hold downs.
7. Make a hydrometer test.
8. Add water to bring the electrolyte to proper level. Do not overfill.

To check for current leakage across the top of the battery, connect the negative lead of the voltmeter to the negative terminal of

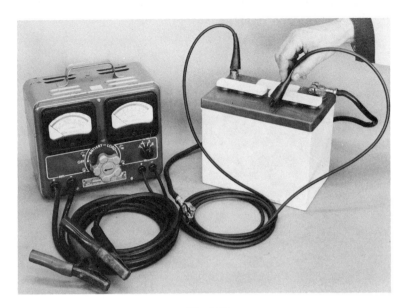

Fig. 3.10.

the battery and move the positive lead of the voltmeter across the top of the battery case (Fig. 3-10). Any voltmeter reading indicates a small leakage. The battery should be cleaned to remove the leakage.

Cleaning the Battery

To prevent battery self-discharge, clean the battery top periodically to remove moisture, grime, and dust. Tighten the vent plugs and wipe the battery top with a rag or brush dampened with ammonia solution or bicarbonate of soda solution. Be careful not to get any soda solution

Fig. 3.11.   Fig. 3.12. *Courtesy of Champion Spark Plug Co.*

Fig. 3.13.

in the battery, as it will tend to neutralize the electrolyte. When the foaming has stopped, flush with clear water.

A special wire brush tool should be used to clean the battery terminals and cables (Figs. 3-11 and 3-12).

The authors also like to use Type A transmission fluid for cleaning batteries. A small amount of transmission fluid placed on a rag and rubbed all over the battery will not only make it look like new but also will remove the surface discharge. (See Fig. 3-13.) Very little fluid is needed for this job and all excess fluid should be wiped off.

Inspecting and Cleaning Cables and Terminals

The battery cables conduct current from the battery to the various automotive circuits. Inspecting the battery cables is relatively simple, but it is just as important as determining the condition of the battery. Corrosion is visible in the form of a white powder around the battery cable and battery terminal.

Fig. 3.14.

Caution: Before servicing any type of battery cable, always disconnect the battery ground cable at the battery post. This will insure against short circuiting. By disconnecting the ground cable at the battery post, the ground circuit is positively "opened."

Poor electrical connections cause many service problems, especially in the starting and charging circuit cables and wiring. The biggest culprit is corrosion between the battery cable terminal and the battery post, where hard scaly corrosion may have formed between the post and cable. This creates a point of high resistance, eventually disabling the cranking, lighting, and accessories operation (Fig. 3-14).

At every tune-up, or when checking out any electrical problem,

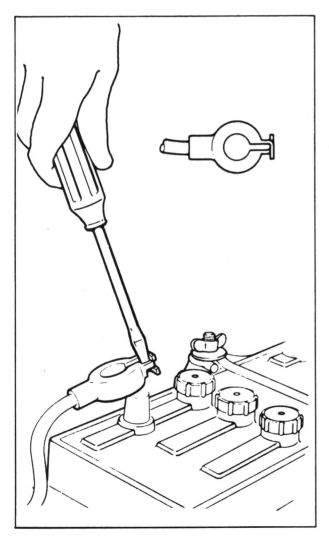

Fig. 3.15. *Courtesy of Champion Spark Plug Co.*

remove the cables and clean cables and posts. Even if they appear clean, you will probably find a buildup of corrosion between the cables and posts. Remove this corrosion, attach the cables, and tighten them securely.

Two different types of battery cables are used. The spring type (Fig. 3-15) can be removed with a screw driver. The bolt-type cable (Fig. 3-16) can be removed with a special tool after the battery bolt and nut have been loosened.

Other notable areas of trouble can be starter and solenoid cables. Shine up the ends of these parts with sandpaper and remove paint or grease where the cables are attached. Reassemble with a shakeproof-type lock washer which will bite into the cable and make a good permanent connection. Remember, physically tight isn't always electrically tight.

On side-terminal batteries (Fig. 3-17), the cable and battery terminals need the same careful preventive maintenance attention as on the post-type batteries. A special brush is available to clean the corrosion on these terminals.

Since the terminals are bolted in place rather than clamped (Fig.

Fig. 3.16.

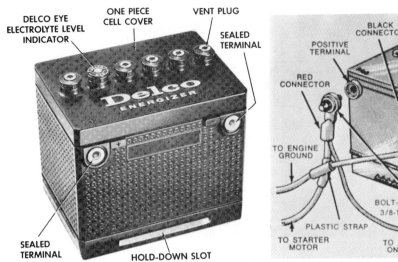

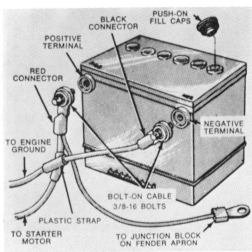

Fig. 3.17. *Courtesy of AC-Delco—General Motors Corp.*

Fig. 3.18. *Courtesy of AC-Delco—General Motors Corp.*

3-18), there are some service requirements that need attention. For example, should the cable bolt terminal get lost or severely corroded, the practice is to replace the cable. The bolts are a specific length and a longer bolt may ruin the battery!

Equally important is the care that must be taken when threading the cable terminal bolt into the battery. To avoid cross-threading or stripped threads, start the bolt into the battery terminal with the fingers before using a wrench. The final specified torque on the bolt is 60–100 in.-lbs.

Note: When replacing any battery clamping bracket, tighten to 20 in.-lb. Additional tightening beyond this recommendation may result in battery distortion.

CHARGING THE BATTERY

There are two basic methods of recharging a battery. One is the slow charge method and the other is the fast charge method.

Before recharging any battery, the cells should be checked and water added if necessary to bring the electrolyte to the proper level. Periodically during the charging process the temperature of the electrolyte should be measured; the electrolyte should never exceed 125°F. If the temperature increases over 125°F, the battery plates may warp and crack. This action could puncture the separator and let

Fig. 3.19.

the positive and negative plates touch, to cause a shorted cell. If the temperature reaches 125°F, decrease or stop the charging rate.

The slow-charge rate should be 7 per cent of the amp-hour rating. A 60 ampere-hour battery would require 4.2 amps of charge. A slow-charge rate of 5 amps for passenger-car batteries is normal. Charging periods of 24 hours or more may be needed to bring the battery to a fully charged condition. The battery is fully charged when the specific gravity does not change for *two* one-hour checks.

The fast-charge method supplies the battery with a high

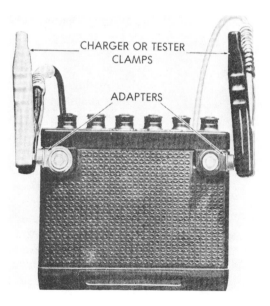

Fig. 3.20.

CHARGER OR TESTER CLAMPS

ADAPTERS

charging rate for a short period of time. Charging rates of 40-60 amps are common for one hour. The high-rate charge can continue until the electrolyte temperature reaches 125°F (use the hydrometer thermometer). Because of the short charging period, the plates are not fully converted to lead peroxide and spongy lead. *This means the battery cannot be fully charged by the fast-charge method.*

If it is necessary to recharge the side-terminal battery or to clean the terminals, unscrew the bolts in the terminal cables. Clean any corrosion products from the face of the terminal on the battery and cables with a wire brush. Install battery charging adapters into the battery terminals (Figs. 3-19 and 3-20). This will give a good electrical connection for the battery charger.

It is very important when charging the battery or jumping the batteries to connect positive to positive and negative to negative to avoid damage to the electrical system.

JUMP STARTING WITH AN AUXILIARY (BOOSTER) BATTERY

Warning: Never expose battery to open flame or electric spark. Battery action generates hydrogen gas, which is flammable and explosive. Don't allow battery fluid to contact skin, eyes, fabrics, or painted surfaces—fluid is a sulfuric acid solution which could cause serious personal injury or property damage. Wear eye protection when working with battery.

The procedures involved in jump starting (Fig. 3-21) are considered important enough to bear repetition here. The need for caution cannot be overemphasized.

1. Set parking brake and place transmission in PARK (neutral with manual transmission). Turn off lights, heater, and other electrical loads.

2. Remove vent caps from both the booster battery and the discharged battery. Lay a cloth over the open vent wells of each battery. These two actions help reduce the explosion hazard always present in either battery when connecting "live" booster batteries to "dead" batteries.

3. Attach one end of jumper cable to the positive terminal of the booster battery (identified by a red color, "+" or "P" on the battery case, post, or clamp) and the other end of same cable to the positive terminal of the discharged battery. Do NOT permit cars to touch each other, as this could establish a ground connection and counteract the benefits of this procedure.

4. Attach one end of the remaining negative cable to the

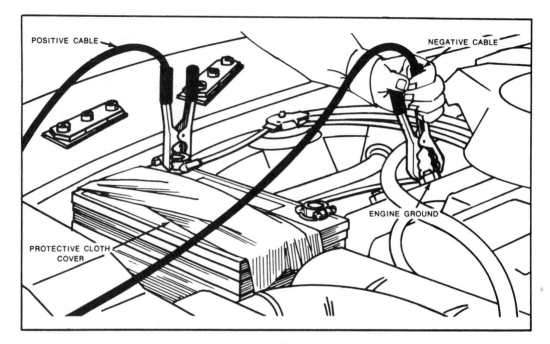

POSITIVE CABLE

NEGATIVE CABLE

ENGINE GROUND

PROTECTIVE CLOTH
COVER

Fig. 3.21. *Courtesy of Ford Motor Corp.*

negative terminal (black color, "—" or "N") of the booster battery and the other end to the negative cable attachment at front of engine of the vehicle (do not connect directly to negative post of dead battery), taking care that clamps from one cable do not inadvertently touch the clamps on the other cable. Do not lean over the battery when making this connection.

Reverse this sequence exactly when removing the jumper cables. Reinstall vent caps and throw away cloths as the cloths may have corrosive acid on them.

Warning: Any procedure other than the above could result in: (1) personal injury caused by electrolyte squirting out of the battery vents, (2) personal injury or property damage due to battery explosion, (3) damage to the charging system or any electronic system of the booster vehicle or of the immobilized vehicle.

To conclude the discussion on batteries, a reprint of an article from *The Battery Man*, November, 1973, summarizes some of the important points stressed in this chapter. Keep in mind that a run down battery affects all of the car's electrical systems.

BATTERY TESTING AND SERVICE

THE BATTERY AND DEPENDABLE CAR PERFORMANCE: A familiar sight today is an auto service truck parked alongside a late model car with the serviceman connecting jumper cables to the car's battery. This is the sign of a "no start" trouble call, which in most cases is a sign of a neglected battery's revenge.

There is one factor that should not be overlooked. With the long-lasting chassis lubrication that is now common, there is much less inspection of under the chassis and the hood. One result is that the battery is less often observed by someone who presumably knows something about batteries. Batteries that need water, have corroded connections, cables in bad shape, racked or broken hold-down frames, etc., are neglected and do not receive the attention that would help keep them in reasonably good condition.

When the service call comes in, the complaint frequently runs something like this, "I tried the starter that it won't turn the engine over," or "The starter just barely turns it over," or "I think the battery is dead." The usual cause of such complaints points directly to a neglected battery. For example:

1. The starter will not crank the engine. This can be caused by a run-down battery, a faulty battery, corroded or faulty battery cables or terminals. Every man in the service business knows that it takes only a very thin layer of corrosion on a battery terminal or inside the cable terminal to keep the current from flowing freely enough to turn over a cranking motor.

2. The starter cranks the engine slowly, but the engine will not start. The battery-related faults just mentioned are often the cause of this complaint. This could also indicate the need for a good tune-up. The combination of a weak cranking circuit and an engine in need of a tune-up can mean trouble for a car owner.

3. Battery is dead (completely discharged). Common causes of this complaint are electrical drains on the battery such as a short circuit, dirty battery case, low electrolyte, a weak cell in the battery, a faulty charging system or inner car lights not shutting off.

Inadequate battery maintenance will eventually lead to "Starting complaints." The heaviest load that the battery has to carry, even under normal starting conditions, is the "starting load." Consequently, hard starting is the first indication that a battery is faulty or run-down.

The average car owner knows very little about a storage battery, much less the care it needs. Therefore, there are more batteries in poor condition than there are in clean, well-kept condition. This gives service men an opportunity to sell needed services and products by simply checking batteries and starting systems whenever they look under the hood.

Two conditions place an extra burden on the battery when cranking the engine. The first is cranking a high compression engine when hot. This requires more current for the starter to crank the engine. The second is cold weather. Near zero temperature reduces the battery's current-producing ability by as much as 60 per cent. Under these two conditions, a faulty or run-down battery will fail to do its job.

Battery maintenance should never be overlooked, because a car is only as dependable as its battery. A car which cannot be started is useless as a means of transportation, therefore, dependability on the part of the battery is extremely valuable and important. Car owners should always be told what a battery needs to keep it in good condition.

Adequate battery service requires a mechanic to ask these questions: (1) Is the battery clean?; (2) Is the electrolyte at the correct level?; (3) Does a load capacity test show that the battery is capable of supplying the current required to crank the engine without losing its charge?; (4) Does a sulphation three minute charge test show that the battery will accept a charge?; (5) Does the specific gravity of the electrolyte show that the battery is charged?; (6) Does a cell voltage test (with battery under charge) show that the battery is free of any weak or defective cells?

ORGANIZED BATTERY SERVICE: An organized battery service program will save time in pinpointing battery related service problems. Repeated success in solving such problems will strengthen your customer's confidence in you. Such a program will include the battery tests suggested here. Testing is the only way to determine the true condition of a battery.

Battery Capacity Test: The battery capacity test (heavy load test) is a quick service area test. It shows whether or not a battery is capable of providing cranking motor current and voltage. It is designed around the requirements for cranking an engine. The power required to crank an engine is the result of amperage (current), voltage and enough cranking time to start the engine. The amount of current a battery is able to put out is directly related to its ampere-hour rating.

In this test, a good battery will produce a current in amperes, equal to 3 times its ampere-hour rating and still maintain a current with a voltage of over 9.6 volts for a period of 15 seconds. For example; a 70 ampere-hour battery should put out 210 amperes for the full time of 15 seconds with voltage above 9.6 volts. The battery may be loaded by means of a carbon plate rheostat.

The rating in ampere hours for batteries is being discontinued and batteries are rated more commonly by "Cold Cranking Power, Amperes for 30 seconds at zero degrees F" and "Reserve Capacity, Minutes of 25 amperes at 80 degrees F." For the purpose of making the capacity test, you can assume 85 ampere hours for larger cars and 75 AH for smaller cars. Three times these values for 15 seconds (in amperes) will give a reasonable capacity test.

To determine whether or not a battery that fails the Battery Capacity Test is serviceable, it should be tested for sulphation.

Three-Minute Charge Test: (To be performed only if previous test fails.) The Three Minute Charge Test is designed around the fact that one of the marks of a sulphated battery is that it won't accept a charge. A battery becomes sulphated from being less than fully charged over an extended period. This will cause the battery to fail the Capacity Test. The Three Minute Charge Test will pinpoint a battery that failed the Capacity Test because of sulphation.

The Three-Minute Charge Test consists of charging a 12-volt battery for three minutes at a rate of no more than 40 amperes. If the battery's voltage climbs above 15.5 volts by the end of the 3 minute period, it is not accepting the charge and should be replaced. *Again, it is important to remember:* This test is not necessary and should not be performed if the battery passes the Capacity Test described previously. It could lead to unnecessary condemnation of serviceable batteries.

A battery that failed the Battery Capacity Test but passed the Three-Minute Charge Test should be charged before being returned to service. During the charging, the internal electrical condition should be checked by a cell voltage test. Before the advent of the sealed battery top, cemented in place and leaving the cells inaccessible for external cell voltage tests, it was a simple matter to check the cell voltage by a properly calibrated voltmeter. Now, however, the sealed battery covers only permit checking the cell voltage by means of the cadmium stick which gives the individual voltages of each positive group of plates and each negative. The negative and positive readings are added algebraically to get the cell voltage.

Cell Voltage Test: Faulty conditions such as a bad cell connection can cause a battery to fail repeatedly. A cell voltage charge test will detect such a condition. This test consists of taking the cell voltage readings with the cadmium tipped cell probes while the battery is being fast-charged at a rate of not over 40 amperes. If the cell voltage readings show a variation of more than 0.1 volt the battery has a non-repairable fault and should be replaced.

A battery that failed the Battery Capacity Test but *has passed both the Three-Minute Charge Test and Cell Voltage Test* can be returned to service after being given a suitable charge with specific gravity being brought up to 1.250 or better.

BATTERY FAILURES: A vehicle that is not properly tuned may place an unreasonable load on the battery due to difficult starting. A worn cranking motor, crankcase oil of wrong viscosity, hot engine drag, etc., may make starting slow with more cranking load than normal, and batteries with some defects, including possible low state of charge, will not deliver the required service.

It is well to repeat our often stated principle that the only dependable and efficient battery is a well charged battery. This leads to the conclusion that to have a well charged battery we must begin with a battery that is in reasonably good condition to take a charge and deliver ample cranking current at the correct voltage.

Review questions

1. Each cell of a 12-volt battery is connected in _____.

2. Battery capacity is determined by _____.

3. If the specific gravity reading of the battery cells differ by over 50 points, the battery should be _____.

4. The specific gravity of a battery is 1.225, and the temperature of the electrolyte is 30°F. What is the true specific gravity reading?

5. The battery capacity test is made by discharging the battery_____

6. The three-minute charge test will determine if a 12-volt battery is sulfated. How is this test made?

7. When you charge a battery, the temperature of the electrolyte should not exceed _____.

8. The battery capacity test should not be made if the specific gravity is less than _____.

9. When slow-charging a battery, the battery is considered fully charged when _____.

10. To remove the surface charge from a maintenance-free battery, connect a _____ ampere load across the terminals for _____ seconds.

11. If the charge indicator on a maintenance-free battery is light, the battery should be _____.

12. If the charge indicator is dark, but has a green dot in the center, the battery is _____.
13. The battery capacity test, on a maintenance-free battery, is made at _____ amps.
14. What are the two basic methods used when charging a battery?
15. The largest load the battery has to carry is called the _____ load.

4

Electrical Power Distribution and Circuit Protection

Automotive electrical circuits can be divided into several major categories. They are defined as:

1. The starting circuit.
2. The ignition circuit.
3. The charging circuit.
4. The chassis lighting and accessory circuits.

The battery and the charging system supply the source of power or hot feed to all the other major electrical circuits, which are the power users. This relationship is illustrated in Fig. 4-1.

All the major circuits that use power are interrelated, because they must tap into the power supply of the battery and charging system. If the performance of the battery and/or the charging system is below standard, then the electrical power users will suffer in their performance. Figure 4-2 shows a basic pictorial wiring diagram typical of the circuitry tie-ins and power distribution used in modern passenger cars. Keep in mind that the wiring diagram is shown in brief form and that variations will be found in different car makes and models. Only the external wire connections are shown, not details of the various circuit components.

Carefully note how the lighting and various accessory circuits pick up their power feed in Fig. 4-2. The headlight switch and the fuse panel take a direct power feed. The exterior and interior lighting of the car—e.g., the hazard warning, stoplight, taillight, and courtesy

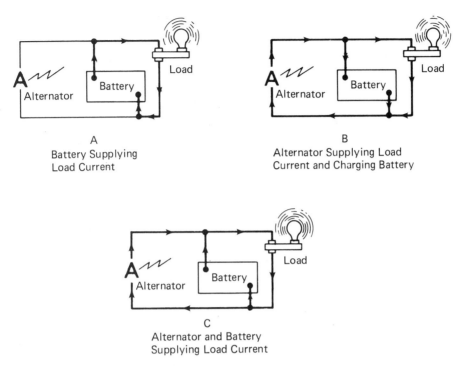

A
Battery Supplying
Load Current

B
Alternator Supplying Load
Current and Charging Battery

C
Alternator and Battery
Supplying Load Current

Fig. 4.1. The battery and the charging circuit.

light circuits—get direct power feed from the fuse panel. These circuits and the headlight circuit will have available power at all times.

To handle accessory circuits and some of the car lighting, the fuse panel gets a second pick-up of power from the ignition switch accessory terminal or terminals. Typical circuits that use this power route are the directional and back-up lights, heater blower, windshield wipers, power accessories, radio, cruise control, etc. These circuits will have available power only when the ignition switch is either in the accessory or ignition "on" position.

FUSE PANEL

A *fuse panel* or *fuse block* is a housing that distributes electrical power to the various lighting and accessory circuits. This distribution is provided with circuit protection against electrical shorts by fuses and circuit breakers located and housed in the front side of the fuse panel, Figs. 4-3, 4-4, 4-5, 4-6, 4-7 and 4-8. The fuse panel for automotive circuits serves the same purpose as the electrical service entrance panel in your home.

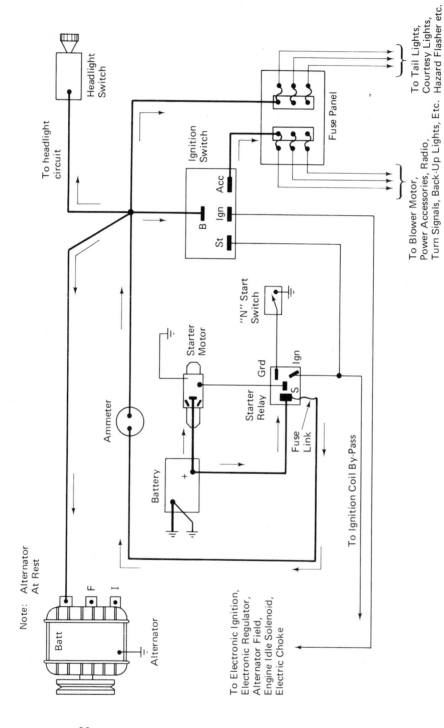

Fig. 4.2. Typical Chrysler power distribution to main circuits.

Headlight Switch

To headlight circuit

Ignition Switch

B   Ign   Acc

St

Fuse Panel

To Tail Lights, Courtesy Lights, Hazard Flasher etc.

To Blower Motor, Power Accessories, Radio, Turn Signals, Back-Up Lights, Etc.

"N" Start Switch

Starter Motor

Starter Relay   Grd   Ign   S

Fuse Link

Battery

+

Ammeter

To Ignition Coil By-Pass

Note: Alternator At Rest

Batt   F   I

Alternator

To Electronic Ignition, Electronic Regulator, Alternator Field, Engine Idle Solenoid, Electric Choke

88

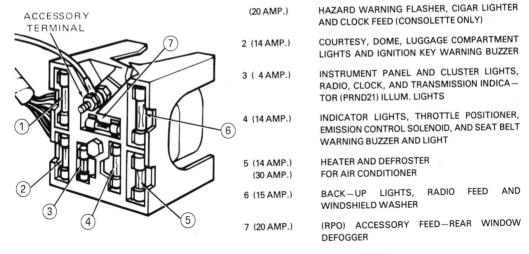

	(20 AMP.)	HAZARD WARNING FLASHER, CIGAR LIGHTER AND CLOCK FEED (CONSOLETTE ONLY)
	2 (14 AMP.)	COURTESY, DOME, LUGGAGE COMPARTMENT LIGHTS AND IGNITION KEY WARNING BUZZER
	3 (4 AMP.)	INSTRUMENT PANEL AND CLUSTER LIGHTS, RADIO, CLOCK, AND TRANSMISSION INDICA— TOR (PRND21) ILLUM. LIGHTS
	4 (14 AMP.)	INDICATOR LIGHTS, THROTTLE POSITIONER, EMISSION CONTROL SOLENOID, AND SEAT BELT WARNING BUZZER AND LIGHT
	5 (14 AMP.) (30 AMP.)	HEATER AND DEFROSTER FOR AIR CONDITIONER
	6 (15 AMP.)	BACK—UP LIGHTS, RADIO FEED AND WINDSHIELD WASHER
	7 (20 AMP.)	(RPO) ACCESSORY FEED—REAR WINDOW DEFOGGER

Fig. 4.3. *Courtesy of Ford Customer Service Division.*

Fig. 4.4. *Courtesy of Ford Customer Service Division.*

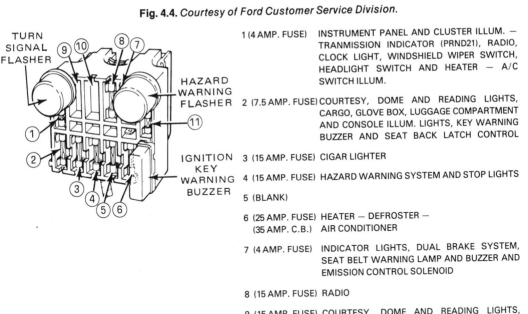

1 (4 AMP. FUSE) INSTRUMENT PANEL AND CLUSTER ILLUM. — TRANMISSION INDICATOR (PRND21), RADIO, CLOCK LIGHT, WINDSHIELD WIPER SWITCH, HEADLIGHT SWITCH AND HEATER — A/C SWITCH ILLUM.

2 (7.5 AMP. FUSE) COURTESY, DOME AND READING LIGHTS, CARGO, GLOVE BOX, LUGGAGE COMPARTMENT AND CONSOLE ILLUM. LIGHTS, KEY WARNING BUZZER AND SEAT BACK LATCH CONTROL

3 (15 AMP. FUSE) CIGAR LIGHTER

4 (15 AMP. FUSE) HAZARD WARNING SYSTEM AND STOP LIGHTS

5 (BLANK)

6 (25 AMP. FUSE) HEATER — DEFROSTER —
(35 AMP. C.B.) AIR CONDITIONER

7 (4 AMP. FUSE) INDICATOR LIGHTS, DUAL BRAKE SYSTEM, SEAT BELT WARNING LAMP AND BUZZER AND EMISSION CONTROL SOLENOID

8 (15 AMP. FUSE) RADIO

9 (15 AMP. FUSE) COURTESY, DOME AND READING LIGHTS, BACK-UP LIGHTS, WINDSHIELD WASHER, POWER WINDOW, RELAY CONTROL, DOOR OPEN WARNING LIGHT, HEATED REAR WINDOW RELAY CONTROL, THROTTLE POSITIONER, POLICE ACCESSORY RELAY CONTROL, PARK BRAKE WARNING LIGHT

10 (BLANK(

11 (20 AMP. C.B.) POLICE ACCESSORY FEED

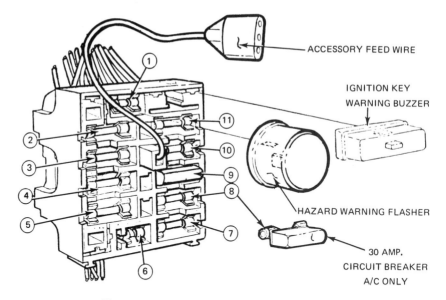

ACCESSORY FEED WIRE

IGNITION KEY WARNING BUZZER

HAZARD WARNING FLASHER

30 AMP.
CIRCUIT BREAKER
A/C ONLY

Fig. 4.5. *Courtesy of Ford Customer Service Division.*

1 (7.5 AMP. FUSE) INDICATOR LAMPS—ENGINE HOT, OIL PRESSURE, DUAL BRAKE, ALTERNATOR INDICATOR, SEAT BELT, AND PARKING BRAKE

2 (15 AMP. FUSE) CIGAR LIGHTER

3 (15 AMP. FUSE) HAZARD WARNING SYSTEM AND STOP LAMPS

4 (15 AMP. FUSE) COURTESY LAMPS, INSTRUMENT PANEL, R.H. AND L.H. DOORS, DOME, GLOVE BOX, CARGO (STATION WAGON ONLY), LUGGAGE COMPARTMENT, CLOCK FEED, DOOR LOCK SOLENOID, KEY WARNING BUZZER AND SEAT BACK LATCH/ RELAY CONTROL

5 (BLANK)

6 (4 AMP. FUSE) INSTRUMENT PANEL AND CLUSTER ILLUMINATION-CLOCK, RADIO, ASH TRAY, HEADLAMP AND WINDSHIELD WIPER SWITCH, HEATER—A/C AND ATC CONTROL

7 (15 AMP. FUSE) BACK-UP LAMPS AND THROTTLE POSITIONER

8 (15 AMP. FUSE) HEATER OR (30 AMP. C.B.) FOR AIR CONDITIONER

9 (8.25 AMP. C.B.) WINDSHIELD WIPER SYSTEM

10 (20 AMP. FUSE) WINDSHIELD WASHER, REAR WINDOW DEFROSTER, RELAY COIL FEED, POWER WINDOW RELAY COIL FEED, POLICE ACCESSORY RELAY COIL FEED, CORNER-ING LAMPS, INTRUSION ALARM SYSTEM AND SPEED CONTROL RELAY.

11 (7.5 AMP. FUSE) RADIO, STEREO TAPE PLAYER

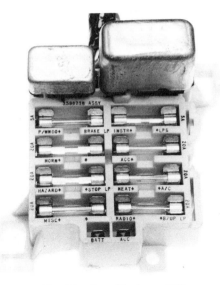

Fig. 4.6. Fuse block pre-1973. (*Courtesy of Chrysler Corporation.*)

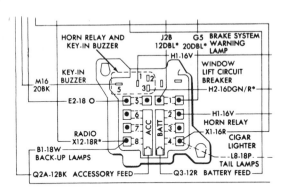

Fig. 4.7. Typical Chrysler block using circuit number codes. (*Courtesy of Chrysler Corporation*)

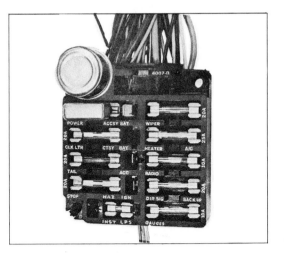

Fig. 4.8. Typical G.M. fuse block. (*Courtesy of Buick Division of General Motors Corporation*)

In reviewing the different panel illustrations, note the various pieces of hardware that might be electrically plugged into or attached to the circuits. It is not uncommon to find that a horn relay, ignition key buzzer, hazard flasher, or directional flasher is plugged into the fuse panel. Each of the circuits leading from the fuse panel is labeled or number-coded at the fuse or breaker insert. Since a fuse usually protects more than one circuit, consult the service manual or car owner's manual to get the complete details of all the electrical loads

Chart 4-1

Typical G.M. Fuse Specifications*

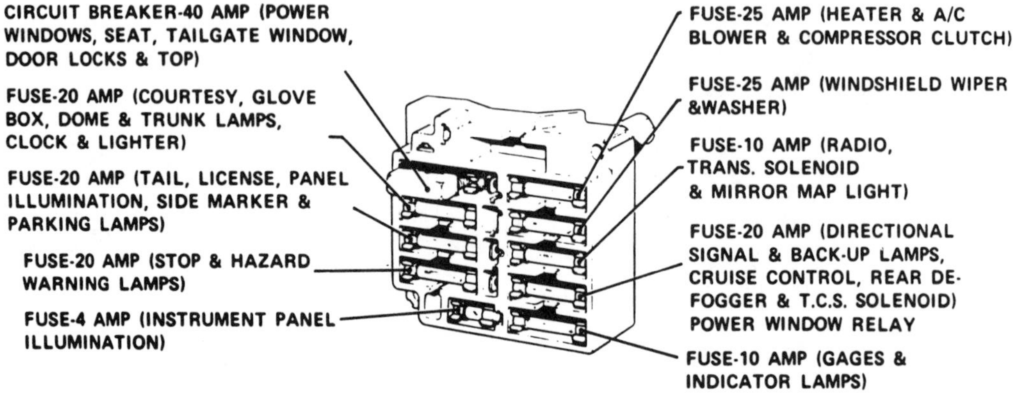

CIRCUIT BREAKER-40 AMP (POWER WINDOWS, SEAT, TAILGATE WINDOW, DOOR LOCKS & TOP)

FUSE-20 AMP (COURTESY, GLOVE BOX, DOME & TRUNK LAMPS, CLOCK & LIGHTER)

FUSE-20 AMP (TAIL, LICENSE, PANEL ILLUMINATION, SIDE MARKER & PARKING LAMPS)

FUSE-20 AMP (STOP & HAZARD WARNING LAMPS)

FUSE-4 AMP (INSTRUMENT PANEL ILLUMINATION)

FUSE-25 AMP (HEATER & A/C BLOWER & COMPRESSOR CLUTCH)

FUSE-25 AMP (WINDSHIELD WIPER &WASHER)

FUSE-10 AMP (RADIO, TRANS. SOLENOID & MIRROR MAP LIGHT)

FUSE-20 AMP (DIRECTIONAL SIGNAL & BACK-UP LAMPS, CRUISE CONTROL, REAR DE-FOGGER & T.C.S. SOLENOID) POWER WINDOW RELAY

FUSE-10 AMP (GAGES & INDICATOR LAMPS)

*Courtesy of Buick Division of General Motors Corp.

Chart 4-2

TYPICAL CHRYSLER FUSE SPECIFICATIONS

CAVITY ONE (1)
  Low Fuel Relay — 20 Amps
  Dual Brake Lamp
  Instrument Panel Gauges
  Air Conditioning Relay
  Seat Belt Lamp
  Seat Belt Relay
  Seat Belt Buzzer
  Window Lift Safety Relay
  Sentry Signal Lamp
  Temperature Gauge
  Fuel Gauge
  Voltage Limiter
  Oil Gauge

CAVITY TWO (2) — 20 Amps
  Trail Lamps
  Parking Lamps
  Side Marker Lamps
  Instrument Lamps (Cavity Five)
  License Lamps
  Headlamp-On Buzzer
  Trailer Running Lamps Relay Coil

CAVITY THREE (3) — 20 Amps
  Stop Lamps

  Front Turn Signal Lamps
  Turn Signal Indicator Lamps

CAVITY FOUR (4) — 20 Amps
  Cigar Lighter (Instrument Panel)
  Map Lamp
  Glove Box Lamp
  Clock
  Ignition Switch Lamp
  Ignition Time Delay Relay
  Trunk Lamp
  Lock Door Indicator Lamps
  Horn (Dual)
  Horn Relay
  Key in Buzzer

CAVITY FIVE (5) — 5 Amps
  Cluster Lamps
  Ash Receiver Lamps
  Stereo Cassette Lamp

CAVITY SIX (6) — 20 Amps
  Speed Control
  Air Conditioning Clutch and
  ETR Valve
  Cornering Lamps

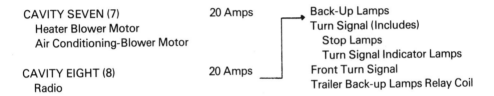

CAVITY SEVEN (7)   20 Amps   Back-Up Lamps
  Heater Blower Motor   Turn Signal (Includes)
  Air Conditioning-Blower Motor   Stop Lamps
                                                     Turn Signal Indicator Lamps

CAVITY EIGHT (8)   20 Amps   Front Turn Signal
  Radio   Trailer Back-up Lamps Relay Coil

IN-LINE FUSES AND CIRCUIT BREAKERS

FUSES   Amps

Rear Defogger or Rear Heater or Rear Air
  Conditioning Blowers 20
Heater and Air Conditioning with Tilt-A-
  Scope Steering Column 20
Automatic Headlamp Dimmer 4
Air Conditioning with ATC Wiring 1
Wheel Slip 1
Electric Deck Lid Solenoid 20
Trailer Tow Package 30
    Back-up Lamps
    Running Lamps
    Electric Brakes

CIRCUIT BREAKERS   AMPS

Concealed Headlamp Relay 5
Power Door Lock/Dome Lamp/Rear Cigar Lighter/Front Seat Back Latch/
  Right Front Door Cigar Lighter/Front and Rear Door Courtesy Lamps/
  Back Lite Lamps 15
Power Windows/Power Seats 30

related to each fuse. This data is already shown in Figs. 4-3, 4-4, and 4-5 for Ford Motor Company. Typical General Motors and Chrysler fuse data appear in Charts 4-1 and 4-2.

By referring to the fuse data, the technician will have complete knowledge of all circuits connected to any one fuse. This is especially helpful when locating a short-circuit. For example, on some vehicles the clock ties in with the courtesy light circuit. If the clock develops a short, it will then blow the courtesy light fuse. If you do not know that the clock ties in with the courtesy light system, you may spend excessive time trying to locate a nonexistent short in the courtesy lights.

Occasionally a single electrical accessory circuit line by-passes the fuse panel and taps an already existing hot line somewhere in the

Fig. 4.9.

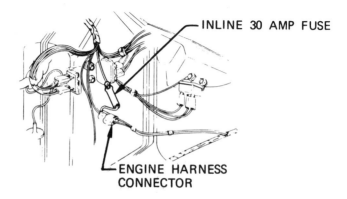

Fig. 4.10. *(Courtesy of Oldsmobile Division of General Motors Corp.)*

wiring system, usually at a connector. For circuit protection, an in-line fuse is used; see Figs. 4-9 and 4-10. In-line fuses may be difficult to find because they are sometimes located in hidden places—e.g., under the dash. Consult the manufacturer's service manual for area location.

Let's take a further look at the fuse panel and see how electrical power enters and leaves. On the back side of the block are two or more 12-volt power leads coming directly from the battery source or from the accessory terminal of the ignition switch. The power leads are then attached to a bus bar (Fig. 4-11).

The *bus bar* is a solid metal strip which distributes power to any number of circuits that are connected to it. In automotive applications, fuse holder clips are riveted to the bus bars; see Fig. 4-11. The power input then comes across the individual fuses as viewed from the front of the fuse panel, Fig. 4-12, for circuit

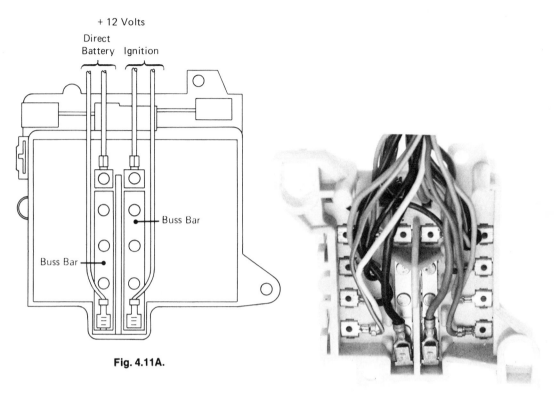

Fig. 4.11A.

Fig. 4.11B.

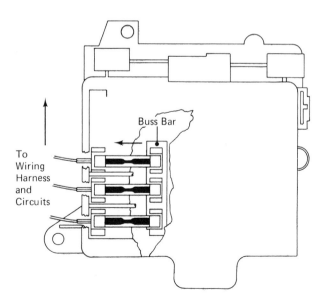

Fig. 4.12.

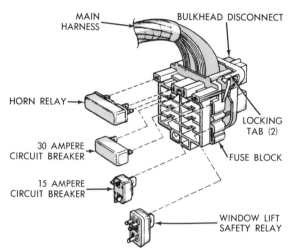

MAIN HARNESS

BULKHEAD DISCONNECT

HORN RELAY

30 AMPERE CIRCUIT BREAKER

15 AMPERE CIRCUIT BREAKER

LOCKING TAB (2)

FUSE BLOCK

WINDOW LIFT SAFETY RELAY

Fig. 4.13. *Courtesy of Chrysler Corp.*

distribution. In Fig. 4-11, the circuit wire leads are shown connected to the fuse outlet clips from the back side of the panel and the wire leads are then carried into the main harness for power distribution. A review of Fig. 4-7, fuse cavity numbers 1 and 5, shows that fuses are not necessarily tied into a bus bar. Some single fuses are built into the fuse panel with their own individual power feed.

Figure 4-13 shows the main harness wiring leads that route into the fuse panel and engine compartment bulkhead connectors. The fuse panel and bulkhead connector are locked together between the firewall.

Fuse panels have several locations on American passenger cars:

1. On the dash firewall inside the car to the left of brake pedal support.
2. Under the dash to the right side of steering column support.
3. Back of the dash on left side.
4. Behind right or left kick pad.

In production year 1974, a swing-down fuse panel was introduced on some car models. The fuse panel swings down from its instrument panel mount to permit easy checking of the panel fuses. On recreation vehicles, the fuse panel is sometimes located right on top of the dash front.

CIRCUIT PROTECTION

To protect the hundreds of feet of wiring in the passenger car, devices such as fuses, circuit breakers, and fuse links are used. These "sentries" of the electrical system are inserted in the wiring system not only to protect the wiring itself from short circuits and burn-outs, but also to protect the wiring circuit components such as switches, relays, and motors. Some of the larger passenger cars may use as many as 10 circuit breakers. The use of 10 fuses also is not uncommon. And as already pointed out, these fuses usually protect more than one circuit. A single fuse may protect a single circuit, or as many as 12 branch circuits.

Fuses

To fuse means to melt. A *fuse* is a protective device of fusible metal set in a circuit so as to be heated and destroyed by any excess current that flows through it.

Automotive fuses use a cartridge-type design. A zinc strip is attached to two metal end caps and is surrounded by a clear glass tube (Fig. 4-14). The narrow section of the zinc strip is the weak link and it is this section of the fuse that opens whenever a short circuit occurs. The wide section of the strip at both ends of the fuse is a heat dissipation feature. When a temporary current overload occurs, the heat is transferred to the fuse holder clips; this slows down the fuse burn-out. Any type of heavy short will cause the solid zinc fuse material to vaporize in microseconds, before serious circuit damage can take place. The end caps are made of brass or copper and are plated with either nickel or cadmium.

Automotive fuses are rated by current capacity. They are quite capable of handling circuits of 12-250 volts. It is the current flow through a fuse that causes it to burn out or "blow," not the circuit voltage. The fuse ratings on automotive applications generally vary from 1 to 35 amps. A 10 per cent overload factor is built into the fuses so that minor "wild current" surges will not cause frequent fuse failure. Figure 4-15 compares two blown fuses, one that resulted from a short circuit and one from a wild current surge. A wild current surge can occur when an electrical circuit is turned on. Before the circuit load takes effect, there can be a microsecond in which the voltage pushes the current through the circuit unrestricted. For example, when the wiper motor circuit is switched on, there will be a current surge until the wiper motor begins to operate.

Automotive fuses are available in a wide range of standard sizes and amperage ratings which have been set by the Society of Fuse Engineers (SFE). In reviewing Fig. 4-14, note that the SFE-type fuses have the same size diameters, but they vary in length according to the fuse rating. It is not possible to interchange an SFE 30-amp fuse with an SFE 4-amp fuse.

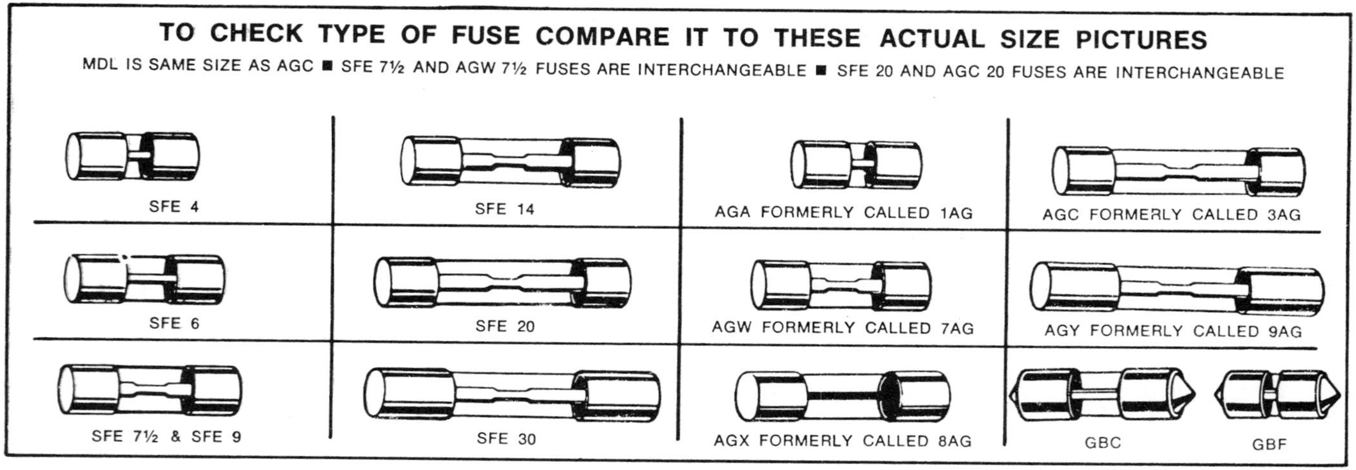

TO CHECK TYPE OF FUSE COMPARE IT TO THESE ACTUAL SIZE PICTURES

MDL IS SAME SIZE AS AGC ■ SFE 7½ AND AGW 7½ FUSES ARE INTERCHANGEABLE ■ SFE 20 AND AGC 20 FUSES ARE INTERCHANGEABLE

SFE 4

SFE 6

SFE 7½ & SFE 9

SFE 14

SFE 20

SFE 30

AGA FORMERLY CALLED 1AG

AGW FORMERLY CALLED 7AG

AGX FORMERLY CALLED 8AG

AGC FORMERLY CALLED 3AG

AGY FORMERLY CALLED 9AG

GBC

GBF

Fig. 4.14. Commonly found fuses that are shown in their actual size. These are the sentries of the electrical system along with circuit breakers.

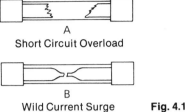

A
Short Circuit Overload

B
Wild Current Surge   **Fig. 4.15.**

The AGA, AGW, AGC, etc., series of fuses also offer a varied range of fuse ratings, but the lengths of the fuses in each series are the same, regardless of the fuse rating. For example, an AGC fuse has a dimension of ¼ in. by 1¼ in., therefore an AGC 5-amp fuse would plug into the same fuse holder clips as an AGC 20-amp fuse. The identifying letters AGA, AGW, AGC, etc., are strictly Bussmann trademarks and have no other meaning.

When you replace fuses, always use a replacement fuse of specified capacity. Variation from this practice can only compound the electrical circuit problem.

An occasional blown fuse may be caused by nothing more than a one-time overload or by a defective fuse itself. Continued blowing of fuses, however, indicates a condition that needs correction.

Some general causes of blown fuses are:

1. Short circuit beyond the fuse (between the fuse and the load) or in the load itself.
2. Internal break in the fuse not caused by heat.
3. Charging voltage too high (if fuse is near capacity at normal voltage).
4. Corrosion on end(s) of fuse (prevents cooling).
5. Overloaded circuit (too many loads operating in parallel).
6. Wrong fuse (too low a capacity for the circuit).

Fusible Links

The *fusible link* is a short piece of insulated wire inserted in series with the circuit; it acts as a fuse. The link is four gauges smaller in size than the circuit wiring it is protecting and is integral with the engine compartment wiring harness. It protects the section of electrical wiring not normally protected by a fuse, but most importantly it prevents the entire wire harness from burning up. The wiring sections are protected between the battery, alternator, fuse panel, ignition switch, and headlight switch—essentially the same power distribution wiring as discussed earlier in the chapter (Fig. 4-2). On some cars the horn circuit is also protected by a fusible link. Figure 4-16 shows the various fuse link installations on Ford Motor Company vehicles.

One type of fusible link is a length of Hyphayon insulated wire which is inserted in the chassis wiring harness with a splice or a connector (Fig. 4-17). Another popular fuse link design incorporates the fusible wire into the insulated battery cable (Fig. 4-18).

When a short circuit occurs, the heat generated by the excessive current will cause the fusible link to heat up and melt, causing an open

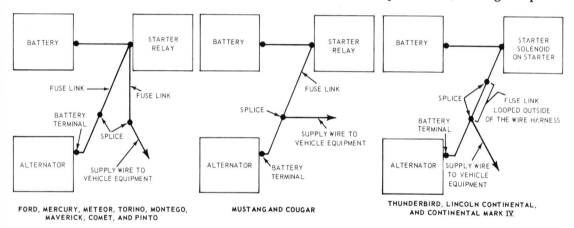

FORD, MERCURY, METEOR, TORINO, MONTEGO, MAVERICK, COMET, AND PINTO

MUSTANG AND COUGAR

THUNDERBIRD, LINCOLN CONTINENTAL, AND CONTINENTAL MARK IV

Fig. 4.16. *Courtesy of Ford Customer Service Division.*

Fig. 4.17 (A).   Welded fuse link splice. (B). Fuse link connector.

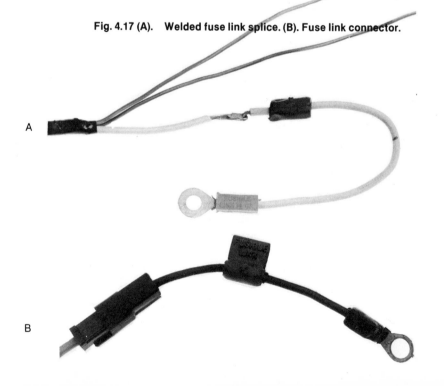

Fig. 4.18.

and thereby protecting the circuit. The insulation on the fusible link is designed to withstand the high melting temperature of the wire. The insulation, however, swells nd gives a bubble effect on its surface, indicating that the fusible link has burned out. On occasion, the burn-out temperature may burst the insulation. In the other extreme, fusible links have been known to melt and not even swell or burst the insulation. Only a continuity test can reveal the true condition.

The number of fusible links that burn out is low. They can, however, be replaced as shown in Chapter 2, Fig. 2-27, 2-28 and 2-29. Naturally, when the fusible link is part of the positive battery cable, the entire cable assembly must be replaced.

Before replacing a fusible link, the problem that caused it must be eliminated. This usually means locating a short circuit to ground. Don't overlook the possibility that a battery charger or booster battery was connected incorrectly.

Circuit Breakers

A *circuit breaker* is a thermal mechanical device that serves a purpose similar to that of a fuse. Circuit breakers are designed to open a circuit when the current flow exceeds the safe limits of the circuit. When a circuit short or overload causes a high current, the excessive temperature acts on a bimetallic strip to cause a deflection of the metal strip; a set of contact points trip open the circuit (Fig. 4-19).

Most automotive thermal circuit breakers are classified as *Type I* or *self-setting* (Fig. 4-19). After a short time (several seconds), the bimetallic strip cools and the points close. If the circuit breaker continues its cycling action, the circuit is shorted and is in need of immediate repair.

On some automotive circuit applications, *remote set* or *noncycling Type II* breakers are used. The design of this breaker is much like the Type I design; however, once the points open they will not reset until the circuit power is switched off. This feature is caused by a heating coil element that comes into play once the contacts open (Fig. 4-20).

In Fig. 4-20, the bimetal strip is shown in series with the protect-

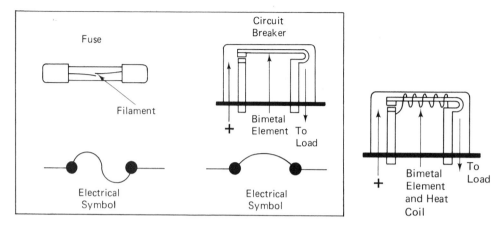

Fig. 4.19.   **Fig. 4.20.**

ed circuit, as in the Type I breaker. The coil of fine wire is in parallel
with the thermal bimetal strip. The bimetal strip and contact points
offer the path of least resistance and carry the full current load as long
as the circuit is operating normally. When a short occurs, the bimetal
strip heats and opens the points; the coil of fine wire is then in series
with the main circuit. The circuit is still protected, though, because
the resistance in the coil is very high, restricting current flow. This
high resistance creates heat, which maintains a high temperature in
the bimetal strip, so that the contact points cannot close again. The
only way Type II circuit breakers can be reclosed is by removing the
source of electricity (disconnect battery), or by turning off the
component that is being protected by the breaker.

Circuit breakers are typically used in protecting the headlight
and the power accessory circuits. In Ford vehicles, additional
breakers are used to protect the taillight, brake light, and horn
circuits. Circuit breakers may be located internally—within electric
motors and switches, or externally—in the fuse block, mounted on a
safety panel above the glove box, or mounted directly at a battery
power junction in the engine compartment.

Review questions

1. Briefly describe how the vehicle power source typically gets
   to the headlight switch, ignition switch, and fuse panel.
2. What wire size is usually used for the power feed in Question
   1?
3. Name some circuits that have a constant power source from
   the fuse panel at all times.

4. Name some circuits that get a power source from the fuse panel when the ignition switch is in the accessory or ignition "on" position.

5. What is the purpose of a fuse panel?

6. Name some typical electrical circuit hardware, other than fuses and breakers, that plug into a fuse panel.

7. What is the purpose of the fuse panel bus bar?

8. Name the three devices that are used for circuit protection.

9. What is a fuse? Briefly describe how it works.

10. How do SFE fuses differ from the AGA, AGW, and AGC fuses?

11. What fuse capacities are interchangeable between SFE, AGW, and AGC?

12. What is a fusible link? Briefly describe how it works.

13. What parts of the automotive wiring are typically protected by the fusible link?

14. What is a circuit breaker? Briefly describe how it works.

15. What is the difference between a self-setting and a remote (noncycling) circuit breaker?

16. Why is the headlight circuit protected with a self-setting circuit breaker? Where is this circuit breaker located?

5

Electrical Test Instruments

Accurate electrical measurements are the basis of electrical diagnosis. The value of these measurements depends upon the accuracy of the meters used and the ability of the technician to connect and read the meters correctly. If you understand how electrical measuring meters work you will find it easy to understand how they must be connected and used when testing electrical circuits.

VOLTMETER

In a *voltmeter* (Fig. 5-1) the windings of the movable coil are connected to the test leads through a high resistance. This resistance unit limits the amount of current flow through the meter.

When the voltmeter is connected across a battery or circuit, current flow through windings of the movable coil produces a magnetic field. The north pole of this magnetic field is fairly close to the north pole of the horseshoe magnet. Since like poles repel, the coil and pointer move anytime current flows through the windings of the coil. The higher the voltage, the greater the current flow through the coil, the stronger the magnetic field around the coil and the greater the movement of the coil.

A voltmeter is always connected across a circuit without disconnecting any wires. In other words, it is always connected in parallel with some part of the circuit. The high resistance built into the voltmeter keeps current flow through the meter low.

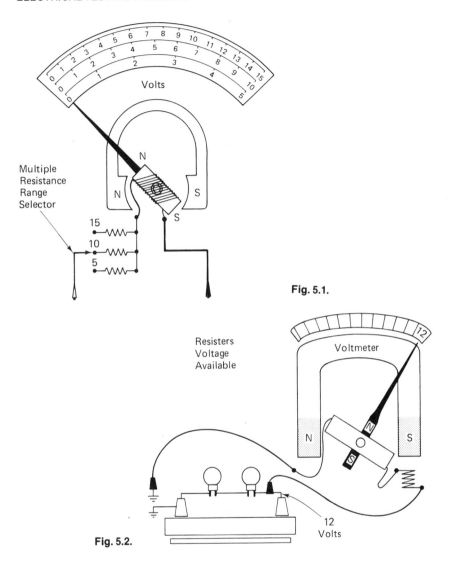

Multiple
Resistance
Range
Selector

Volts

Fig. 5.1.

Resisters
Voltage
Available

Voltmeter

12 Volts

Fig. 5.2.

A voltmeter measures the voltage difference between the two terminals the meter leads are connected to. It measures the voltage drop between two points in the circuit (Fig. 5-2).

If one voltmeter lead is connected to a terminal in a circuit and the other lead is connected to a good ground, the voltmeter will register the voltage available at that terminal. In the example (Fig. 5-3), voltmeter 1 measures available voltage across the battery. If the circuit is electrically tight, voltmeters 2 and 3 should read battery voltage.

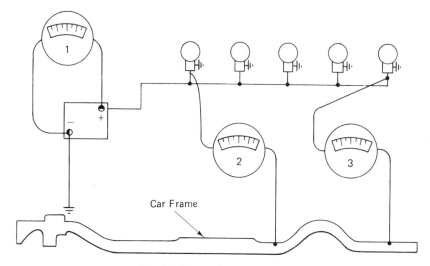

Fig. 5.3. Measuring voltage.

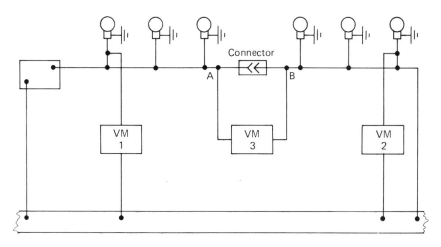

Fig. 5.4.

Figure 5-4 shows how a voltmeter can be used to locate excessive current resistance. If voltmeter 1 measures 12 volts but voltmeter 2 only reads 9 volts, that is an unwanted voltage drop. Voltmeter 3 connected across the connector could confirm a bad electrical connection at the connector. Voltmeter 3 would measure 3 volts, the voltage difference between point A and point B.

AMMETER

Like a voltmeter, an *ammeter* has a permanent horseshoe magnet and a movable coil with pointer (Fig. 5-5). However its internal circuitry is entirely different. The movable coil windings of an ammeter are connected to the external test leads through a low-resistance shunt. The internal meter connections are made so that the movable coil is connected in parallel with the shunt (Fig. 5-6).

When an ammeter is connected into a circuit, most of the current flows through the low resistance of the shunt and only a small amount flows through the movable coil. An ammeter must always be

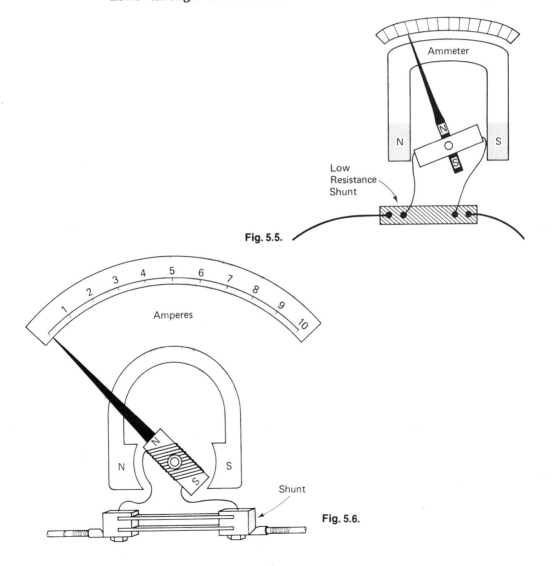

Fig. 5.5.

Fig. 5.6.

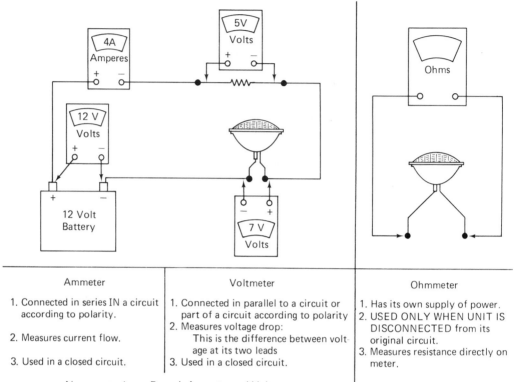

Ammeter	Voltmeter	Ohmmeter
1. Connected in series IN a circuit according to polarity.	1. Connected in parallel to a circuit or part of a circuit according to polarity	1. Has its own supply of power.
	2. Measures voltage drop: This is the difference between voltage at its two leads	2. USED ONLY WHEN UNIT IS DISCONNECTED from its original circuit.
2. Measures current flow.		
3. Used in a closed circuit.	3. Used in a closed circuit.	3. Measures resistance directly on meter.

Always use a Large Enough Ammeter and Voltmeter

Fig. 5.7.

connected directly into the circuit *in series* so that all the current flowing in the tested circuit will flow through the ammeter. That means that you must disconnect at least one wire and break into a circuit in order to connect an ammeter correctly. Never connect an ammeter into a circuit unless there is enough resistance in the circuit you are testing to limit the amount of current flow through the meter.

For example, suppose you connect an ammeter into a 12-volt circuit having a lamp in it with a 6-ohm resistance. Ohm's law will tell you that the resistance of this lamp will let only 2 amps flow through the circuit. This will not damage an ammeter rated at 2 amps. However, if the resistance were less than 6 ohms, the ammeter would have to have a capacity of more than 2 amps. The ammeter itself has a very low resistance so we must depend on the external circuit to protect the meter. Figure 5-7 shows how the voltmeter, ammeter, and ohmmeter can be used.

If an ammeter is connected across a circuit, full battery voltage will push too much current through the low-resistance shunt and the coil windings and damage them.

OHMMETER

Ammeters and voltmeters are designed to indicate values in a circuit when current is flowing. To test the condition of a unit when it is *disconnected* from the circuit, an *ohmmeter* is used (Fig. 5-8).

When the probes are together, the circuit is complete, causing the meter needle to deflect. The variable resistance is then used to calibrate the meter to read zero. Zero in full scale deflection indicates

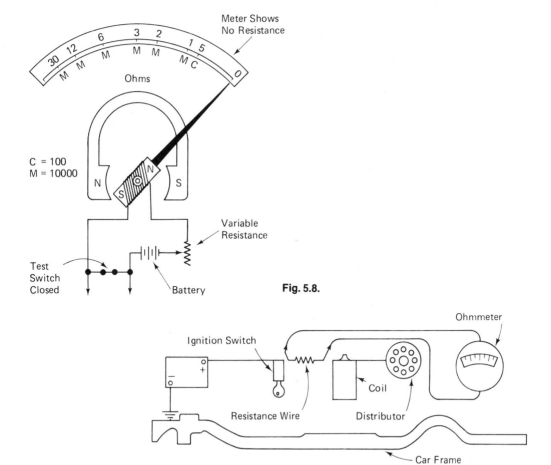

Fig. 5.8.

Fig. 5.9.   Ohmmeter

no resistance between the test probes. When the probes are held apart, the needle moves to the maximum resistance side of the scale. This reading indicates that the resistance between the probes is so high that no current will flow through the circuit.

The ohmmeter has its own supply of electricity. These batteries have a known voltage and are used to send a "test" current through the electrical components being tested. An ohmmeter is never connected into or across a hot circuit. The circuit being tested must be dead (Fig. 5-9).

VARIABLE RESISTOR

A *variable resistor* (*rheostat*) is designed to allow its internal resistance to be changed (Fig. 5-10). A rheostat is made by using a coil or high resistance wire and a movable contact. One lead is connected to one end of the resistance coil and the other lead is connected to the movable contact.

As the contact moves along the coil, away from the open connection, a greater length of resistance wire is included in the circuit (Fig. 5-11). The resistance of the rheostat depends on the position of the movable contact.

JUMPER WIRE

Although a *jumper wire* is not a true test instrument, it is a very effective testing device when properly used. A jumper wire is nothing more than a piece of stranded, insulated electrical wire, with sufficient current capacity.

A jumper wire may be used as a substitute for any nonresistive component, such as a switch. It should never be used in such a manner that it would short circuit a hot lead to ground.

In Fig. 5-12, the motor operates when the jumper wire is connected between points A and E. Notice that we are going through the resistance unit (motor) and not to ground. When we move the wire from E to D the motor still will operate, proving that the circuit is still in good condition.

When we move the jumper wire from D to C the motor will not operate, indicating that the switch is bad and should be replaced.

TEST LIGHT

There are two basic types of *test light:* The probe light and the self-powered test light.

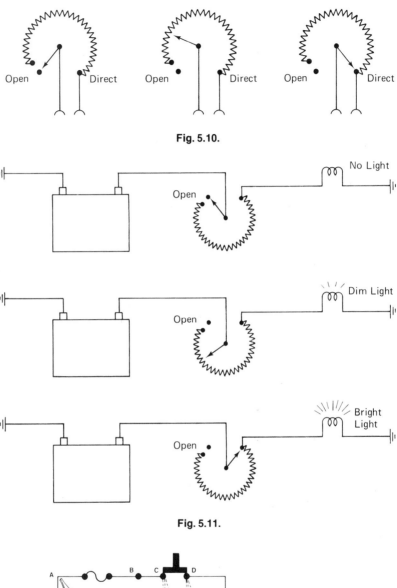

Fig. 5.10.

Fig. 5.11.

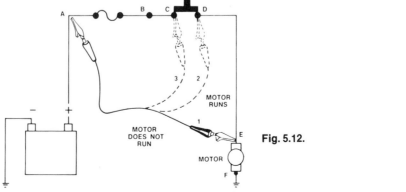

Fig. 5.12.

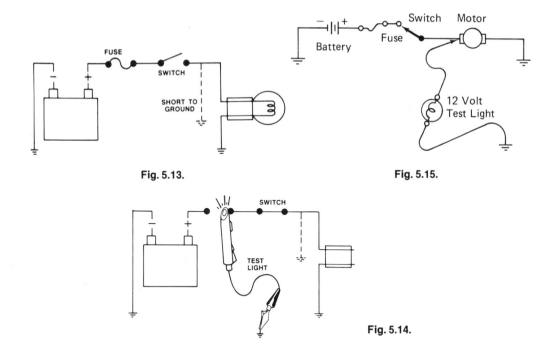

Fig. 5.13.   **Fig. 5.15.**

Fig. 5.14.

A probe test light does not have a power supply built in—it uses the circuit power supply. It tests for power and continuity.

A self-powered test light is used as a continuity tester only. Because of the built-in power supply, it cannot be used as a tester for power.

In Fig. 5-13, the fuse will blow when the switch is closed because the short to ground is bypassing the resistance unit (bulb). With a self-powered test light, as shown in Fig. 5-14, connect to the cold side of the fuse holder, close the switch, and remove the bulb. Removing the bulb removes a ground connection.

If the test light still lights, it indicates that another ground exists and must be found.

Figure 5-15 shows a probe test light that test for power at different places in the circuit.

Review questions

    1. A voltmeter is always connected in _____.

    2. A voltmeter measures _____.

    3. An ammeter is always connected in _____.

    4. When an ammeter is connected, most of the current flows through the _____.

5. A zero full-scale deflection on an ohmmeter indicates

   _____.

6. The power source is supplied to an ohmmeter by

   _____.

7. Ohmmeters should never be used to check for

   _____.

8. A rheostat is used to _____.

9. A jumper wire is used to _____.

10. A self-powered test light can be used to test for

    _____.

6

*Reading Electrical Wiring Diagrams**

Wiring diagrams are a valuable diagnostic tool. When they are properly teamed with the use of electrical measuring instruments, circuit test lights, and jumper test wires, the most difficult circuit problems can be quickly isolated and repaired.

Although a wiring diagram shows many circuits, the technician can select the one circuit with the problem and determine how it is routed in the vehicle and related to other branch circuits. The following example illustrates how important a wiring diagram can be.

> The left front directional light filament has no power at the light socket. You find that the wire color code at the steering column multiple connector does not match the wire color at the light. Further confusion sets in when you find that the one simple wire run between the steering column and light socket gets buried in a harness.

Trying to find the source of the circuit problem by the fumble method can be a long drawn-out process. The real solution to the problem is to consult the manufacturer's wiring diagram. It identifies the wire connectors in the circuit line that can be used for power test points. It also indicates the color code change that might take place at a connector or within a harness. When you know the correct color

*Based on training publications of the Ford Motor Company and Chrysler Corporation.

code of a wire, it is easy to trace it through the one or more wire harnesses in which it travels.

Electrical wiring diagrams aren't difficult to read—they just look that way. Every piece of wire in an automobile—including switches, fuses, breakers, flashers, motors, connectors, splices, etc.—is presented on a piece of paper in the form of a road map. As with any other type of map, you must have some understanding of what you are reading before it will mean anything.

The wiring diagrams and the actual layout of the wiring on the car don't really have much physical similarity. When tracing a circuit on the diagrams you can expect to find components, connectors, and switches in the correct sequence between battery and ground, but not in the same relative positions as in the vehicle. A modern wiring diagram, however, is coded to show where every component, connector, and switch is located on the vehicle. This is just one more reason why it is important to understand how to read a wiring diagram. Otherwise, locating components, connectors, and switches in circuits not familiar to you could become an extremely time-consuming job. For example, if you needed to replace a turn-signal flasher, where would you find it? On the fuse panel, left side of the glove box, right side of the ash tray, left side of the brake pedal support bracket, etc.?

In the past, automotive wiring diagrams were not standardized and it was difficult to adjust to each diagram scheme. There were too many wires shown on one page and it often was necessary to flip back and forth between the several schematics that made up and illustrated the electrical system. They also lacked data for locating components and connectors on the car; this is still a problem with some wiring diagrams.

The modern trend is to feature the entire electrical system on one schematic. It may be a multiple-page diagram, but the schematic continues from page to page with no need for flipping back and forth.

Let us concentrate on how to read the newer wiring diagrams. You'll find that much of the information can be related to automotive wiring diagrams that still use the traditional layout schemes of previous years.

CIRCUIT SYMBOLS

To follow and read electrical circuits, you must be familiar with a number of traditional symbols used in automotive wiring diagrams (Figs. 6-1 and 6-2). These symbols are especially helpful when you view detailed schematics that are used to show what goes on electrically within switches, motors, relays, etc. (Fig. 6-3).

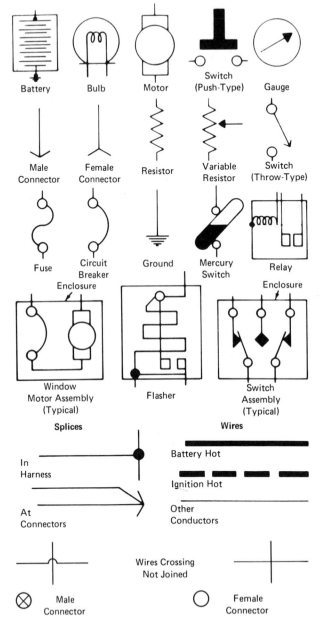

Fig. 6.1. Common electrical symbols. *(Courtesy of Ford Customer Service Division.)*

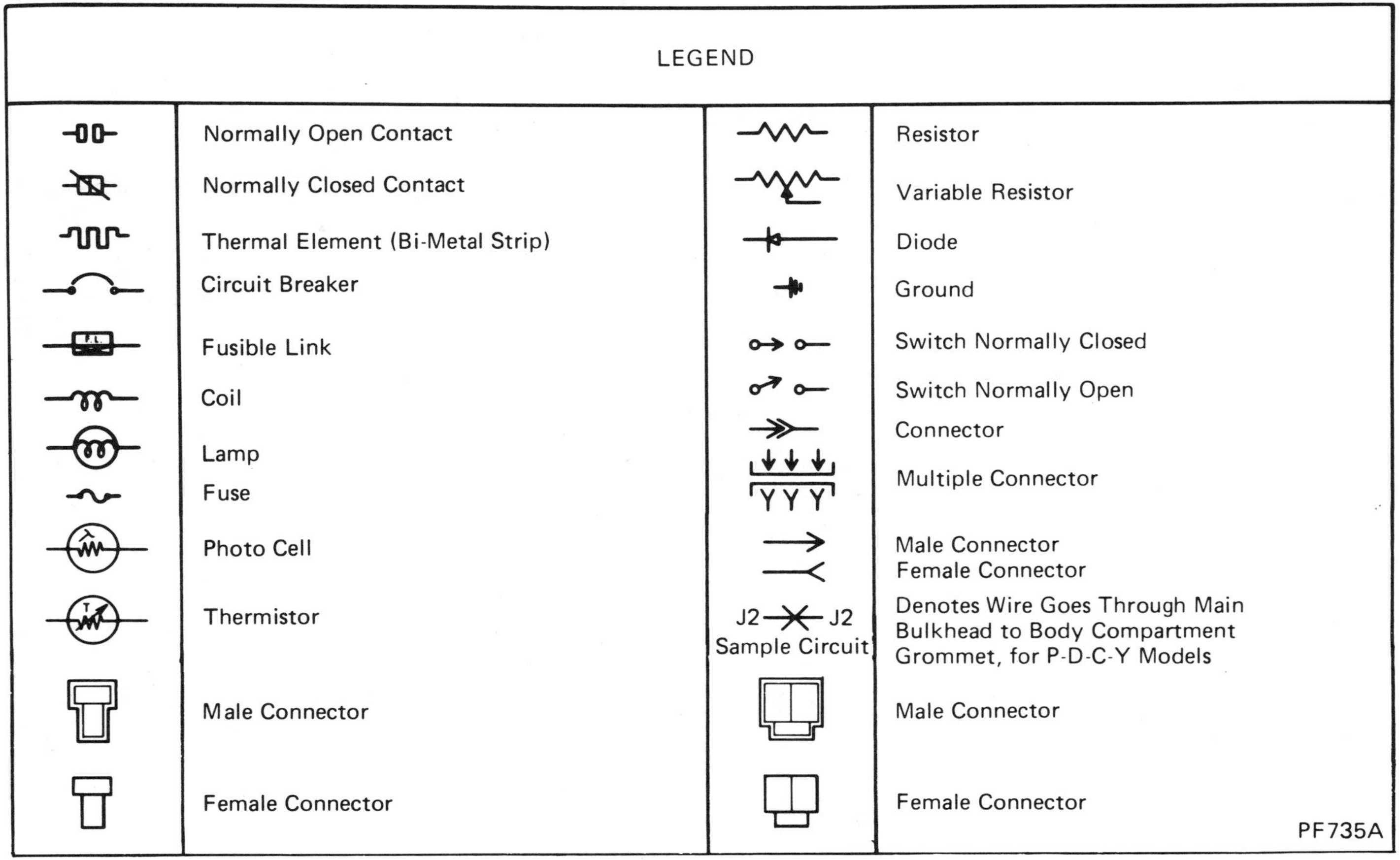

LEGEND

Symbol	Description	Symbol	Description
	Normally Open Contact		Resistor
	Normally Closed Contact		Variable Resistor
	Thermal Element (Bi-Metal Strip)		Diode
	Circuit Breaker		Ground
	Fusible Link		Switch Normally Closed
	Coil		Switch Normally Open
	Lamp		Connector
	Fuse		Multiple Connector
	Photo Cell		Male Connector
			Female Connector
	Thermistor	J2 ── ✕ ── J2 Sample Circuit	Denotes Wire Goes Through Main Bulkhead to Body Compartment Grommet, for P-D-C-Y Models
	Male Connector		Male Connector
	Female Connector		Female Connector

PF735A

Fig. 6.2.

117

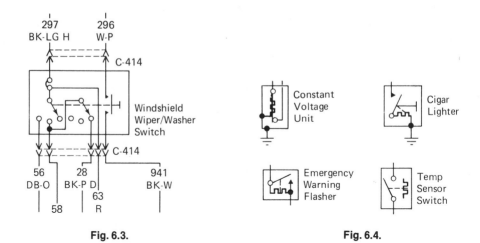

Fig. 6.3.   Fig. 6.4.

Some of the symbols in Figs. 6-1 and 6-2 are of special interest—e.g., the thermal element symbol that is used in such components as the constant-voltage regulator, cigar lighter, emergency warning flasher, and turn signal flasher (Fig. 6-4). A thermal element contains a coil of high-resistance fine wire that gives off heat when current flows through it.

WIRE CONNECTIONS

All the wires in a wiring diagram are represented by straight lines. The wires may be joined in a harness by crimping or soldering and these points are called splices. The symbol for a harness splice is a large solid dot, Fig. 6-1. Sometimes a splice is made at a connector, this symbol is also illustrated in Fig. 6-1.

For location in the wiring harness on the car, splices are sometimes coded (Fig. 6-5). This makes it possible to refer to a code chart for the specific location information. Figure 6-6 shows an application of a splice at a connector.

Somewhere along the route in a diagram, wire lines are found to cross other lines and these intersections should not be confused with harness splice points. Figure 6-1 shows the difference between a splice and wires crossing but not joined.

The joining of wires by connector terminals is represented by pointers (Fig. 6-2). Where connector terminals on the diagram are joined by a broken line, this means that all the terminals are in a single multiple connector. For drawing convenience, additional terminals located in the same connector are found elsewhere on the diagram (Fig. 6-7). They are identified by the same connector code number.

For location on the car, connectors are coded so that reference can be made to a diagram section on connector graphics which also shows the shape of the connector and the wire connections (Figs. 6-8 and 6-9).

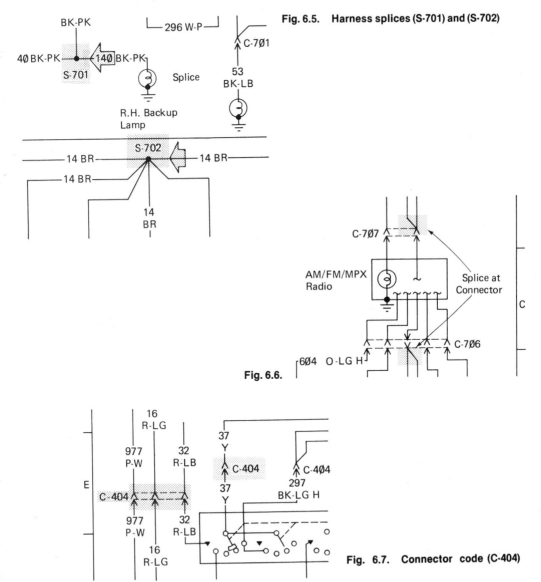

Fig. 6.5.   Harness splices (S-701) and (S-702)

Fig. 6.6.

Fig. 6.7.   Connector code (C-404)

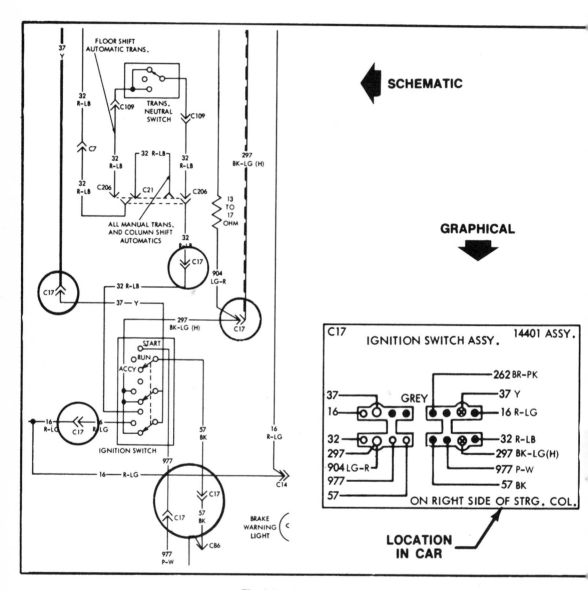

Fig. 6.8. *Courtesy Ford Corp.*

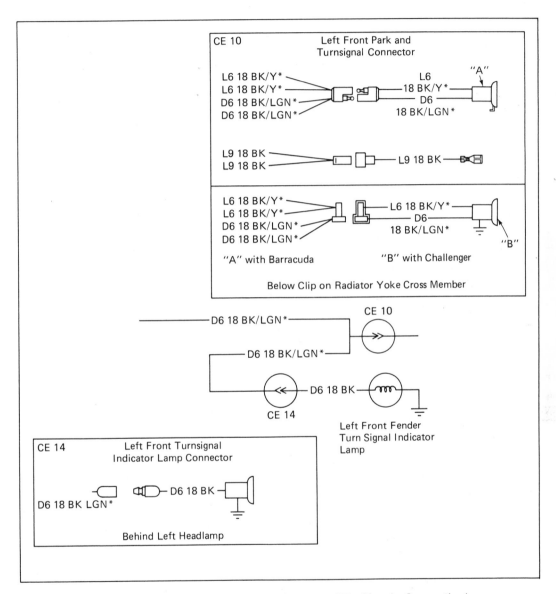

Fig. 6.9. Connector code graphics. *(Courtesy of The Chrysler Corporation.)*

Optional Wiring

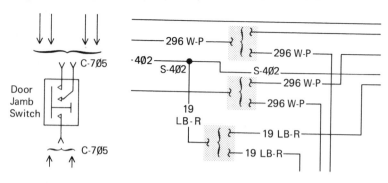

Fig. 6.10.   Fig. 6.11.

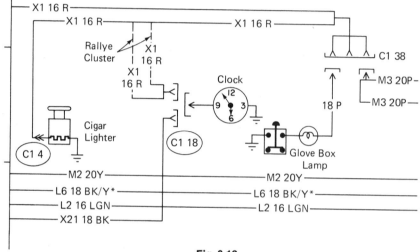

Fig. 6.12.

OPTIONAL WIRING

Optional wiring means that a circuit can be routed or completed in two or more different ways depending on the car model and attached accessories. Optional wiring is shown by putting a bracket around the optional wires and facing the bracket toward the matching wire or wires. In Fig. 6-10, the car will have one or the other of the wire routes shown.

Other techniques for showing optional wiring include using wavy lines at the wire ends (Fig. 6-11), or hash marks (Fig. 6-12).

WIRE AND CIRCUIT IDENTIFICATION

To help the technician follow the wires and circuits that are shown in the diagram, the wires are coded by a combination of letters, numbers, colors, and gauge sizes.

Circuit Codes

The first part of the wire code identifies the individual circuit or portion of the circuit to which the wire is related. The circuit wire is coded by either numbers or combinations of letters and numbers and

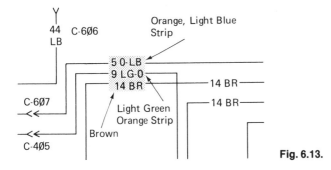

Fig. 6.13.

Fig. 6.14. *Courtesy Ford Corp.*

CAR STANDARD WIRE COLOR CODE CIRCUIT

CIRCUIT	DESCRIPTION	COLOR
1	HORN SWITCH CONTROL	DK BLUE BASE
2	RH FRONT TURN SIGNAL LAMP	WHITE-LT BLUE STRIPE
3	LH FRONT TURN SIGNAL LAMP	LT GREEN-WHITE STRIPE
4	ALTERNATOR REG. "S" TERM. TO ALTERNATOR "S" TERM.	WHITE-BLACK STRIPE
5	RH REAR TURN SIGNAL LAMP	ORANGE-LT BLUE STRIPE
6	HORN RELAY TO HORN	YELLOW-LT GREEN HASH
7	SEAT SWITCH ARM TERM. TO RELAY FIELD TERM.	LT GREEN-YELLOW DOT
8	TURN SIGNAL FLASHER FEED	ORANGE-YELLOW STRIPE
9	LH REAR TURN SIGNAL LAMP	LT GREEN-ORANGE STRIPE
10	STOPLAMP SWITCH FEED	LT GREEN-RED HASH
11	ELECTRONIC SWITCH TO IGNITION COIL NEG. TERMINAL	DK GREEN-YELLOW DOT
12	HEADLAMP DIMMER SWITCH TO HIGH BEAMS	LT GREEN-BLACK STRIPE
13	HEADLAMP DIMMER SWITCH TO LOW BEAMS	RED-BLACK STRIPE
14	HEADLAMP SWITCH TO TAIL LAMPS AND SIDE MARKER LAMPS	BROWN BASE
15	HEADLAMP SWITCH TO HEADLAMP DIMMER SWITCH	RED-YELLOW STRIPE
16	IGNITION SWITCH TO IGNITION COIL "BATT." TERMINAL	RED-LT GREEN STRIPE
17	LOW OIL PRESSURE WARNING LAMP TO LOW OIL PRESS. SENDING UNIT	WHITE BASE
18	SEAT SWITCH TO RELAY FIELD TERMINAL	ORANGE-YELLOW DOT
19	INSTRUMENT PANEL LAMPS FEED	LT BLUE-RED STRIPE
20	DISTRIBUTOR ELECTRONIC CONTROL FEED	WHITE-LT BLUE HASH

CHRYSLER WIRING DIAGRAM CIRCUIT CODES

The Code letter will designate its particular circuit throughout the entire wiring diagram. The codes are as follows:

A1- Battery Circuit to Ammeter.
A2- Battery Circuit to Ground.
B-- Back Up Lamp Circuit.
C-- Air Conditioning and Heater Circuits (Including Rear Units).
D-- Emergency, Stop Lamp and Turn Signal Circuits.
E-- Instrument Panel Cluster, Switches and Illumination Circuits.
F-- Radio Speakers and Power Seat Circuits.
G-- Gauges and Warning Lamp Circuits.
H-- Horn Circuit.
J-- Ignition System Run Circuit.
J1- Ignition Switch Feed Circuit.
J3- Ignition Switch Start Circuit.
L-- Lighting Circuit (Exterior Lights).
M-- Lighting Circuit (Interior Lights).
P-- Brake Checking Circuit.
Q2 Accessory Buss Bar Feed (Fuse Block).
Q3- Battery Buss Bar Feed.
R3- Alternator Circuit to Electronic Voltage Regulator (Field).
R6- Alternator Circuit to Ammeter (Feed).
S-- Starter Motor and Starter Relay Circuit.
T-- Trunk Lamp Circuit.
V-- Windshield Wiper and Washer Circuit.
W-- Power Window Circuit.
X-- Radio, Cigar Lighter, Lamp Grounds, Clock, Speed Control, Power Antenna, Deck Lid and Door Locks.

Fig. 6.15. *Courtesy of The Chrysler Corporation.*

will designate the particular circuit throughout the entire wiring diagram.

Figure 6-13 shows a portion of a Ford wiring diagram with attention given to wire identification. By referring to the diagram circuit and color code chart, Fig. 6-14, we find that wire 5 is the right rear turn signal circuit, wire 9 is the left rear turn signal circuit, and wire 14 is the taillight circuit.

Chrysler wiring diagrams use letter codes to identify the circuit wiring; see Fig. 6-15.

Size and Color

The last part of the wire code shows the wire size and color of the wire insulation as it appears in the car. For example, 18 BK means 18 gauge/black. On some diagrams only the color is given and the wire size is omitted.

A car manufacturer usually furnishes a primary color chart for identification of abbreviated letter designations as they relate to the color code. Some examples are shown in Fig. 6-16.

Most wires are one solid color, such as brown (BR). The solid primary colors, however, do not give enough variety to identify all the wires. Therefore, a second code is added to the primary color to indicate striping. For example, the wire color code BK-P means black with a purple stripe. If the BK is followed by an asterisk, BK*, it indicates simply a black wire with a stripe.

The Ford Motor Company uses for further variety dots or hash marks in addition to stripes (Fig. 6-17). If the second color code is followed by a letter D or H, the second color is in dots or hash marks. In the example BK-W H, the wire is black with white hash marks. Figures 6-18 and 6-19 show wire identifications that can be found in wiring diagrams.

Fig. 6.16 *Courtesy General Motors and The Chrysler Corporation.*

GENERAL MOTORS
WIRE IDENTIFICATION

SYM	COLOR
AL	Aluminum
BLK	Black
BLU LT	BLUE LIGHT
BLU DK	BLUE DARK
BRN	BROWN
GLZ	GLAZED
GRN LT	GREEN LIGHT
GRN DK	GREEN DARK
GRA	GRAY
MAR	MAROON
NAT	NATURAL
ORN	ORANGE
PNK	PINK
PPL	PURPLE
RED	RED
TAN	TAN
VLT	VIOLET
WHT	WHITE
YEL	YELLOW

SINGLE OR DOUBLE STRIPED CABLES
EXAMPLE:
WHITE WITH BLACK STRIPE . . WH/BLK

	WIRE COLOR
18	BRN

WIRE GAUGE

CHRYSLER
WIRING COLOR KEY
PRIMARY COLORS

BK	BLACK
BR	BROWN
T	TAN
R	RED
PK	PINK
O	ORANGE
Y	YELLOW
DG	DARK GREEN
LG	LIGHT GREEN
DB	DARK BLUE
LB	LIGHT BLUE
P	PURPLE
*	STRIPED WIRE
Y*	YELLOW W/STRIPE

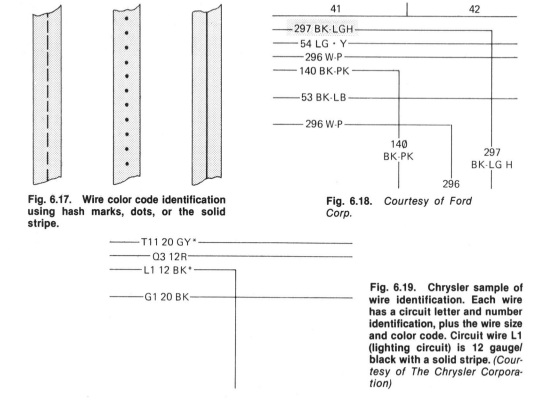

Fig. 6.17. Wire color code identification using hash marks, dots, or the solid stripe.

Fig. 6.18. *Courtesy of Ford Corp.*

Fig. 6.19. Chrysler sample of wire identification. Each wire has a circuit letter and number identification, plus the wire size and color code. Circuit wire L1 (lighting circuit) is 12 gauge/black with a solid stripe. *(Courtesy of The Chrysler Corporation)*

One word of caution on wire colors. The color of a wire on one end of a circuit may not be the same as it is on the other end. The wire can enter a splice in the loom with one color and come out of the splice wearing a different color. Occasionally a wire of one color enters a connector, and the circuit comes out of the matching terminal of that connector with another color. In some instances, a single wire enters one side of a terminal connector, and two wires, each a different color, come out of the other side at the matching terminal.

This color changing again points out the need for using a wiring diagram.

SWITCHES

Switches are usually drawn in a schematic form. Schematic drawings present the switch circuit in it simplest form so that the circuit itself can be easily traced through the switch. The symbols within the switch show all the contact points and the movable contacts that do the switching.

Switches are drawn in their normal at-rest position. Most switches will be shown in an open position since they are normally open. Figure 6-20 shows a stoplight switch, with the movable contact away from the fixed contacts and in the open circuit position. A study of the stoplight switch as it is drawn should make it obvious that when the switch control is pushed, the movement closes the circuit (Fig. 6-21).

Again using the stoplight switch illustration, Fig. 6-20, notice that the fixed contacts in the switch are represented by triangle points. Triangle point contacts indicate that the switch is spring loaded and the contact is only momentary. As soon as the operator releases the control, the spring load opens the switch, in this case the brake pedal. Spring-return switches are also used for the glove box light and courtesy lights.

Round contact point symbols indicate that the switches are not spring returned. An example is the headlight switch, which remains where the operator puts it (Fig. 6-22).

The headlight switch is also an example of a ganged-type switch. In Fig. 6-22, notice the hashed line connecting the two movable contacts. This shows that the two are ganged or mechanically connected so that they move together. The left half of the switch operates the headlights, the right half the parking lights and taillights.

The contacts are easy to identify by following two simple rules: (1) the diagram shows the switch in its "at rest" or "off" position, and

Fig. 6.20.

Fig. 6.21.

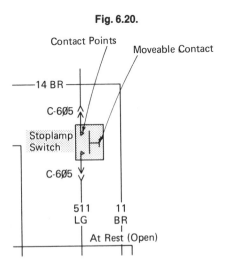

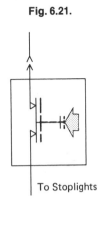

(2) the contacts move in the same order as the switch operates on the car. In Fig. 6-23, with the lights off, both movable contacts lead to dead ends. The first "on" position is for parking lights (Fig. 6-24). Notice that the headlight switch still is at a dead end, but the parking light switch makes contact with the circuit wire. With the switch in the last position, electrical contact is made with the headlight circuit while the parklight switch maintains contact with its circuits (Fig. 6-25).

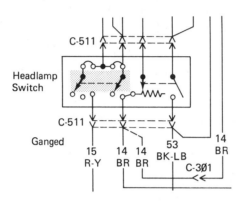

Fig. 6.22. *Courtesy Ford Corp.*

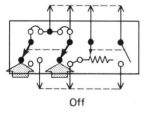

Off

Fig. 6.23.

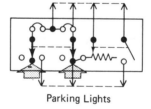

Parking Lights

Fig. 6.24.

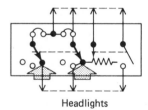

Headlights

Fig. 6.25.

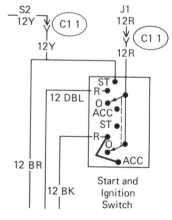

Fig. 6.26. *Courtesy The Chrysler Corporation.*

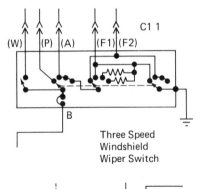

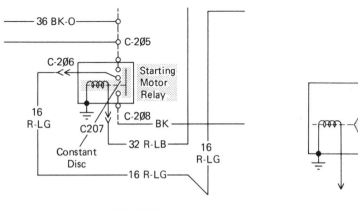

Fig. **6.27.** *Courtesy The Chrysler Corporation.*

Three Speed
Windshield
Wiper Switch

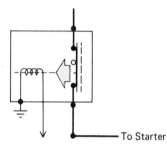

Fig. 6.28.

Fig. 6.29.

Other examples of gang switches are the ignition and the wiper motor, Figs. 6-26 and 6-27.

It is important to recognize how an electromagnet application, as used in a solenoid or relay, is usually represented in a wiring diagram. Figure 6-28 is a schematic view of a starter relay with its electromagnetic coil, fixed contacts, and movable contact disc. The broken line in the schematic indicates that the relay contact disc is actuated by the pull of the coil's magnetism. The coil is also shown in a nonenergized position, which in this case means that the contact disc is in the open position. When the coil is energized, it pulls on the iron stem (broken line) attached to the disc. This action closes the circuit to the starter (Fig. 6-29).

HARNESS LAYOUTS

An important part of reading a wiring diagram is to transfer the diagram information to the actual wiring on the car. This can be done easily once you know the wiring path of the circuit you're working with.

In general, the routing of the harnesses is quite similar among the various car makes and body styles. There are some variations, which usually include extra wiring, but these are easy to pick up once you know how the standard wiring runs throughout the car.

These typical harness runs are illustrated in Chapter 2, and it is important that you give them special attention.

TRACING ELECTRICAL CIRCUITS

Tracing electrical circuits in a wiring diagram and relating them to the automobile can be as easy or as difficult as you make it. It becomes easy when you have a planned approach and follow it. Here are some tips that should help you unwind a circuit from most wiring diagrams:

1. You're usually interested in just one circuit and not the whole wiring diagram. Don't let all those lines and symbols frighten you. Locate the circuit load component you're interested in, concentrate on it, and follow it back to its source of power.

2. Fundamentally, all electrical wiring diagrams use a common or standard set of electrical symbols. Learn these basic symbols.

3. The diagram wiring usually has a color and circuit code system that makes it easier to follow and identify an individual circuit not only in the wiring diagram but also on the vehicle. With a little effort, any of the coding systems can easily be self-taught in a few minutes. In some cases, the wires are shown in their actual color.

4. If a diagram location index is provided for locating circuit components, be sure to use it. Locating circuit components in a wiring diagram not familiar to you can become a difficult task.

5. Get acquainted with the car manufacturer's diagram layout. In most cases, you will find that diagrams run in a continuous, logical sequence. The diagram for the whole car may be printed on one large master sheet or it may involve several continuous pages. Sometimes the chassis wiring is covered on several separate diagrams. For example, one car manufacturer divides its chassis wiring into three separate diagrams:

   (a) front end lighting and engine compartment

   (b) instrument panel

   (c) body and rear lighting

   This means that when you're tracing a circuit it will usually involve transferring between diagrams.

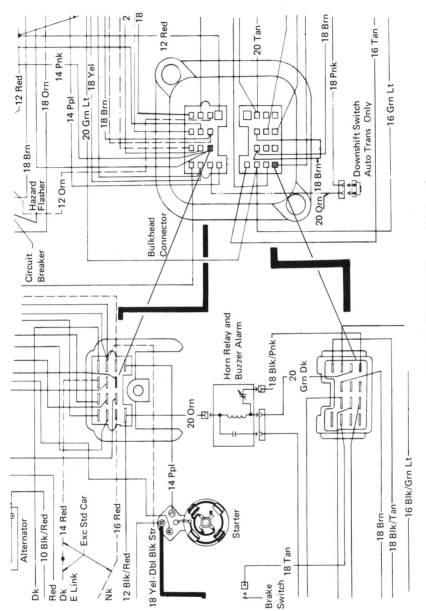

Fig. 6.30. *Courtesy of Pontiac Division of General Motors Corp.*

131

6. You may find it difficult to trace a circuit through diagram multiple connectors that are not number- or letter-coded. Fig. 6-30 shows the connector ends of the engine harness and front-end lighting harness that must be matched to the bulkhead connectors. To correctly match the connector halves, simply place them side by side as two pages in a book and fold them together. Note how the matched terminals are illustrated in the bulkhead connectors, Fig. 6-30.

7. The individual power-accessory circuits such as windshield wipers, seats, windows, etc., are sometimes shown separately from the main chassis wiring diagram (Fig. 6-31). It is not

Fig. 6.31.   Six-way power seat circuit. *Courtesy of Fischer Body—General Motors Corp.*

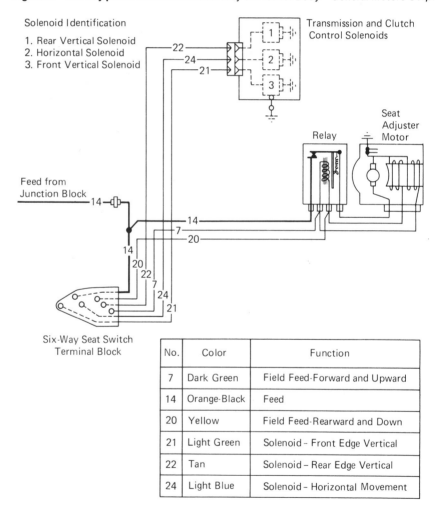

No.	Color	Function
7	Dark Green	Field Feed-Forward and Upward
14	Orange-Black	Feed
20	Yellow	Field Feed-Rearward and Down
21	Light Green	Solenoid – Front Edge Vertical
22	Tan	Solenoid – Rear Edge Vertical
24	Light Blue	Solenoid – Horizontal Movement

ALPHABETICAL INDEX

NAME	ZONE LOCATION
Lamps: (continued)	
License Lamp	C42
Right Back-Up Lamp	D42
Right Rear Side Marker Lamp	C42
Right Tail, Stop, and Turn Signal Lamp	D42
Rear End Lighting (J):	
Left Back-Up Lamp	D46
Left Rear Side Marker Lamp	C46
Left Tail, Stop, and Turn Signal Lamp	C45
License Lamp	C45
Right Back-Up Lamp	D46
Right Rear Side Marker Lamp	D46
Right Tail, Stop, and Turn Signal Lamp	D45
Reverse Gear Indicator Lamp	D67
Starter and Ignition Switch Lamp	C40
Seat Belt Warning Lamp	B10
Trunk Lamp	D32
Turn Indicator Lamps: Left	B34
Right	B35

Fig. 6.32.

uncommon to find the accessory circuit wiring details in the car manufacturer's body service manual.

Now let us use the knowledge gained in this chapter and follow a simple circuit in an actual wiring diagram. We will examine the backup lamp circuit in the Chrysler Barracuda and Challenger, and you'll have a chance to work with the new-style wiring diagram featured in this chapter.

We'll start by looking in the alphabetical index for component location in the diagram and follow through on the Challenger. In Fig. 6-32, the index lists the backup lamp zone location as D 46 for both the left and right sides. In the wiring diagram, find the backup lights by following across the top of the diagram to index number 46 and then up or down to the letter D (Fig. 6-33). Now you can trace the circuit back to a fuse or splice or to a common ground or common switch.

Looking at the circuit detail, Fig. 6-33, note that the lamps are grounded directly at their sockets and that each backup lamp is connected to its power source with individual connectors in the body section. These are coded CB 3 and reference must be made to the body compartment connector graphics (CB), which shows the shape of each connector and it's location in the vehicle (Fig. 6-34).

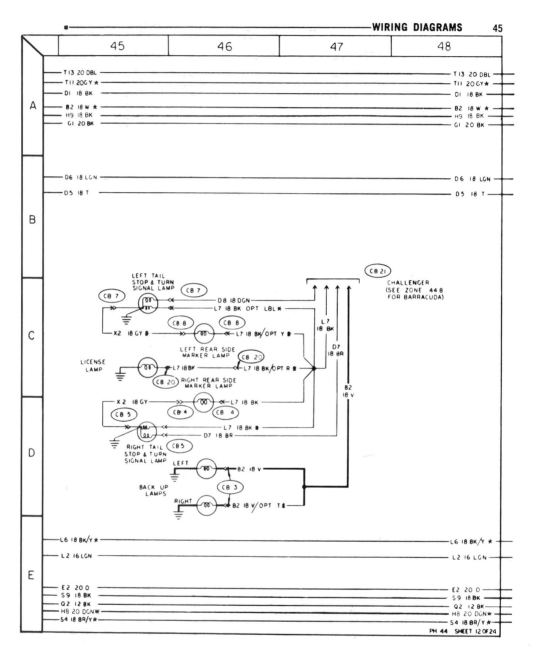

Fig. 6.33.

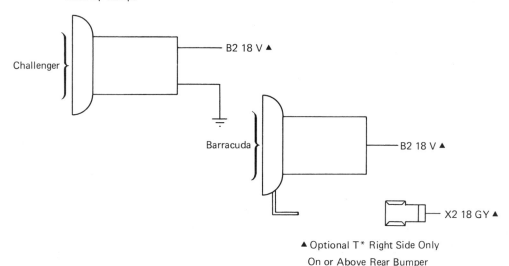

Back Up Lamps

Challenger

B2 18 V ▲

Barracuda

B2 18 V ▲

X2 18 GY ▲

▲ Optional T* Right Side Only
On or Above Rear Bumper

Fig. 6.34. Connector Graphics

By continuing to follow the circuit power to the source of origin, we see that the lamps are joined at a common point or splice somewhere in the wiring harness and the circuit is brought out to a multiple body connector CB 21, Fig. 6-33. The connector graphics are shown in Fig. 6-35.

Notice in the wiring diagram, Fig. 6-33, that the backup circuit is coded B 2, and the standard wiring is 18 gauge and color-coded violet. An optional wire color code, tan with a tracer, also could be used.

At CB 21 in the diagram, Fig. 6-33, reference is made to the Barracuda at zone location 44 B, Fig. 6-36. It can readily be seen that the rear lighting circuits of the Challenger and Barracuda are slightly different; however, they both plug into the body wiring at the common connector CB 21. Basically, the Barracuda rear lamp sockets are grounded by a common wire ground at CB 1 rather than directly to the vehicle body.

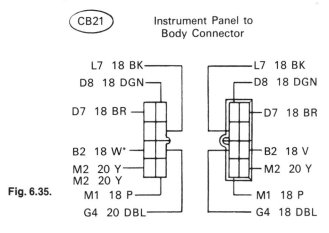

CB21   Instrument Panel to
Body Connector

L7 18 BK
D8 18 DGN
D7 18 BR
B2 18 W*
M2 20 Y
M2 20 Y
M1 18 P
G4 20 DBL

L7 18 BK
D8 18 DGN
D7 18 BR
B2 18 V
M2 20 Y
M1 18 P
G4 18 DBL

Fig. 6.35.

Left Side Cowl

Note that CB 21, Fig. 6-36, the backup circuit wire changes color from a violet to a white wire with a tracer. Following B 2 18W* leads us to the backup lamp switch and the circuit fuse, Fig. 6-37.

Fig. 6.36. *Courtesy of the Chrysler Corporation.*

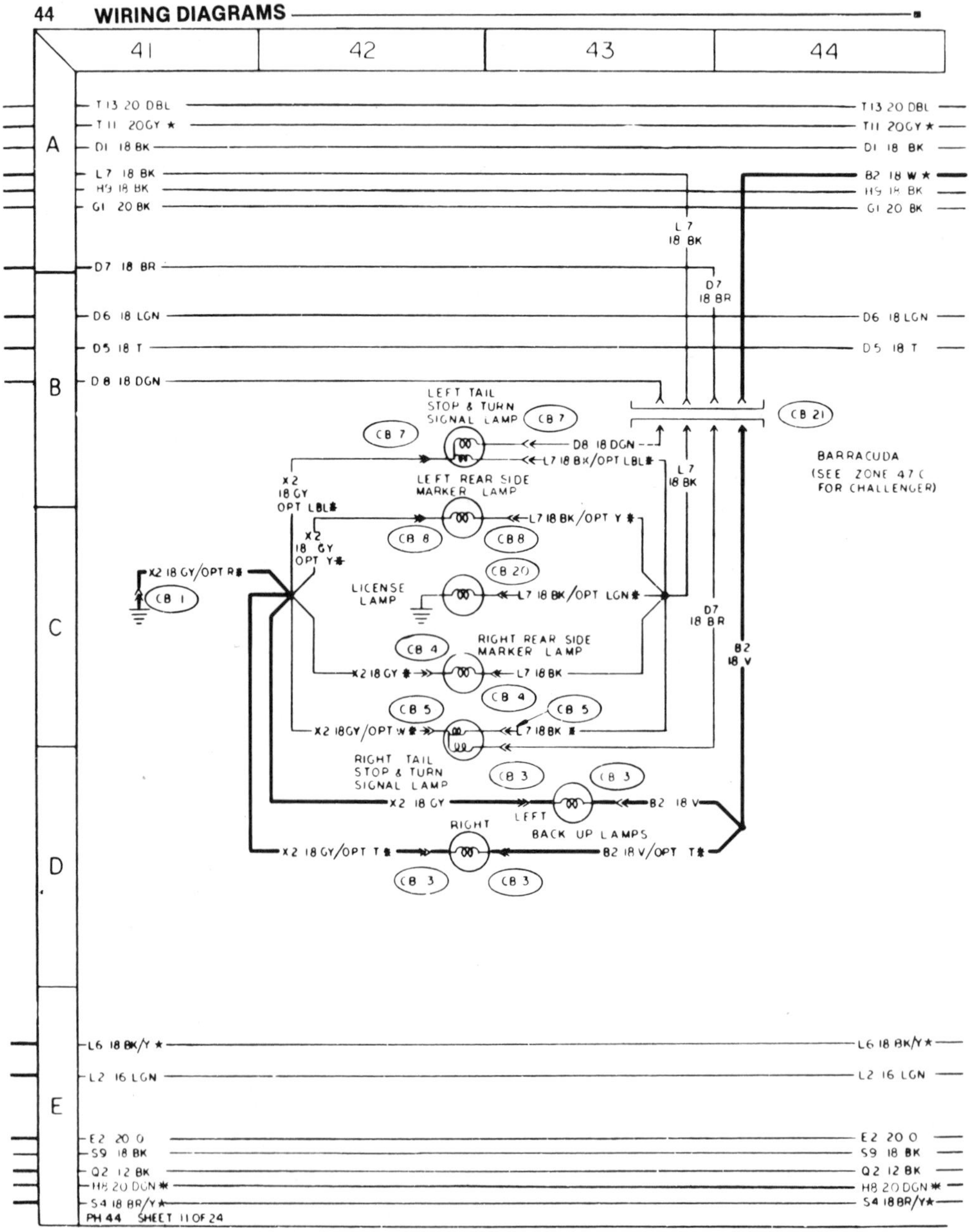

B-J—Master Wiring Diagram

Notice that connector CE 2, Fig. 6-37, can be located in the engine compartment connector graphics (CE) and is plugged into a bulkhead disconnect, Fig. 6-38. The circuit wire had transferred from inside the car body (under the dash panel) to the engine compartment.

Fig. 6.37.

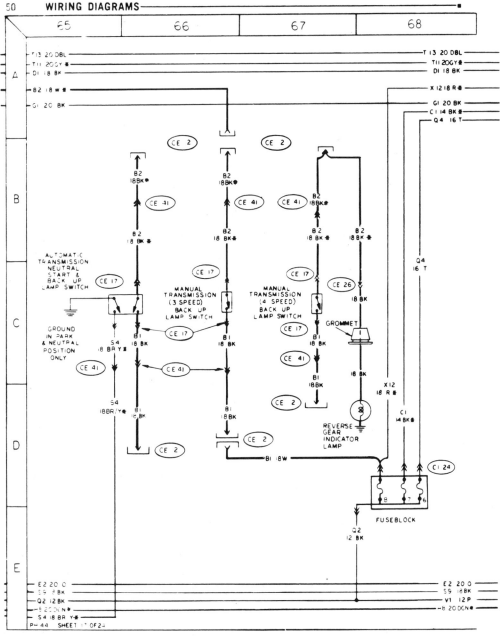

B-J—Master Wiring Diagram

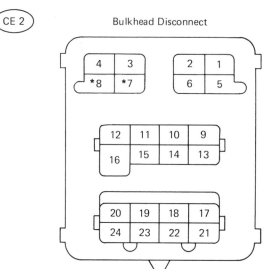

CE 2   Bulkhead Disconnect

1. V3 18 BR	13. D6 18 BK/LGN*
2. V4 18 R	14. L3 16 R
3. S4 18 BR/Y*	15. L4 16 V*
4. C5 14 DGN	16. A1C 1OR
5. V6 18 DBL	17. G6 20 GY
6. V5 18 DGN	18. R6B 12 BK
* 7. B2 18 BK*	19. V10 18 BR
* 8. B1 18 BK	20. C2 18 DBL
9. S2 18 Y	21. G2 20 V
10. L6 18 BK/Y*	22. J3 14 BR
11. D5 18 B/T*	23. J2 16 DBL*
12. H2 16 DGN/R*	24. P5 20 BK

Dash Panel — Left Side, Below W/Wiper Motor

Fig. 6.38. *Courtesy of The Chrysler Corporation.*

CE 17   Transmission Switches

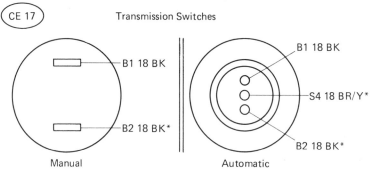

Lower Left Side of Transmission

Fig. 6.39. *Courtesy of The Chrysler Corporation.*

The wiring diagram also shows that connector CE 2 will plug into one of three circuit routes, depending on the transmission application; 4-speed, 3-speed, or automatic. If you are looking for the backup lamp switch for the first time, connector graphic CE 17 will give you the information (Fig. 6-39).

Once the circuit goes through the switch, it routes itself back to the fuse block through connector CE 2 at a bulkhead disconnect; see Fig. 6-38 for CE 2 graphics. Note again the change in the wire color code between the engine compartment and the fuse block, Fig. 6-37; it changes from black to white. The fuse block is coded CI 24 for reference to instrument panel compartment (CI), Fig. 6-40.

In the fuse block, the **Q2 12 BK** is a hot wire feed from the ignition switch to a bus bar. The **X 12 18 R*** wire, which shares the same fuse with the backup circuit, leads to the radio and also furnishes a power tap for the directional light circuit. The actual reference to the Q and X circuits can be found in the circuit code index, Fig. 6-41.

Fig. 6.40. *Courtesy of The Chrysler Corporation.*

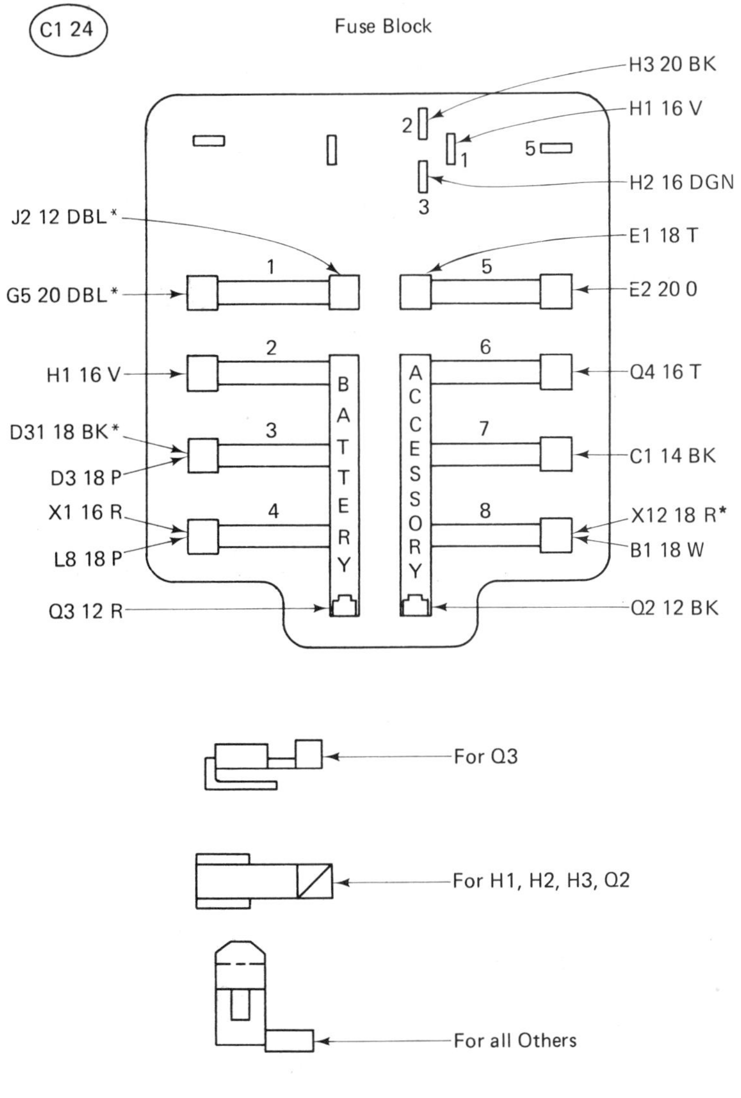

Center of Dash Panel on Bulkhead

A1- Battery Circuit to Ammeter.
A2- Battery Circuit to Ground.
B-- Back Up Lamp Circuit.
C-- Air Conditioning and Heater Circuits (Including Rear Units).
D-- Emergency, Stop Lamp and Turn Signal Circuits.
E-- Instrument Panel Cluster, Switches and Illumination Circuits.
F-- Radio Speakers and Power Seat Circuits.
G-- Gauges and Warning Lamp Circuits.
H-- Horn Circuit.
J-- Ignition System Run Circuit.
J1- Ignition Switch Start Circuit.
J3- Ignition Switch Start Circuit.
L-- Lighting Circuit (Exterior Lights).
M-- Lighting Circuit (Interior Lights).
P-- Brake Checking Circuit.
Q2- Accessory Buss Bar Feed (Fuse Block).
Q3- Battery Buss Bar Feed.
R3- Alternator Circuit to Electronic Voltage Regulator (Field).
R6- Alternator Circuit to Ammeter (Feed).
S-- Starter Motor and Starter Relay Circuit.
T-- Trunk Lamp Circuit.
V-- Windshield Wiper and Washer Circuit.
W-- Power Window Circuit.
X-- Radio, Cigar Lighter, Lamp Grounds, Clock, Speed Control, Power Antenna, Deck Lid and Door Locks.

Fig. 6.40. *Courtesy of The Chrysler Corporation.*

Review questions

1. Identify the following wiring diagram schematic symbols.

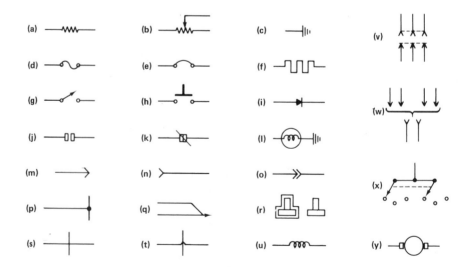

2. Identify the following wiring diagram color codes:

a. BK   b. W   c. LGN   d. O   e. V   f. Y
g. DBL   h. R   i. P   j. PK   k. BR   l. LG
m. LB   n. GY   o. T   p. ORN   q. GRN   r. PPL
s. WHT   t. PNK

3. Identify the following connector codes for Chrysler cars:

a. CE   b. CI   c. CB

4. Identify the meaning of the following wire code letters and numbers:

Chrysler: D 31 18 BK*
Ford: 54 LG-Y; 297 BK-LG H

5. Select a passenger car and locate the following electrical components in the related wiring diagram and then on the car. Use manufacturer's wiring diagram.

a. Hazard Flasher (emergency warning)
b. Turn Signal Flasher
c. Brake Light Switch
d. Horn Relay
e. Fusible Link
f. Neutral Start Switch
g. Backup Light Switch
h. Fuse Panel

6. Select a passenger car and trace the complete backup light circuit on the car using the related wiring diagram. Be sure to locate the circuit fuse and all circuit connectors. Use manufacturer's wiring diagram.

7

Electrical Diagnosis *

The difficulty with electricity is that you can't see it and you can't hear it. In addition, the hideaway manner in which much of automotive electrical wiring is routed and the obscure location of some electrical components and wire connectors often make the diagnosis of electrical problems look like one big headache. It is a headache only if you continuously use a shotgun approach and have no logical step-by-step plan. Without a systematic electrical troubleshooting plan you may find yourself spending hours trying to locate the cause of a light not burning or a motor not turning. You may never even find a solution to the problem.

There is no such thing as an electrical problem that can't be solved when you adopt a systematic troubleshooting plan. There are basic skills and knowledge, however, that you need before you can use any troubleshooting plan:

1. You must have a basic knowledge of electrical circuits and electrical properties.
2. You must be able to locate components and specific wires on a wiring diagram and on the car.
3. You must have the ability to make and interpret tests, such as for power and continuity and for location of shorts and

*This chapter is based on training publications of the Ford Motor Company.

142

opens. This involves the use of a test light, ohmmeter, voltmeter, ammeter, jumper wires, and rheostat.

4. You must learn how to deal with the problem by using simple tests first and more complex tests later in the procedure.

5. You must be able to think in terms of what is right with the problem circuit before concluding what is wrong. Try this approach and you'll like it.

That's what this chapter is all about—to help you develop your own systematic plan to isolate any electrical complaint. Electrical circuit test methods will be reviewed and then you'll be introduced to a technique called *common point diagnosis*.

TESTING METHODS

The systematic approach to troubleshooting requires that you be familiar with some basic testing procedures. Let's get acquainted with them as they will be valuable as you search out circuit troubles.

Visual Inspection

Visual inspection can always be considered a test method. When wisely used, it offers a quick check of the easy-to-see part of a circuit and may quickly reveal the problem; visual inspection alone can solve over 50 per cent of electrical problems. After all, the object is to "find it and fit it," as quickly as possible.

Even mechanics who don't fully understand electrical circuits can often solve front and rear lighting problems by finding a loose or

Fig. 7.1. *Courtesy Peticolas.*

corroded connection, a frayed or broken wire, a poor ground, or a burned-out bulb or corroded bulb socket.

The classic example of where visual inspection pays off is in rear lighting problems such as no lights, intermittent lights, dim lights, or blown fuses. The luggage compartment often takes a beating from vacation suitcases, boxes, golf clubs, etc. This is also hard on the wiring for the rear lights. Another source of rear wiring abuse is the amateur installation of trailer lighting by car owners. Lifting up the trunk lid and inspecting the wiring condition can reveal the cause of many rear lighting problems (Fig. 7-1).

Substitution

Where the symptoms indicate that a circuit component is highly suspect, and it can be substituted easily, replacing the component is the fastest method of troubleshooting. If the "known" good part remedies the circuit problem, then the removed part must be defective. Substitution works well on quick testing of light bulbs, turn-signal and hazard flasher units, relay and switch units (Figs. 7-2 and 7-3). Using a jumper wire as a substitute ground medium for light socket, relay, or switch jumper wire is also a good practice (Fig. 7-4).

Fig. 7.2.   Light bulb substitution. *(Courtesy Peticolas.)*

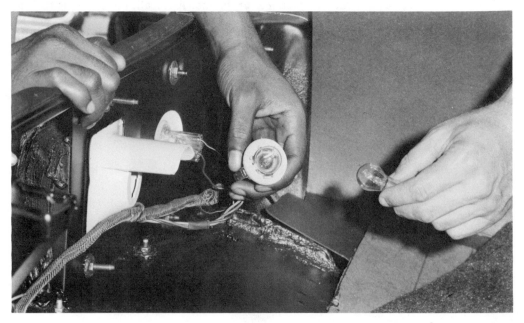

Fig. 7.3.   Flasher bulb substitution.
(Courtesy Peticolas)

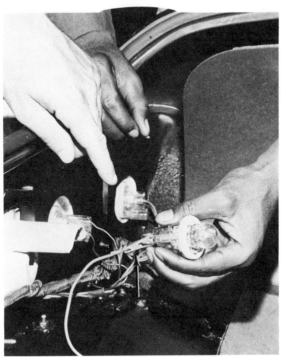

Fig. 7.4. Ground substitution with jumper wire. *(Courtesy Peticolas.)*

Open Circuit

A jumper wire, a 12-volt test light, or a voltmeter can be used to test for an open circuit. A jumper wire provides a means of temporarily by-passing circuit components such as switches, breakers, fuses, relays, or sections of the circuit wire itself. In Fig. 7-5, the jumper wire is connected across a switch component suspected of being open. If the circuit operation is restored, the switch is open.

Another practice is to "jump" directly from a battery hot source to the input connection of a load component to see if the component is operational. This separates the load from the circuit. In Fig. 7-6, if the motor operates, the open circuit can be found by moving the motor end of the jumper toward the power source at exposed check points. If the motor fails to operate then the jumper wire can be used to check out the motor ground.

In testing for an open, you are actually searching for a point or section of the circuit where the power stops. Testing for power is done with a 12-volt test light instrument or a voltmeter; the light is easier to use. Tests for power are made at feed-wire connectors and terminals that should be hot. Keep in mind the limitations of a test

Fig. 7.5.

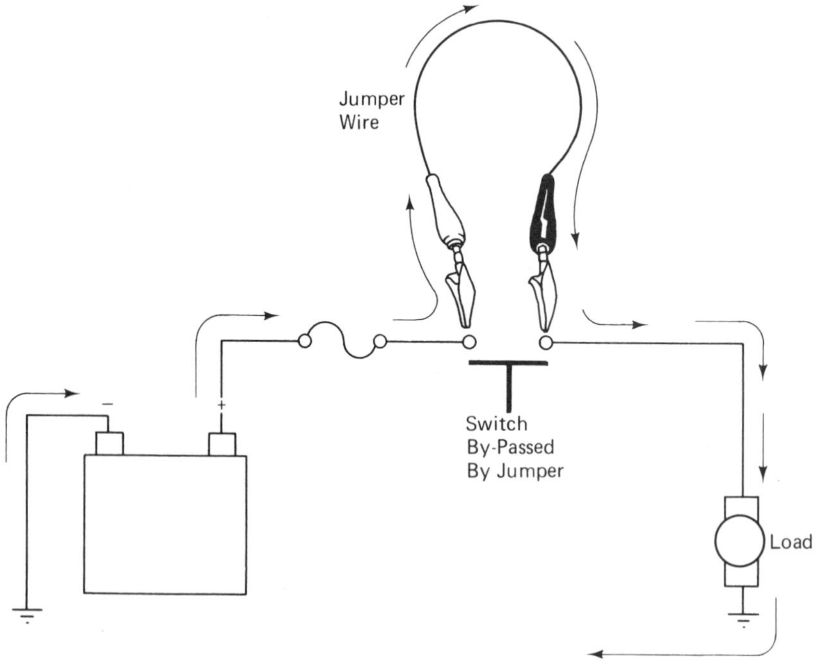

Jumper Wire

Switch By-Passed By Jumper

Load

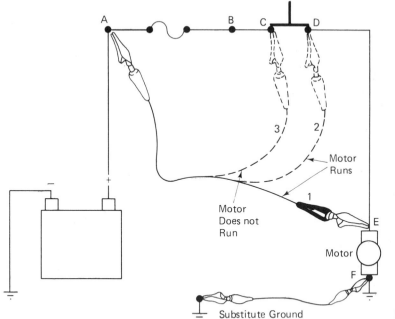

Motor Runs

Motor Does not Run

Motor

Substitute Ground

Fig. 7.6.

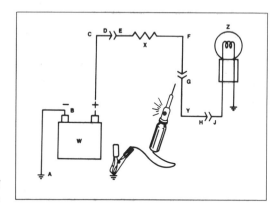

Fig. 7.7. *Courtesy Ford Customer Service Division.*

light; it will tell you if you have power or if you don't, but it will not tell you how much power you have.

Figure 7-7 illustrates the use of a test light. Like a jumper test, the test for power can be performed at successive points to isolate the open in the circuit. For example, the test light in Fig. 7-7 glows when the probe is placed at point G, but it does not glow at point H. The open circuit has now been traced to the wire section Y.

On light bulb problems, the test light offers a quick method of

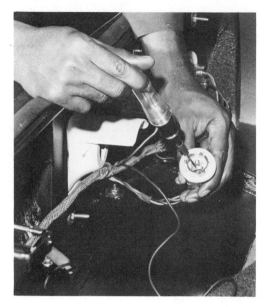

Fig. 7.8.   Testing for power in the light socket. (*Courtesy Peticolas.*)

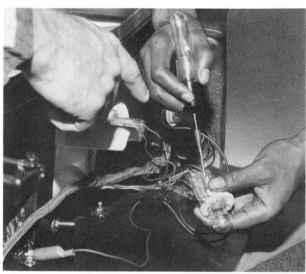

Fig. 7.9.   Testing for power in the hot line to the socket. (*Courtesy Peticolas*)

checking for power in the socket and for power in the hot line to the socket (Figs. 7-8 and 7-9).

Short Circuit

A short circuit can drive a mechanic up the wall. But with calm thinking, a careful plan, and a few tricks of the trade, a short-circuit problem can easily be isolated and repaired. It is not necessary to burn out a dozen fuses or smoke the wiring.

To locate a short, you must keep the circuit excited and the circuit load component disconnected. Figure 7-10a illustrates a short circuit; in Fig. 7-10b, a self-powered test light at the fuse block keeps the circuit short excited without smoking the wire. In place of a self-powered test light, a 5-amp circuit breaker jumper, or even a voltmeter can be inserted in series into the fuse block (Fig. 7-11). If the circuit has a short the test light will glow, the breaker will trigger, or the voltmeter will read 12 volts.

The following procedure based on using the self-powered test light will isolate a short circuit (Fig. 7-12). The same procedure can also be applied when using a test breaker or a voltmeter.

1. Using a wiring diagram, determine the location of all the wire connectors in the circuit.

2. Remove the load component (in this case the light bulb).

3. Unplug the connector farthest from the test light (connector D in Fig. 7-12) and observe if the light still glows. If the light goes out, the short is between the connection and the load component.

4. Continue opening connectors toward the test light. When the light goes out, the short is in that section of wire just beyond

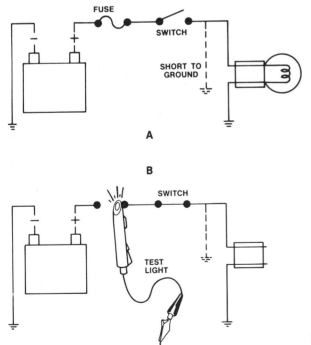

A

B

Fig. 7.10. *Courtesy Ford Customer Service Division.*

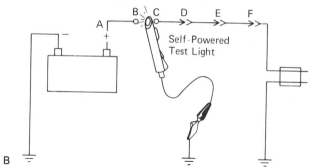

Fig. 7.11. *Courtesy Champion Spark Plug.*

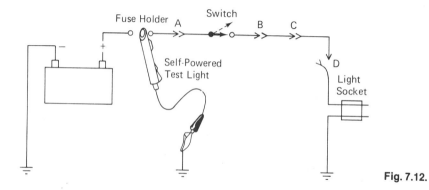

Fig. 7.12.

the "no glow" test point. For example, in Fig. 7-12, if the test light glows with connector C separated but does not glow when B is separated, then wire section B-C is shorted to ground.

It should be obvious that if the test light glows with the circuit switch open, the short circuit problem is between the fuse and the switch.

Continuity

A continuity test is made with an ohmmeter or a self-powered test light, and is used for detecting opens in wire sections, fuses, relay contacts, switches, etc.

The following continuity test procedure is based on using the self-powered test light. The same procedure can be applied when using an ohmmeter.

1. Disconnect the part being tested from the circuit. Circuit power must always be isolated from the test part.
2. Clip the lead to one terminal and touch the light tip to the other.
3. If the light glows, there is continuity. If not, the component is open (Fig. 7-13).

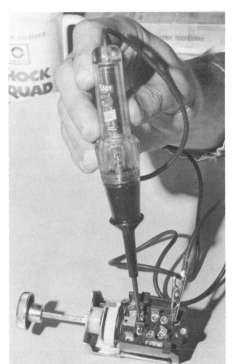

Fig. 7.13. Testing headlight switch for continuity. *(Courtesy Peticolas.)*

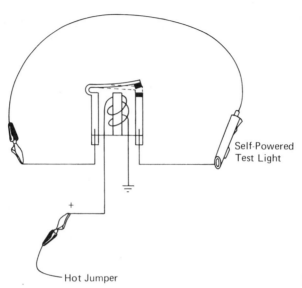

Self-Powered
Test Light

Hot Jumper

Fig. 7.14.

Figure 7-14 shows a continuity test on a "normally open" relay. The light should glow when the relay coil is energized because the points are closed. If the light glows when the coil is not energized, it indicates that the relay points are struck closed.

Voltage Drop

An often overlooked test in working with electrical lighting and accessory circuits is the V.D. or voltage drop test. Although voltage drop was discussed in Chapter 1, let us review it once more.

Voltage drop is simply defined as voltage lost. In any electrical circuit, all of the applied voltage is used up by the time it goes from the battery positive post, all the way through the circuit, and back to the negative post. If the voltage at the battery is 12.5 volts, then all 12.5 volts are used somewhere in the circuit (Fig. 7-15). It would be ideal to have all the applied battery voltage available to be used up by the circuit load (Fig. 7-16). This ideal is never reached, however, because there is always normal built-in circuit resistance that uses some of the voltage before it actually gets to the load. This normal

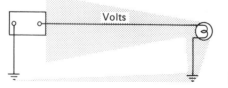

Volts

Fig. 7.15.

resistance occurs at wire connections and switch contacts, and is also a result of the internal resistance of the circuit wire (Fig. 7-17). What is left over is used by the circuit load. In all instances, voltage drop is the result of resistance.

When an electrical circuit exceeds its normal resistance, then more than normal voltage is lost on its way to the working component. Without adequate applied voltage, the working component malfunctions. In the example shown, Fig. 7-18, a poor connection drops or uses 2.5 volts of the battery pressure before it gets to the motor. This means that the applied voltage to the motor is 10 volts. In this situation, the motor would lug and operate at a speed slower than normal.

Let's see how we can use a voltmeter to detect and isolate excess voltage drop. It can get a little tricky, so we'll start by showing you some of the common testing errors that are made and then we'll discuss correct procedures. *Keep in mind that any voltage drop testing must take place with power applied to the circuit.*

In the voltage drop example, Fig. 7-18, if the motor connector were disconnected and the power feed wire attached to a voltmeter, the test reading would be 12.5 volts and the voltage drop would not show up (Fig. 7-19). Another misleading reading occurs when the

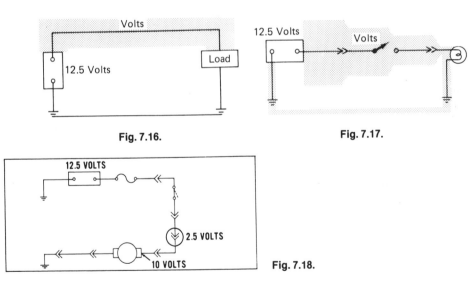

Fig. 7.16.

Fig. 7.17.

Fig. 7.18.

Fig. 7.19. *Courtesy Ford Customer Service Division.*

voltmeter is hooked into the wire connector at the motor with a closed circuit (Fig. 7-20). The meter reads 10 volts and indicates the voltage that must be used by the rest of the circuit, but it doesn't indicate how much voltage is being lost in the ground side of the circuit (Fig. 7-21). From the example shown in Fig. 7-21, the motor really has only 8 volts to work on since 4.5 volts are used up at excessive resistance points in the circuit.

The best way to test for voltage drop is to connect a voltmeter in parallel with the circuit to the operating component. On the power feed side of the circuit, connect the positive lead of the voltmeter to the positive post of the battery and the negative lead into the circuit wire at the selected test point. The voltmeter in Fig. 7-22 is connected to show the total amount of voltage loss on the power feed side of the circuit. For the ground side, connect the negative lead of the voltmeter to the negative post of the battery and the positive lead into

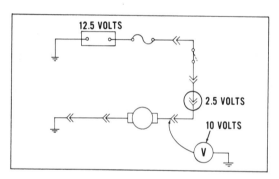

Fig. 7.20.

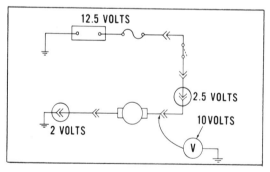

Fig. 7.21.

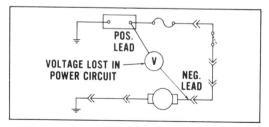

Fig. 7.22.

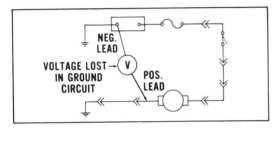

Fig. 7.23.

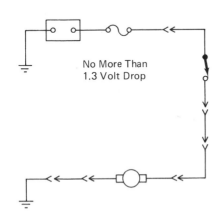

Fig. 7.24.

Fig. 7.25.

the circuit test point. The voltmeter in Fig. 7-23 is connected to show the total amount of voltage loss on the ground side of the circuit.

For lighting and accessory circuits, any total voltage drop over 1.3 volts is unacceptable (Fig. 7-24). The circuit in Fig. 7-25 shows an unacceptable total voltage drop of 1.6 volts. As a standard rule, the ground side of the circuit should not exceed 0.2 volt, and preferably should be zero.

There are three places in the lighting and accessory circuits where the voltage drop specification is a little tighter. The maximum allowable voltage drop between the battery and following points is 0.5 volts:

1. Fuse panel.
2. Headlight switch.
3. Windshield wiper motor.

Battery Drain

A battery that continuously runs down may be subject to an undetected electrical drain from one of the lighting or accessory circuits. To test for battery drain, connect a low-reading ammeter in

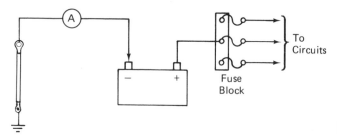

Fig. 7.26.

series between the negative battery post and battery cable (Fig. 7-26). If a significant battery drain exists, the ammeter will read a current draw above .5 amps.

Where do you start to look for the problem? As a guideline, start with some easy checks and highly suspect areas. For example, walk around the car to make sure that all the exterior lights are out; a switch stuck in the closed position could keep the brake lights on. Examine the interior lighting with attention to concealed lights in the glove box, luggage compartment, and under the hood. Remove them one at a time to test for correct switch operation. Does the ammeter read zero when the glove box door, trunk lid, or hood is closed?

In many cars the clock shares a common circuit fuse with the courtesy lights and rates very high as the cause of battery drain. The wind up points in the clock have a habit of sticking closed. In this case, since the disconnect to the clock is usually difficult to get at, pull the fuse to verify with the ammeter that a drain does exist. The clock is also a major suspect when blown fuses continuously occur.

On accessories such as power windows a switch may fail to open when it is released. When the window is in the full-up or full-down position, the car operator fails to suspect this condition. Again, remove the accessory breaker or fuse to determine a drain condition with the meter.

Once you've confined the problem to one area you'll have to use your own imagination to pinpoint the problem. Don't forget to use a wiring diagram to help in your planning.

What would you do if all the fuses and breakers were removed and the test meter still showed a current draw on the battery?

COMMON POINT DIAGNOSIS

Various electrical test methods have been discussed and now you're ready for electrical diagnosis. It will be your job to use whatever test method is needed to help diagnose and isolate the problem.

The purpose of any diagnosis is to give a procedure that will enable you to fix the problem quickly and accurately the first time.

Once you've developed such a procedure, you'll avoid the needless aggravation of false starts. As a matter of fact, you'll really enjoy working with electrical circuits.

Let's introduce you to *common point diagnosis,* a procedure that pinpoints the most probable cause of a problem in a multiload circuit (a circuit with more than one operating component or a circuit made up of several branch circuits). It confines the problem to a small section of a large circuit, before any electrical tests are made.

Common point diagnosis includes a five-step total diagnosis procedure:

1. Verify the complaint.
2. Locate the component on the wiring diagram.
3. Locate common points and common circuits.
4. Try the components on common circuits to isolate the trouble before or after the common point.
5. Perform electrical tests to further isolate the problem.

Before we show how common point diagnosis works in the analysis of a simple complaint, it might be wise to discuss how to verify a complaint. Start by operating the defective circuit to see if it really doesn't work, as described by the customer or the repair order. This sounds very basic, but it is an often overlooked item. While verifying the complaint, be sure to observe all of the symptoms. If related or branch circuits are tied into the system complaint, they should also be tested for proper operation.

Time should be spent not only on verifying what doesn't work, but also what does work. Put a new twist in your diagnosis by concentrating on what is right about the problem circuit before thinking about what is wrong.

Troubleshooting Exercise I

Now we're ready to go through the five-step diagnosis procedure to see how easy it is. For our test case we'll take a complaint of an air-conditioning system that doesn't cool on a Ford Motor Company passenger car. Keep in mind that the following procedure is adaptable to any car and any wiring diagram.

Step 1 Verify Complaint. To verify the complaint, turn on the air conditioning and note the symptoms. In this case the blower works normally, but the air remains warm after several minutes of operation (Fig. 7-27). It is also noted that the engine appears to lack a compressor load and an

Fig. 7.27. *Courtesy Peticolas.*

Fig. 7.28. *Courtesy Peticolas.*

		Noise Suppr
Alternator	A-1	Capacitor
Alternator Regulator	F-2	Radio AM
Battery	B-3	Radio AM/FM
Blower Motor Resistor A/C	E-53	Radio Nois
Blower Motor Resistor Htr.	E-51	Chok
Cigar Lighter	E-24	Radio Spe:
Clock	E-23	AM
Constant Voltage Unit	E-22	AM/FM,
		Seat Belt
Distributor 6 Cylinder	D-4	
Distributor 8 Cylinder	F-4	Starting M
Electric Choke	D-5	Switches
Emission Heater	F-50	A/C Blow
Emission Control Solenoid	D-7	A/C Clutch
Flashers		Backup
Emergency Warning	C-24	Defogger
Turn Signal	C-40	

Fig. 7.29.

under-the-hood inspection reveals that the compressor clutch is not engaged. The pulley is turning, but the compressor driveshaft is not, an indication that the compressor clutch solenoid is not holding (Fig. 7-28).

Step 2   Locate on Schematic. Locate the inoperative component, the air-conditioning clutch solenoid, on the diagram. On Ford Motor Company vehicles, components are easily located in the wiring diagram from a location index code. The location code in this case is found to be F-54 (Fig. 7-29). Once the clutch solenoid is located in the wiring diagram, Fig. 7-30, the circuit can be traced back to a common point.

Step 3   Locate Common Point. In our example, by tracing back on the circuit, a common point is found with the blower circuit at the blower switch. If the blower works, there is power to the switch (Fig. 7-31).

Step 4   Try Common Component. Since the blower motor works, it can be concluded that there is power to the switch. Therefore the trouble must be somewhere between the blower switch and clutch solenoid (Fig. 7-32). Without making one electrical instrument test we have confined the problem on paper to a specific area. We're now ready for the next step, in which we apply our paper work findings to the car.

Step 5   Make Electrical Tests. Using the wiring diagram, again check the locations of the connectors in the isolated trouble area. Note in Fig. 7-32 that each connector has a code number and the locations can be checked out with the wiring diagram connector graphics. Connector C-809 is easily accessible and is a bullet connector in the engine compartment located near the compressor (Fig.

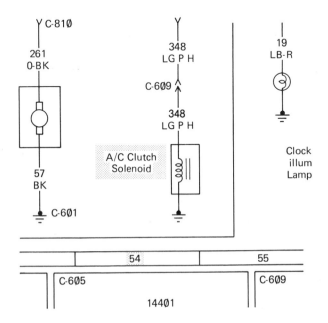

Fig. 7.30. *Courtesy Ford Customer Service Division.*

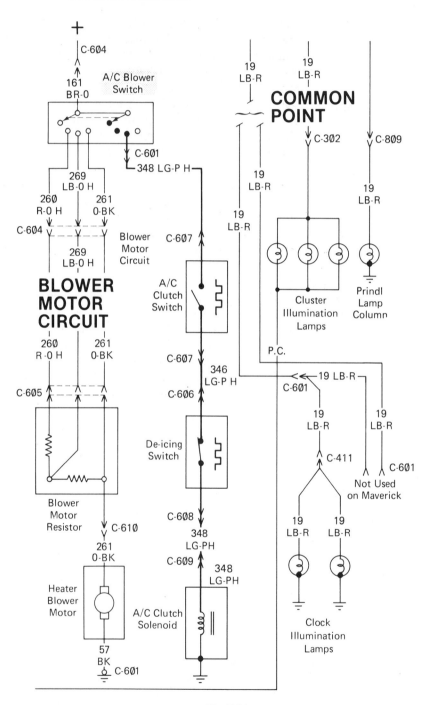

Fig. 7.31.

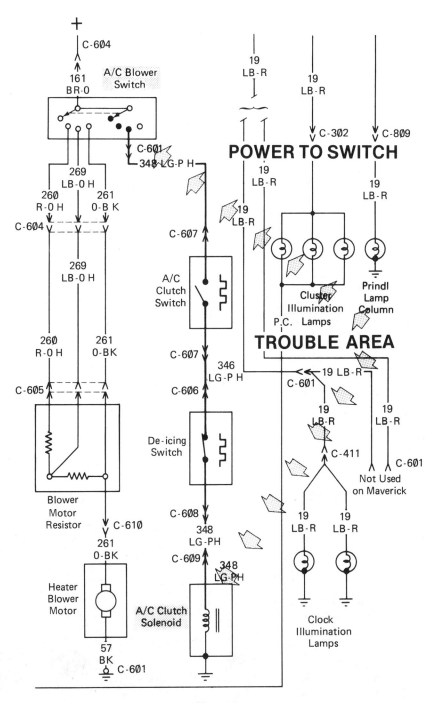

POWER TO SWITCH

TROUBLE AREA

Fig. 7.32.

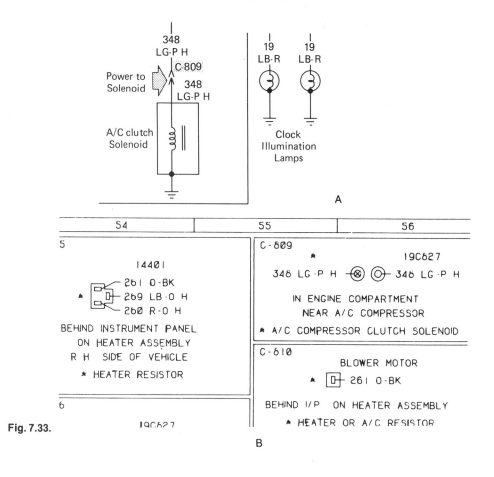

Fig. 7.33.

A

54	55	56

A

B

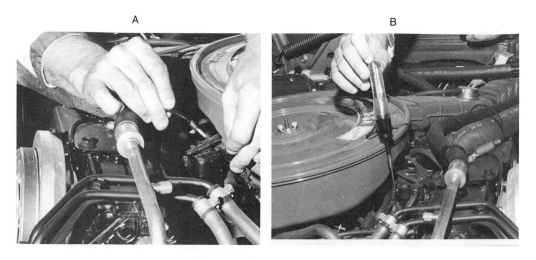

Fig. 7.34. *Courtesy Peticolas.*

7-33). Power to the solenoid is from the female end of the connector. With a test light it is found that there is no power at this connector (Fig. 7-34). The next logical step is to proceed to the next connector point, which is at the deicing switch connector, C-808. The connector graphics tells us that connector C-808 is located under the instrumental panel on the evaporator case and that there are two test points (Fig. 7-35). Using the test light again for a quick power check at these two test points, it is found that there is power to the switch, but no power from the switch (Fig. 7-36). From these test indications it can be concluded that the switch is probably at fault. A positive check of the switch with a continuity test verifies that it is open and should be replaced (Fig. 7-37).

Now wasn't that easy? All it took was a diagnostic process that proceeded in a logical order, effective use of a wiring diagram, and some good common sense.

Fig. 7.35. *Courtesy Ford Customer Service Division.*

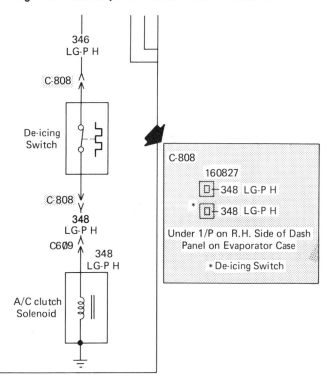

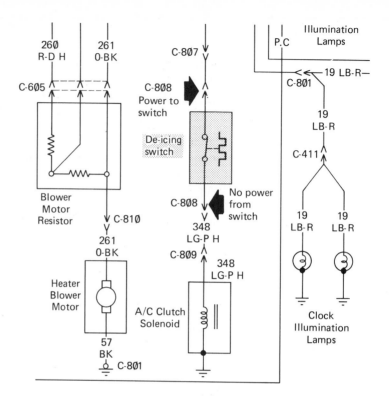

Fig. 7.36.

Fig. 7.37.   Test for Continuity.

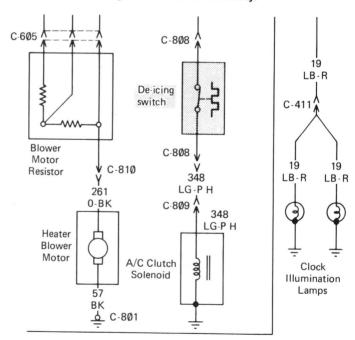

Don't forget to back up your diagnosis with two more steps:

Step 6   Repair the defect.

Step 7   Operate the circuit to check that the repair was successful in correcting the complaint.

Troubleshooting Exercise II

Let's take one more problem and show you how a voltage drop test can apply to an actual situation. We'll make it easy and use the same customer complaint as in Troubleshooting Exercise I—"No Cooling-Fix A/C." Only this time we're going to use a situation that calls for some different thinking.

Step 1   Verification of the complaint proves that there is no cooling. It also indicates that the blower is working and discharging air from the ducts. Visual inspection of the compressor shows that the clutch solenoid is not engaged, Fig. 7-28.

Step 2   Locate the malfunctioning component and circuit in the wiring diagram, as in Troubleshooting Exercise I, Figs. 7-29 and 7-30.

Step 3   Locate the circuit common points in the wiring diagram. In this case there is a common point with the blower motor at the blower switch, as in Troubleshooting Exercise I, Fig. 7-31.

Step 4   Try the common component. Since the blower already works, it proves that there is power to the switch and that the trouble is between the blower switch and the clutch solenoid, as in Troubleshooting Exercise I, Fig. 7-32.

Step 5   Now here's where we'll change the conditions. We're still going to test for power to the clutch solenoid, connector C-809, as in Troubleshooting Exercise I, Figs. 7-33 and 7-34. Only this time the test light indicates that there is power to the solenoid connector (Fig. 7-38). A good technician will then consider the ground side of the solenoid and use a jumper wire to run a known good ground contact. The clutch solenoid, however, still fails to engage. From the above testing we conclude that the problem is in the clutch.

Step 6   Make the repair and replace the clutch.

Step 7   Finally, check that the air-conditioning system has cold air and is working properly.

Fig. 7.38. *Courtesy Peticolas.*

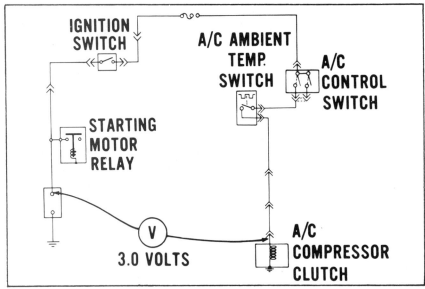

Fig. 7.39. *Courtesy Ford Customer Service Division.*

You're all done, right? Wait a minute! Something caused that clutch to fail! Could it be that the clutch failed because of excessive circuit voltage drop? What if the applied voltage to the solenoid were so low that it failed to develop its normal holding power and had to work extra hard to do its job? If the applied voltage is low, the solenoid cannot draw enough current in its coil windings for the required holding power under heavy compressor load. The clutch slips and develops heat that burns the solenoid windings. This condition may not always be obvious during a check-out of the air-conditioning system.

Let's do a complete job and check the circuit for excessive voltage drop. Keep in mind that the total voltage drop on the insulated side and ground side of the circuit must not exceed 1.3 volts.

To run this check we'll start with the insulated side of the circuit. This requires that the voltmeter positive lead be connected to the positive post of the battery and the negative end to the power feed at the clutch solenoid connector (Fig. 7-39). This hookup parallels

Fig. 7.40.(A)   *Courtesy Peticolas.* **(B)** *Courtesy Ford Customer Service Division.*

A

B

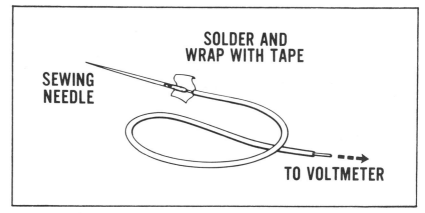

the entire circuit to the clutch and will read the voltage drop measured between the voltmeter leads. To tap the voltmeter leads properly into the circuit, an ice pick can be used at the battery post and a needle probe at the wire connector (Fig. 7-40). Remember that voltage drop testing must be done on a closed circuit. In this problem the voltage drop is 3.0 volts, much too high (Fig. 7-39). The problem must be located and fixed or the new clutch will fail in a short time.

Using the wiring diagram as a guide, move the positive or negative meter lead to a new connector test point, one that is easy to get at. To save time it is a good move to split the circuit in half in this problem and measure the voltage drop between the fuse and the clutch (Fig. 7-41). The meter reads 2.7 volts. That means that most of the drop is occurring within this area and is not between the battery and fuse.

Let's move the negative voltmeter lead to the connector coded C-10, which is located at the bulkhead connector in the engine compartment and is easily accessible (Fig. 7-42). The wire is color-coded black with yellow hash marks at the connector. The voltmeter reading remains 2.7 volts. The problem still hasn't been located but the problem area is gradually getting confined.

Figure 7-43 summarizes the remaining test hookups that finally pinpoint the problem to a bad connection at C-10. The voltmeter reads 2.4 volts across the connection. The positive lead hookup of the voltmeter to the female side of connector C-10 must be made behind the fuse panel.

Fig. 7.41. *Courtesy Ford Customer Service Division.*

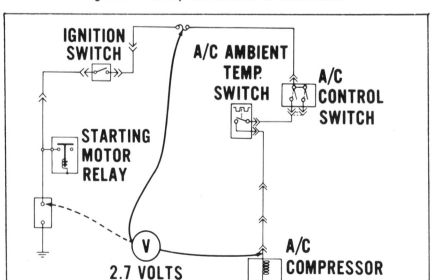

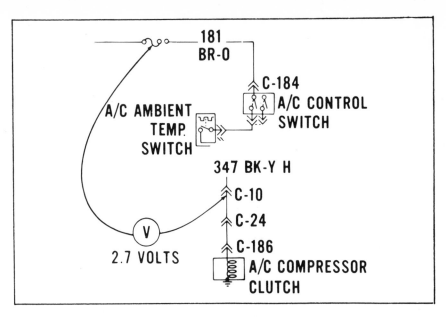

Fig. 7.42.

Fig. 7.43.

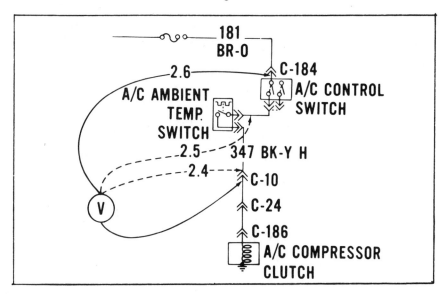

Review questions

1. Why is *visual inspection* an important part of any diagnosis?
2. When would you use *substitution* as a test method for solving a circuit problem?
3. Name two methods that can be used in testing for power in a circuit.

4. What *doesn't* a test light tell you about the circuit power?
5. Define the following terms:
   a. Closed circuit
   b. Open circuit
   c. Short circuit
   d. Voltage drop
6. What four methods can be used to keep a short circuit safely excited while tracking down the problem?
7. How does the use of an electrical wiring diagram help in locating a circuit short or open?
8. What is the purpose of a continuity test?
9. Name two instruments that can be used for testing continuity.
10. Why is it important that the test part of a continuity test be isolated from its power source?
11. Why is it important to have the power source applied to the circuit when measuring the voltage drop of the test part?
12. What is the maximum allowable voltage drop for most lighting and accessory circuits (insulated side *plus* ground side)?
13. What is the maximum allowable voltage drop for the ground side of a lighting or accessory circuit?
14. What is the maximum allowable voltage drop between the battery and the fuse panel, headlight switch, or windshield wiper motor?
15. Why is the ammeter hooked in series between the negative battery post and cable rather than between the positive battery post and cable for a battery drain test?
16. Why can't a voltmeter be hooked in series between the battery negative post and cable for a battery drain test?
17. What is a common point diagnosis?
18. What is the value of an electrical wiring diagram in common point diagnosis?
19. List the five-step procedure for a complete common point diagnosis.
20. Select a passenger car and locate on a related wiring diagram all the circuits that have a common point with the back-up light system.

8

Lighting Circuits

Are you in the dark about this part of a car's electrical system? The average mechanic is not prepared to solve lighting circuit problems much more complicated than replacing a light bulb or a fuse. But lighting circuits are easy to understand and are fun to work with, and to be able to troubleshoot, you must know how the circuit works. This knowledge can be the first step in opening an entire new frontier for you. Car manufacturers claim that mechanics with a lighting and accessory circuit background are the most needed and the least available.

It is not uncommon for the lighting system of many modern passenger cars to contain 50 or more lamp bulbs and hundreds of feet of wiring. Coupled to these are protective devices such as fuses and circuit breakers, switches, wire connectors and harnesses, and a variety of other components that might be necessary to complement the circuit design.

Not too many years ago the typical lighting system used in a passenger car consisted only of those lights required by law: headlights, taillights, and license plate light. In today's car an array of interior and exterior lights have been added for safety and for driver convenience. These include parking lights, stoplights, side-marker lights, back-up lights, dash instrument lights, trunk light, courtesy and dome lights, glove box light, turn-signal and hazard warning lights, etc. Figure 8-1 shows the multitude of light bulbs used for vehicle illumination and discusses some lighting facts and figures related to service.

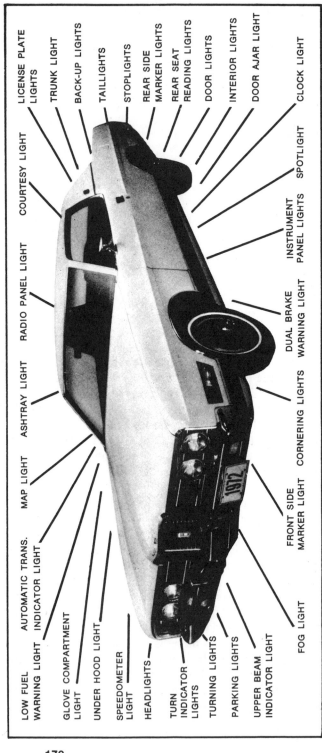

LOW FUEL WARNING LIGHT

AUTOMATIC TRANS. INDICATOR LIGHT

GLOVE COMPARTMENT LIGHT

UNDER HOOD LIGHT

SPEEDOMETER LIGHT

HEADLIGHTS

TURN INDICATOR LIGHTS

TURNING LIGHTS

PARKING LIGHTS

UPPER BEAM INDICATOR LIGHT

FOG LIGHT

FRONT SIDE MARKER LIGHT

CORNERING LIGHTS

DUAL BRAKE WARNING LIGHT

INSTRUMENT PANEL LIGHTS

SPOTLIGHT

MAP LIGHT

ASHTRAY LIGHT

RADIO PANEL LIGHT

COURTESY LIGHT

LICENSE PLATE LIGHTS

TRUNK LIGHT

BACK-UP LIGHTS

TAILLIGHTS

STOPLIGHTS

REAR SIDE MARKER LIGHTS

REAR SEAT READING LIGHTS

DOOR LIGHTS

INTERIOR LIGHTS

DOOR AJAR LIGHT

CLOCK LIGHT

Fig. 8.1. A modern American produced passenger car showing a multitude of light bulbs used to illuminate everything from the roadway to the ashtray. Statistics show that nearly 80 percent of all older model cars have some kind of lighting defect or problem, 50 percent of which consist of burned out or mis-aimed headlights. Others include burned out small bulbs, fuses and turn signal flashers, damaged or broken lenses, and corroded, rusted or damaged connectors or housings. *(Courtesy of Ford Customer Service Division.)*

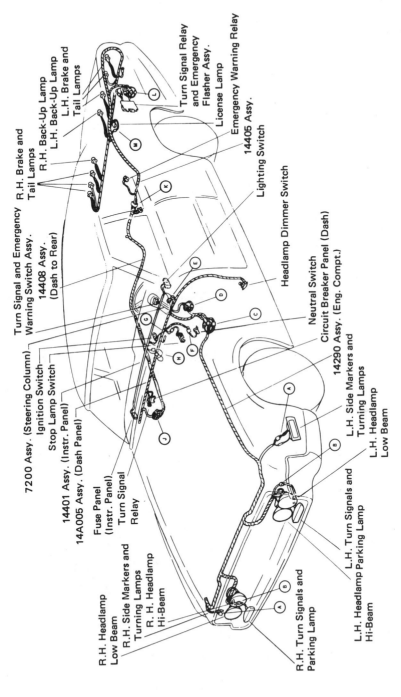

R.H. Headlamp
Low Beam

R.H. Side Markers and
Turning Lamps

R. H. Headlamp
Hi-Beam

R.H. Turn Signals and
Parking Lamp

L.H. Headlamp Parking Lamp

L.H. Turn Signals and
Turning Lamps

L.H. Side Markers and
Turning Lamps

L.H. Headlamp
Low Beam

L.H. Headlamp
Hi-Beam

14290 Assy. and
Circuit Breaker Panel (Eng. Compt.)

Neutral Switch

Headlamp Dimmer Switch

Lighting Switch

14405 Assy.

Emergency Warning Relay

License Lamp

Turn Signal Relay
and Emergency
Flasher Assy.

L.H. Back-Up Lamp

R.H. Back-Up Lamp

L.H. Brake and
Tail Lamps

R.H. Brake and
Tail Lamps

Turn Signal and Emergency
Warning Switch Assy.

14408 Assy.
(Dash to Rear)

7200 Assy. (Steering Column)
Ignition Switch
Stop Lamp Switch

14401 Assy. (Instr. Panel)

14A005 Assy. (Dash Panel)

Fuse Panel
(Instr. Panel)

Turn Signal
Relay

Fig. 8.2. Courtesy of Ford Customer Service Division.

173

Figure 8-2 illustrates the typical routing of interior and exterior wiring in a passenger car. Although lighting system layouts and circuits usually follow a basic pattern in all the car makes and models, some small variations do exist. If you are not totally familiar with a light circuit on a specific car, it is a good policy to check for details in the service manual wiring diagram. The various exterior and interior light circuits will be explored individually in this chapter and will be presented as they appear in most car applications.

LIGHT BULBS

If you are going to work with lighting circuits, you should be aware of some general facts about light bulbs that will make your service more exact and may even turn you into a salesman. Burned-out bulbs are easy to sell as well as easy to replace.

Light bulbs, unlike many other parts and units of a car, have a service life measured in hours of actual use. Rough usage, severe driving conditions, and excessive line voltage shortens the number of service hours that the bulb functions. If the voltage on the bulb is 6 per cent higher than normal, bulb life will be reduced by more than 50 per cent.

The problem with light bulbs is that they make no noise and produce no "fuss" when they burn out. A car owner is usually not aware that a bulb has burned out in the exterior lighting, and this can affect highway safety. Therefore, every mechanic should always make it a standard practice to give every vehicle he services a safety-light check. The average car owner is usually agreeable to having a bulb replaced, the wiring repaired, terminals cleaned, or a fuse replaced. Have you checked *your* exterior car lighting lately? How do you know that all the light bulbs are functioning?

Each automotive light bulb is identified by a common bulb trade number used industry-wide by the various manufacturers of light bulbs. For example, a 1034 double-filament bulb always has that number, whether it is produced by Guide Lamp, Westinghouse, General Electric, or Tung-Sol. The bulb trade number is printed on the bulb for easy identification.

It is important that the correct light-bulb number or substitute number be used for replacement. An incorrect bulb can cause a dim light complaint, or it can cause a turn-signal complaint in which the signal flashes are too rapid or too slow. Do not always assume that the bulb you remove is the correct one for replacement. When in doubt, always consult the service manual or parts catalog.

Chart 8-1 presents some of the common bulb trade numbers you

CHART 8-1

BULB CHART

Bulb Trade Number	Candle Power	Current @ Rated Voltage	Bulb Trade Number	Candle Power	Current @ Rated Voltage
53X	1	.12 Amps	1178	4	.69 Amps
67AF	4	.59 Amps	1195	50	3.00 Amps
90	6	.58 Amps	1196	50	3.00 Amps
90	15	1.04 Amps	1232	4	.59 Amps
97	4	.69 Amps	1445	1.5	.15 Amps
158	2	.24 Amps	1815	1.4	.20 Amps
161	1	.19 Amps	1816	3	.33 Amps
211	12	1.02 Amps	1891	2	.24 Amps
212	6	.74 Amps	1892	1.3	.12 Amps
256	1.6	.27 Amps	1893	2	.33 Amps
257	1.6	.27 Amps	1895	2	.27 Amps
631	6	.63 Amps	4001	26,000	2.93 Amps
1003	15	.94 Amps	4002	21,000 Low 14,000 Hi	3,91,2.93 Amps
1004	15	.94 Amps	4405	50,000	2.34 Amps
1034	32-4	1.80-.51 Amps	4412	35 Watts	2.74 Amps
1073	32	1.80 Amps	4414	18 Watts	1.41 Amps
1076	32	1.80 Amps	4415	35 Watts	2.73 Amps
1095	4	.51 Amps	4416	30 Watts	2.34 Amps
1141	21	1.44 Amps	4435	75,000	2.34 Amps
1142	21	1.34 Amps	4475	30 Watts	2.34 Amps
1155	4	.59 Amps	6012	21,000 Low 32,000 Hi	3.12,3.91 Amps
1156	32	2.10 Amps	6013	21,000 Low 32,000 Hi	3.12,3.91 Amps
1157	32-4	2.10-.59 Amps	6112	21,000 Low 14,0000 Hi	3.91,2.93 Amps

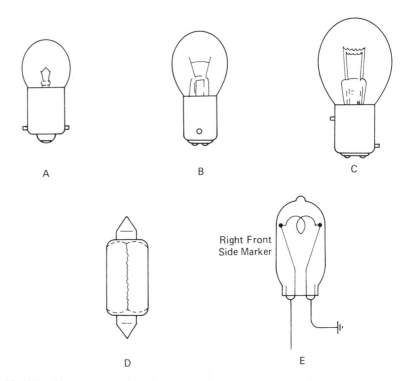

A   B   C

Right Front
Side Marker

D   E

Fig. 8.3. Here are five of the most popular types of small bulbs used in American passenger cars. "A" is a single contact bayonet base type. The light bulb filament is grounded through its socket retainer. "B" is a double contact bayonet base type. The base of the bulb is insulated from the filament. The filament is in series to the contacts and is usually grounded at a switch. "C" is the double contact-duel filament bayonet base type. Each filament is in series to one hot contact and the bayonet base ground. This bulb handles two separate circuits and has offset indexing bugs to locate the bulb in its socket properly. It is primarily used in front and rear exterior lighting for stop-lights, parking lights, tail-lights, turn signals, etc. "D" is the cartridge type small bulb which is often used in dome lights and the other areas that require a shallow socket because of limited bulb space. "E" represents the wedge base small bulb in popular use in printed circuit applications and in some side marker lighting. All the bulb types illustrated fit into a compatible bulb socket, which receives, retains, and positions a bulb correctly for its intended application and for making electrical contact. *(Courtesy of S.A.E.)*

will encounter in automotive applications. A bulb number may be followed by the letters *A* or *NA*. The letter *A* means paint-coated amber and *NA* natural amber.

Small Bulbs

Small bulbs, also known as miniature bulbs, are used for the majority of lights in an automobile (other than headlights, fog lights, and road lights). These smaller type bulbs are available in the basic designs shown and discussed in Fig. 8-3.

FIBER OPTICS

Fiber optics is a method of providing illumination by a single light source acting at a distance from the objects to be illuminated. The single light source is transmitted to the object to be illuminated by a special type of optical cable consisting of strands of plastic material known as polymethyl-methacrylate. These strands are sheathed by a transparent polymer that acts to insulate the bouncing light rays as they travel within the strands; the cable is further enclosed in a flexible opaque outer sleeve. The fiber cable acts as a light conductor; light rays produced by the light source travel in a zig-zag path by internal reflections along the cable and produce a source of illumination at the other end of the cable (Fig. 8-4). The light intensity at the cable exit can be increased by simply increasing the number of fiber strands. The fiber cable itself can be bent and twisted in any number of positions and can be used for short or long runs without affecting the light conductance.

Fiber optics can provide a lighted area wherever desired, particularly in places where ordinary small bulbs would be inaccessible for service replacement. On a limited basis fiber optics applications are found on instrument faces, dash lighting over switches, and even in the front and rear lighting of some vehicles.

Fig. 8.4.

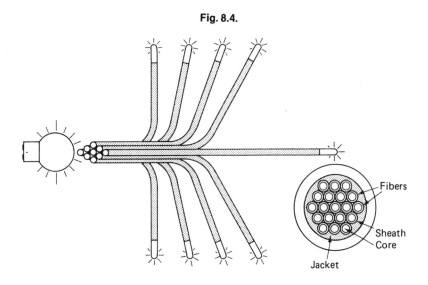

HEADLIGHTS

Headlight bulbs have remained basically the same since the introduction of the sealed beam in 1939. The "safety" legislation of 1940 made sealed-beam headlights a legal requirement in all the states and still regulates current production for both headlights and auxiliary lighting. The few changes that have taken place have been limited to minor modifications in the lens structure and a modest increase in candlepower. For increased visibility, the four-light system on large passenger cars was introduced in 1958.

As most of us realize, car headlights have not produced the optimum illumination necessary for present highway cruising speeds. A car is often moving faster than what the headlights can illuminate. One must realize, however, that car manufacturers have been hindered in their ambition to give better lighting up front. In the 1940s, the use of high-intensity lights was abused by a significant number of car owners so that light intensity and glare became a road safety hazard. Various state legislatures passed laws regulating the power of the headlights, and regulating the number and use of auxiliary lights. In some states auxiliary lights were banned entirely. Because each state has its own regulations, car manufacturers are limited to designing a headlight system that will satisfy all legal requirements.

The U.S. Department of Transportation has recently considered upgrading automobile headlighting systems. They have proposed new regulations permitting an increase in candlepower from the current

Fig. 8.5.

Headlighting Systems
Present Systems

2 Beam – 2 Lamp (7")   2 Beam – 4 Lamp ($5\frac{3}{4}$")

Proposed Systems

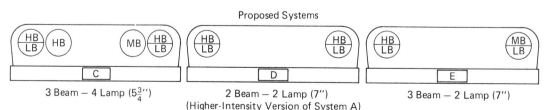

3 Beam – 4 Lamp ($5\frac{3}{4}$")   2 Beam – 2 Lamp (7")   3 Beam – 2 Lamp (7")
(Higher-Intensity Version of System A)

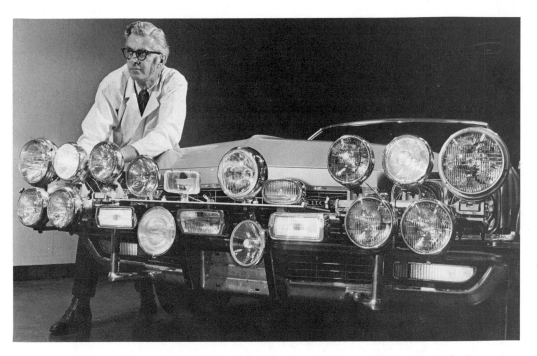

Fig. 8.6. Lighting equipment being tested here may appear as improvements in the future. *(Courtesy of Guide Lamp Division of General Motors Corp.)*

75,000 to a maximum of 200,000. The regulations also call for any of three types of improved headlighting systems:

1. An improved two-lamp, two-beam system.
2. A two-lamp, three-beam system.
3. A four-lamp, three-beam system.

Figure 8-5 compares the present and proposed headlighting systems.

The three-beam system gives the following advantages:

1. The total forward version on low beam is less intense and more spread out to provide better roadway illumination in urban area traffic.
2. The mid-beam light is superimposed toward the center of the road and seeing distance approaches that of the current two-lamp and four-lamp high beams with glare no greater than that of present low beams. This is useful on high-speed freeways and rural roads, even with heavy oncoming traffic.
3. The high beam adds concentrated light to the right and center

of the roadway, increases illumination, and keeps glare at the level of present high beams. The high-beam filaments of the outboard supply "surround" light to enable motorists to see traffic signs on the side of the roadway.

The test vehicle in Fig. 8-6 clearly indicates that car manufacturers are prepared to accept the challenge to provide better headlighting systems.

A sealed-beam headlamp is a special self-contained glass unit made up of (1) an inner glass parabolic reflector sprayed with

Fig. 8.7. *Courtesy of General Electric Lamp Division.*

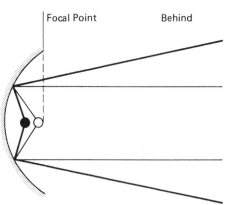

Fig. 8.8.

Focal Point   Behind

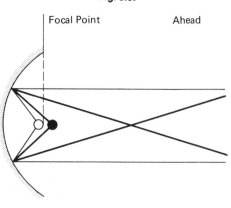

Fig. 8.9.

Focal Point   Ahead

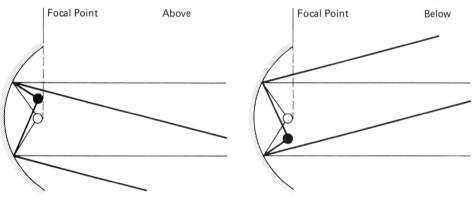

Fig. 8.10.   Fig. 8.11.

vaporized aluminum to give a reflecting surface comparable to that of silver and (2) an outer glass lens (Fig. 8-7). The glass lens is fused to the glass reflector and the inside is filled with argon gas. Precision-positioned bar filaments are employed for the illumination source and a prefocused beam. A bar filament may produce no more than 50 candlepower; however, the parabolic reflector intensifies this light output into a power beam of 20,000 candlepower. The lens action of the outer glass directs the reflected light to form the required beam pattern.

It is important that the parabolic reflector reflect parallel beams of light only. This is accomplished by accurately placing the filament at the focal point of the reflector. Figures 8-8 and 8-9 illustrate how the light rays will be dispersed should the filament be located behind or ahead of the focal point. If the filament is behind the focal point, the reflected rays will diverge. If the filament is ahead of the focal point, the light beams will narrow to a point where they cross and separate.

If the light filament is above the focus, the major portion of the beam will be tilted down. If it is below the focus, the major portion of the beam will be tilted up. This effect is shown in Figs. 8-10 and 8-11. Note, however, that the beams are in a parallel projection. Filaments are deliberately offset in this manner to control the beam and to make it move up and down in a two-filament headlight. The lower filament is used for the high beam and the upper filament for the low beam.

If the light beam did not pass through the lens, a bright circular beam would be projected and road illumination would be limited. A broad flat beam is desired and this is accomplished by passing the light through concave flutes or prisms in the front cover glass (Fig. 8-12). This spreads the circular beam horizontally.

The circular beam can also be controlled vertically (Fig. 8-12). It

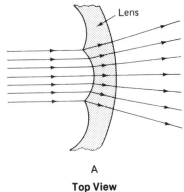
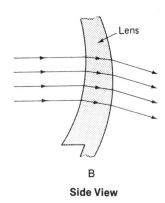

A

Top View

Fig. 8.12.

B

Side View

Fig. 8.13.

is important that the glaring upper part of the beam be deflected below the eye level of oncoming traffic. This, too, is accomplished by prisms or flutings in the cover glass (Fig. 8-13).

The shape of the reflector, the type of lens, and the position and shape of the filament all influence the design beam of a headlight.

Headlights are classified as Type-1 or Type-2. Type-1 bulbs have a single filament centered in the reflector so that the light is reflected straight ahead; they are used as the inboard lights in a four-lamp dual sealed-beam roadlighting system and provide for part of the upper beam pattern in conjunction with the Type-2 bulb located on the outboard.

Type-2 bulbs have double filaments. One filament is slightly above the reflector focal point and the other is slightly below. The upper filament provides the low beam and the lower filament the upper beam. The low beam carries the higher candlepower.

In a four-lamp dual sealed-beam roadlighting system the Type-1 and Type-2 bulbs each have a standard 5 3/4-inch diameter. Both high-beam projections from the bulbs are aimed into a single effective up-front pattern for maximum lighting on open-road driving. For traffic driving, a low-beam pattern is furnished by the Type-2 bulb only.

On vehicles using a two-lamp dual sealed-beam roadlighting system, two similar 7-inch Type-2 bulbs are used, one on each side of the vehicle, providing for upper and lower beams.

It is difficult to interchange or mix-up Type-1 and Type-2 5 3/4-inch bulbs during installation for the following reasons:

1. For easy identification, the bulb type number is clearly molded on the top of the front lens (Fig. 8-14).

2. The seating lugs on the back of the reflector flange, Fig. 8-15, are located at different angles for Type-1 and Type-2 bulbs, and will not permit installation of the bulb, in other than their own retainers. These lugs also insure that the bulbs will be set in their correct position within the headlamp assembly.

3. A Type-2 bulb has three terminal connectors and a Type-1 bulb two terminal connectors. One terminal always leads to a chassis ground.

Fig. 8.14(A).

Type 1

Fig. 8.14(B).

Type 2

Type-1 and Type-2 sealed beams are also identified by their bulb trade numbers which are stamped on the back of the reflector.

5¾ inch	Type 1	(5001) or (4001)
5¾ inch	Type 2	(4000) or (4002)
7 inch	Type 2	(6014) or (6012)

Figure 8-16 shows a typical headlight housing assembly. When a sealed beam bulb is replaced, the retainer ring can be removed without having to tamper with the adjustment screws for the vertical or horizontal bulb aim. Recent assembly design changes now make it

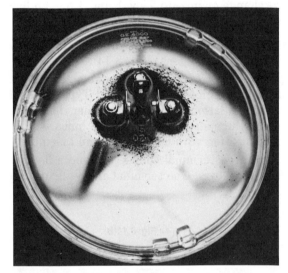

Fig. 8.15.

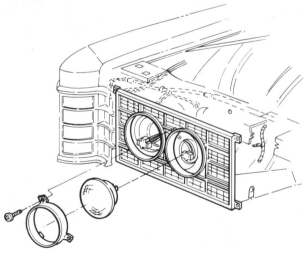

Fig. 8.16. *Courtesy of Ford Customer Service Division.*

Fig. 8.17.

possible to adjust the headlight aim without removing the headlight door or cover trim (Fig. 8-17).

> *Note:* Tampering with the headlight adjustment screws when replacing a seal beam is a common error made by novice mechanics.

Headlight Aiming

Headlight aiming is a critical service item on cars. Safety-lane check data show that headlight adjustment is the leading single item found to be faulty. We will discuss headlight aiming only briefly, because details of equipment and aiming procedures can be found in most manuals.

It is interesting to note the results of some recent research evaluating the accuracy of headlamp aim or adjustment using four current methods: visual, optical, photoelectric, and mechanical. Mechanical aimers were assessed to be the most accurate of the four methods; in addition, they are available at reasonable cost and are portable. To use this type of equipment, aiming lugs are provided on the sealed-beam headlamps to properly orient the aimers to the lens (Fig. 8-18). Figures 8-19 and 8-20 show examples of a mechanical-type spirit cross car aimer, a popular technique; it is available from several equipment manufacturers. The least accurate method tested was visual aiming, in which an aiming screen is placed 25 feet in front of the vehicle and the headlight pattern is then projected on the screen. Although this method is still promoted in some service manuals, it fails to produce accuracy because even skilled test drivers are unable to exactly center the vehicle to the screen, and this is essential to obtain precision with this method. Future developments may provide for the actual headlight aiming by the driver from a dash control.

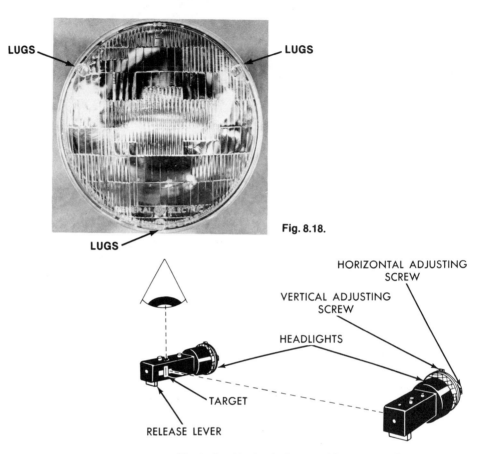

LUGS

LUGS

Fig. 8.18.

LUGS

HORIZONTAL ADJUSTING
SCREW

VERTICAL ADJUSTING
SCREW

HEADLIGHTS

TARGET

RELEASE LEVER

Fig. 8.19.   Mechanical type spirit cross car aimer.
(Courtesy of The Chrysler Corporation.)

Fig. 8.20.   Compensating for floor-level mechanical aimers.
(Courtesy of The Chrysler Corporation.)

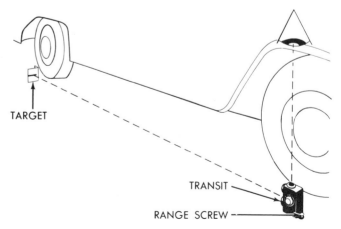

TARGET

TRANSIT

RANGE SCREW

Fig. 8.21.

After replacing a sealed-beam unit it is always a good practice to recommend a headlight aim check to the customer.

Available on some car makes and models are headlight designs of rectangular shape to accommodate low-profile body styling, Fig. 8-21.

Headlamp Switch

The headlamp switch is an operator-actuated device for control of various vehicle light sources. Its primary function is to control headlights, parking lights, taillights, and certain marking lights. A secondary function may be to control various accessory and instrument lights. Circuit breakers may be incorporated for circuit overload protection.

The switch is a "push-pull" type that includes a rheostat for controlling the brightness of the instrument panel lights, and a detent position for the dome and courtesy light circuit (Fig. 8-22). The switch knob "push-pull" positions control the light circuits as follows:

1. Parking Position (knob pulled out to the first notch) turns on the parking lights, taillights, license light, side marker lights, and instrument panel lights. The rheostat, controlled by turning the knob, must be set properly for the instrument panel to turn on.

2. Driving Position (knob pulled out to last position) turns on the headlights while the other lights remain as in the parking position.

3. Dome Light Position (knob turned fully counterclockwise) turns on the dome and courtesy lights regardless of the in or out position of the switch.

Incorporated in every light switch is at least one thermal circuit

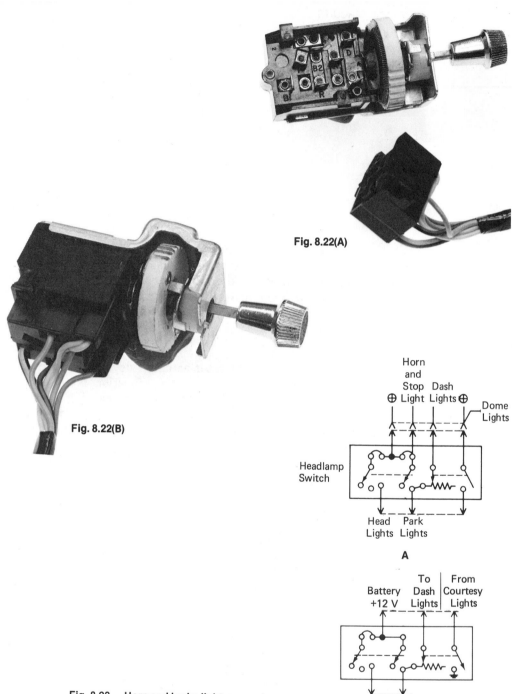

Fig. 8.22(A)

Fig. 8.22(B)

Horn
and
Stop Dash
⊕ Light Lights ⊕
Dome
Lights

Headlamp
Switch

Head Park
Lights Lights

A

To From
Battery To Dash Courtesy
+12 V Lights Lights

To To
Headlights Taillights

B

Fig. 8.23. Horn and brake light power does not always tap from the light switch. (Shown in "OFF" position.) (A) Ford; (B) American Motors, Chrysler, General Motors.

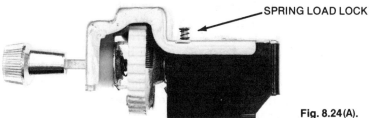

Fig. 8.24(A).

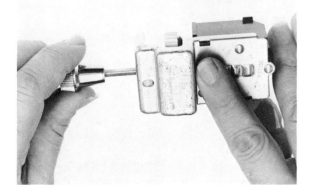

Fig. 8.24(B).

breaker connected in series to the headlight circuit. Should a short occur in the headlight circuit, it protects the wiring and prevents a sudden loss of light power. The thermal breaker produces a vibrating action and resulting light flicker which serves as a warning that a short circuit exists. The thermal breaker at least permits partial headlight operation during short circuit conditions, whereas a fuse would blow and leave the car with no lights.

Some light switches are designed with two thermal circuit breakers. The second circuit breaker protects the parking light circuit and may also include the brake light and horn circuits. The dual breaker switch is used by the Ford Motor Company (Fig. 8-23).

Fig. 8-24a is a picture of a light switch assembly. To remove the light switch from the dash board, you first must remove the control knob stem. Pull the control knob stem all the way out until it stops, then push in the spring loaded lock (Fig. 8-24b) and pull the stem completely out of the switch. To replace the stem, insert the stem into the switch and push it all the way in. The stem will lock in place automatically.

Headlight Circuit

In a four-lamp dual sealed-beam circuit (Fig. 8-25), the power comes into the headlight switch and goes through a circuit breaker inside the headlight switch to a dimmer switch (Fig. 8-26). The dimmer switch can be in either the high beam or the low beam position. If the high beam is selected, the current will travel to the inboard and outboard lights and also to the high-beam indicator on the dashboard. The indicator light informs the driver that the high beams are on. With the dimmer switch on the low-beam selection, the circuit power feeds the low-beam filaments on the outboard lights only.

A two-lamp sealed-beam circuit is shown in Fig. 8-27; it works in a manner similar to the four-lamp circuit just described.

Fig. 8.25.   High Beam

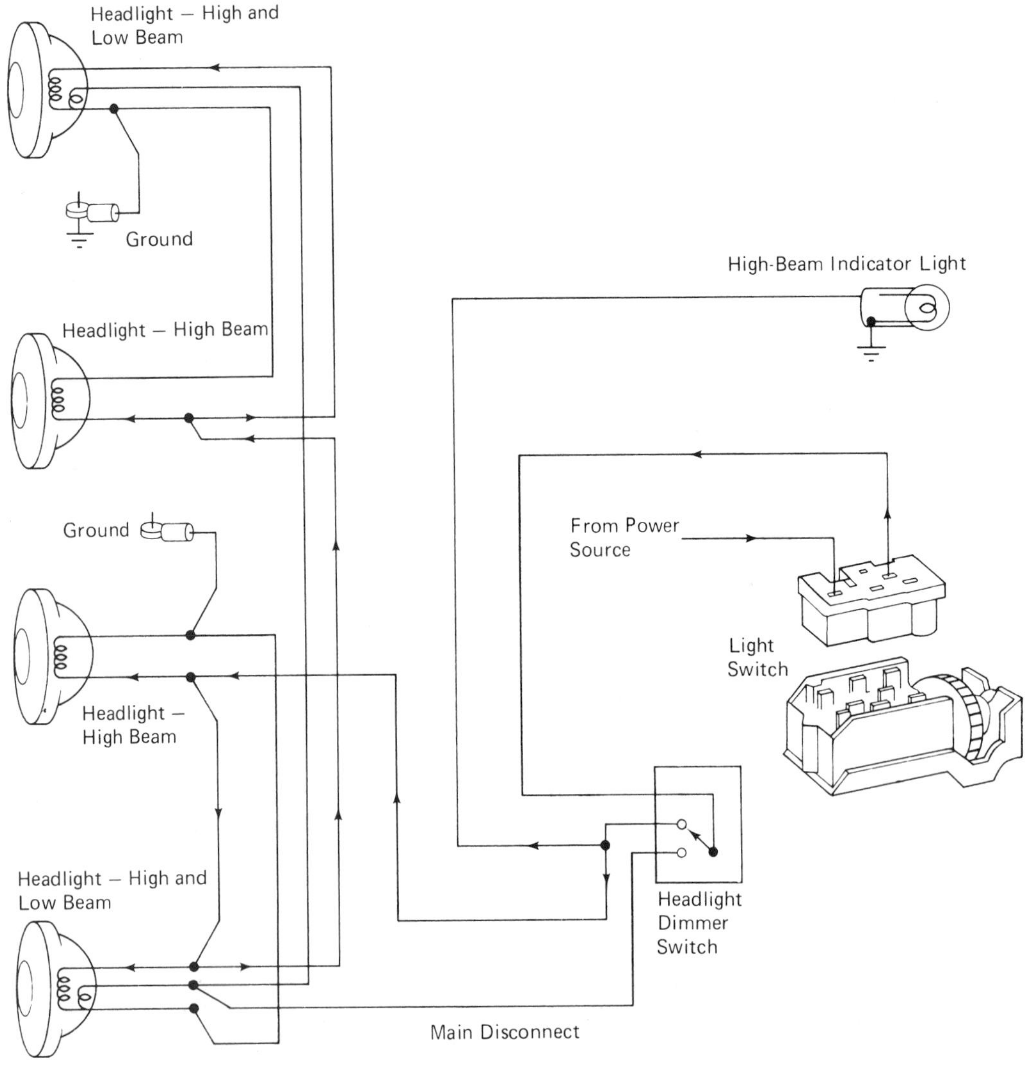

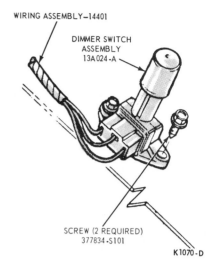

WIRING ASSEMBLY—14401

DIMMER SWITCH
ASSEMBLY
13A024-A

SCREW (2 REQUIRED)
377834-S101

K1070-D

Fig. 8.26. *Courtesy of Ford Customer Service Division.*

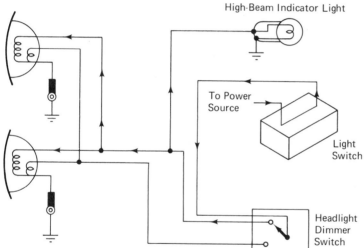

High-Beam Indicator Light

To Power
Source

Light
Switch

Headlight
Dimmer
Switch

Fig. 8.27.

PARKING LIGHTS AND TAILLIGHTS

The parking lights and taillights are steadily burning, low-intensity lights. These light circuits are energized whenever the headlight switch is in the park or the driving position.

The parking lights are mounted on the left and right front of the vehicle to mark the vehicle when parked. They also serve as a reserve front position marking system in case of a headlight failure. The taillights are used simply to designate the rear of the vehicle.

Parking lights and taillights usually use a double-contact dual-filament light bulb number 1157 or 1034. The bulbs contain a high current filament used for the turn signal and stoplight operation, and a low current filament for the parking light and taillight operation.

Circuit power is supplied from the fuse panel or from a circuit breaker in the headlight switch (Ford). Since both the parking lights and taillights are tied into the same circuit, they share the common circuit protection. Figure 8-28 shows the power distribution of a complete parking and taillight circuit.

A typical wiring harness routing of the parking lights and taillights is illustrated in Fig. 8-29.

SIDE MARKER LIGHTS

For added nighttime driving safety, exterior automobile lighting now includes side marker lights. An amber-lensed light is used on the left and right sides of the vehicle front and a red-lensed light on the left and right sides of the vehicle rear. These lights glow continuously

Fig. 8.28.

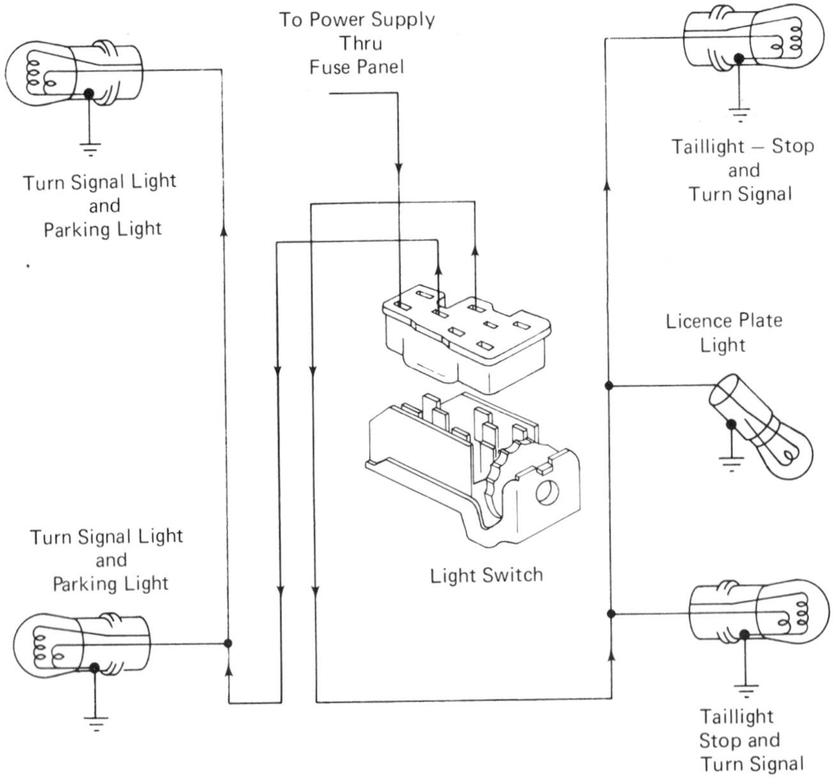

To Power Supply
Thru
Fuse Panel

Turn Signal Light
and
Parking Light

Turn Signal Light
and
Parking Light

Light Switch

Taillight – Stop
and
Turn Signal

Licence Plate
Light

Taillight
Stop and
Turn Signal

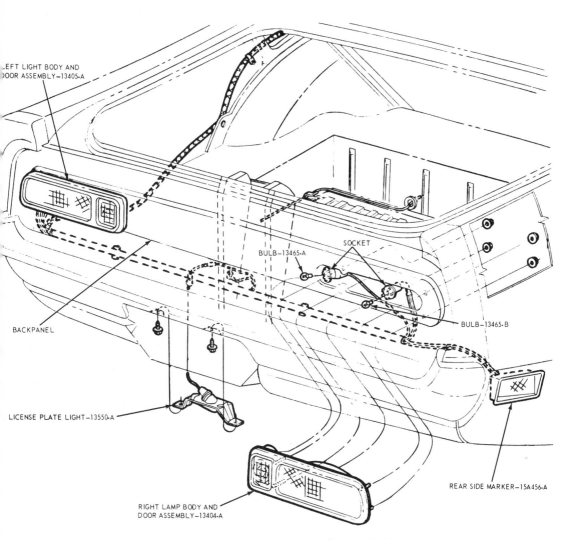

LEFT LIGHT BODY AND
DOOR ASSEMBLY–13405-A

SOCKET

BULB–13465-A

BULB–13465-B

BACKPANEL

LICENSE PLATE LIGHT–13550-A

RIGHT LAMP BODY AND
DOOR ASSEMBLY–13404-A

REAR SIDE MARKER–15A456-A

Fig. 8.29. *Courtesy of the Ford Customer Service Division.*

when the park lights or headlights are on. Typical wiring circuits are shown in Figs. 8-30 and 8-31; note that the front side marker lights either have a direct ground to the body sheet metal or are connected across the turn signal and park light circuits.

In Fig. 8-31, the front side marker lights will flash when the turn signal is activated. One side of each marker light is connected to the parking light circuit, the other to the turn signal circuit (Fig. 8-32). When power is applied to the parking light circuit, with the turn signal switch off, the parking lights and the side marker lights shine.

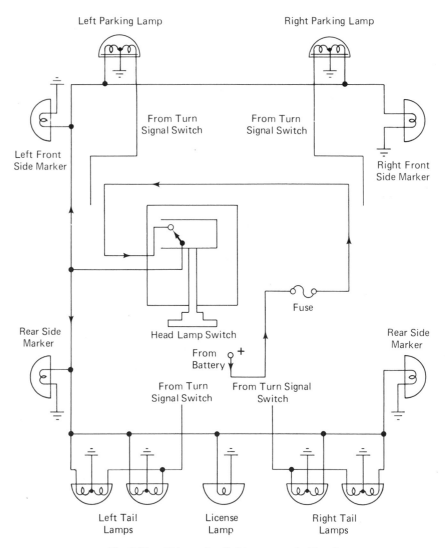

Fig. 8.30.   Side marker lights—grounded front.

(The side marker lights are grounded through the turn signal bulb filaments.) The current passing through the side marker lights is not enough to light the turn signal light (Fig. 8-33).

When the turn signal lights are on with the parking lights off, the side market lights are grounded through the parking light bulb filaments. The turn signal lights and the side marker lights flash simultaneously (Fig. 8-34).

If the parking lights are on when the turn signal light comes on, equal power is applied to both sides of the marker lights. The side marker lights will not shine (Fig. 8-35). But when the turn signal flasher shuts off power to the turn signal light, with the parking ights on, the side marker lights shine (Fig. 8-36). In other words, if the parking lights are on when the turn signal switch is actuated, the side marker lights and the turn signal lights flash alternately.

Fig. 8.31.   Side marker lights—insulated front.

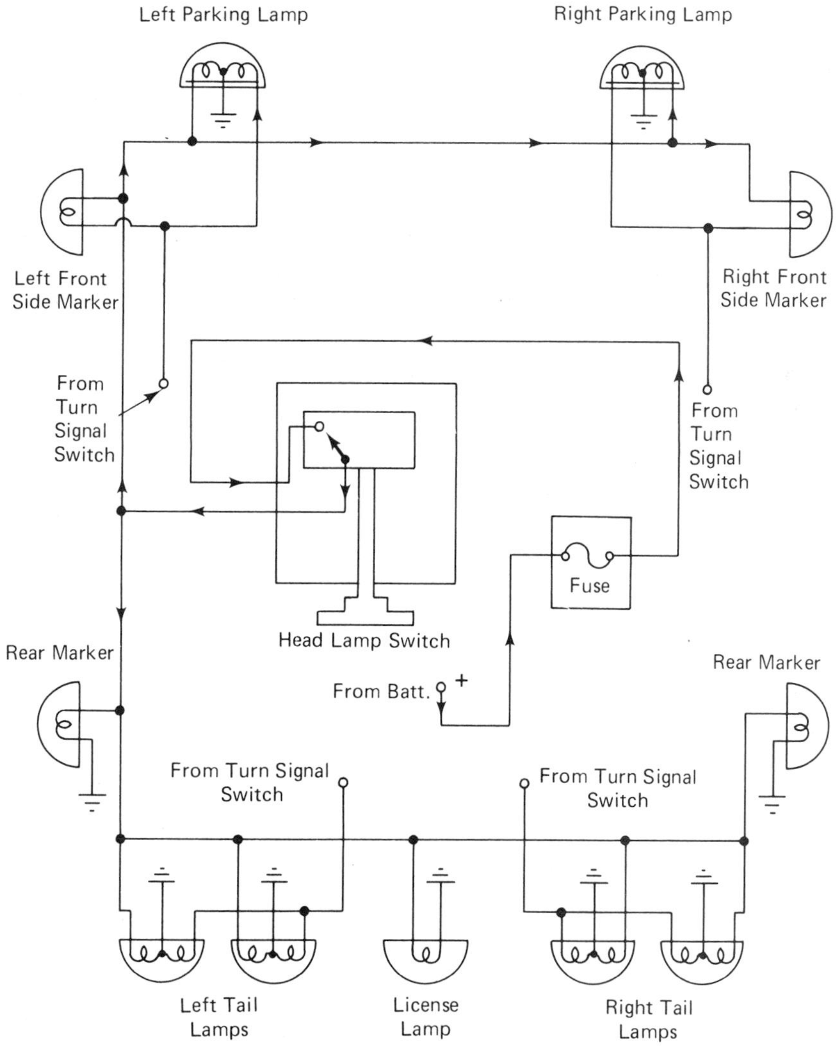

Left Parking Lamp

Right Parking Lamp

Left Front
Side Marker

Right Front
Side Marker

From
Turn
Signal
Switch

From
Turn
Signal
Switch

Fuse

Rear Marker

Head Lamp Switch

From Batt.   +

Rear Marker

From Turn Signal
Switch

From Turn Signal
Switch

Left Tail
Lamps

License
Lamp

Right Tail
Lamps

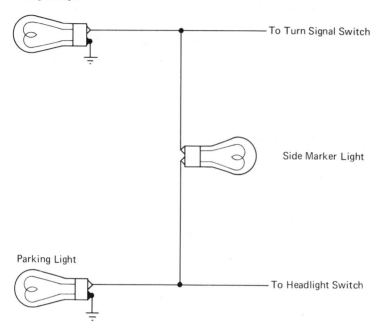

Turn Signal Light

To Turn Signal Switch

Side Marker Light

Parking Light

To Headlight Switch

Fig. 8.32. *Courtesy of Ford Customer Service Division.*

Fig. 8.33. *Courtesy of Ford Customer Service Division.*

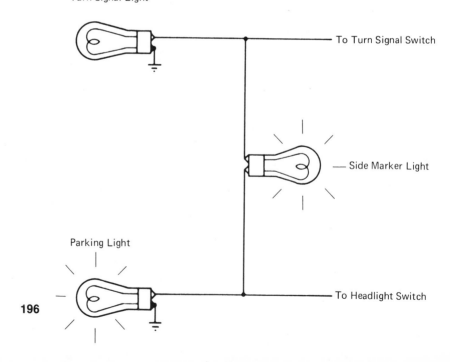

Turn Signal Light

To Turn Signal Switch

Side Marker Light

Parking Light

To Headlight Switch

196

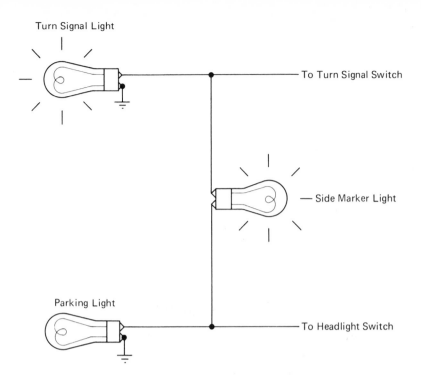

Turn Signal Light

To Turn Signal Switch

Side Marker Light

Parking Light

To Headlight Switch

Turn Signals "On" — Parking Lights "Off"

Fig. 8.34. *Courtesy of Ford Customer Service Division.*

Fig. 8.35. *Courtesy of Ford Customer Service Division.*

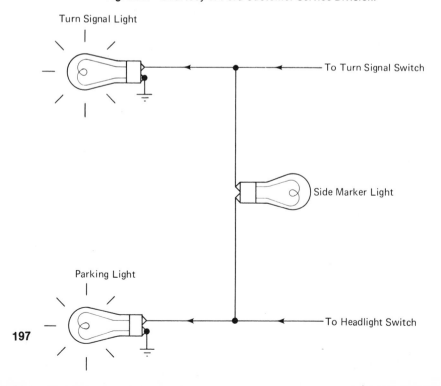

Turn Signal Light

To Turn Signal Switch

Side Marker Light

Parking Light

To Headlight Switch

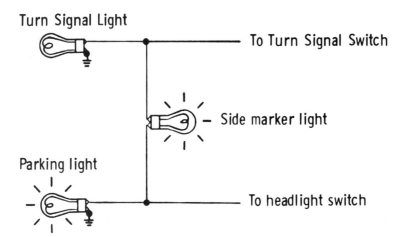

Turn Signal Light

To Turn Signal Switch

– Side marker light

Parking light

To headlight switch

Fig. 8.36.

Fig. 8.37.

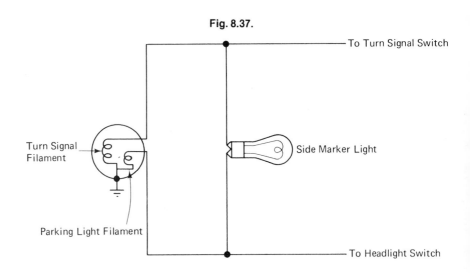

To Turn Signal Switch

Turn Signal Filament

Side Marker Light

Parking Light Filament

To Headlight Switch

Figure 8-37 shows the turn signal and park light filaments assembled into one dual-filament light bulb (1157 or 1034).

INSTRUMENT PANEL LIGHTS

The instrument panel lights provide indirect lighting to illuminate the speedometer, instrument gauges, heat-defroster controls, air-conditioner controls, ash tray, clock, and transmission control dial.

The instrument panel lights are controlled by the headlight switch, which incorporates a knob-operated rotating rheostat to adjust the light brightness. The circuits are protected by a fuse (generally 4 amps).

Using Fig. 8-38 as a reference, we can trace the instrument

Fig. 8.38.   *Courtesy of Buick Division of General Motors Corp.*

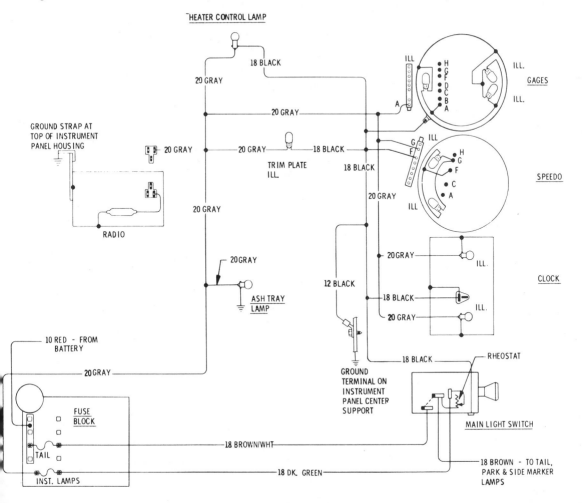

panel light circuit. Starting with the taillight fuse, power enters into the headlight switch to a common point shared by both the taillight and instrument panel light circuits. Since the common point acts as the power pick-up for the instrument panel lights, the power flow will pass through the headlight switch rheostat and to the fuse block, where the circuit is fused and power is passed on to the lights.

From the above discussion it should be obvious that perfectly working instrument panel lights won't work if the taillight fuse is blown.

On some Chrysler cars using a throw-type headlight switch, a separate instrument panel dimmer switch is mounted on the dash. The circuit, however, remains basically the same.

COURTESY LIGHTS

Courtesy lights illuminate the floor area of the automobile when the doors are open. They operate, along with the dome light, from the headlight switch and/or from a door jamb switch. It is not uncommon to find the courtesy, dome, trunk, and glove box lights linked to the

Fig. 8.39.   Typical dome light wiring—insulated switch circuit.

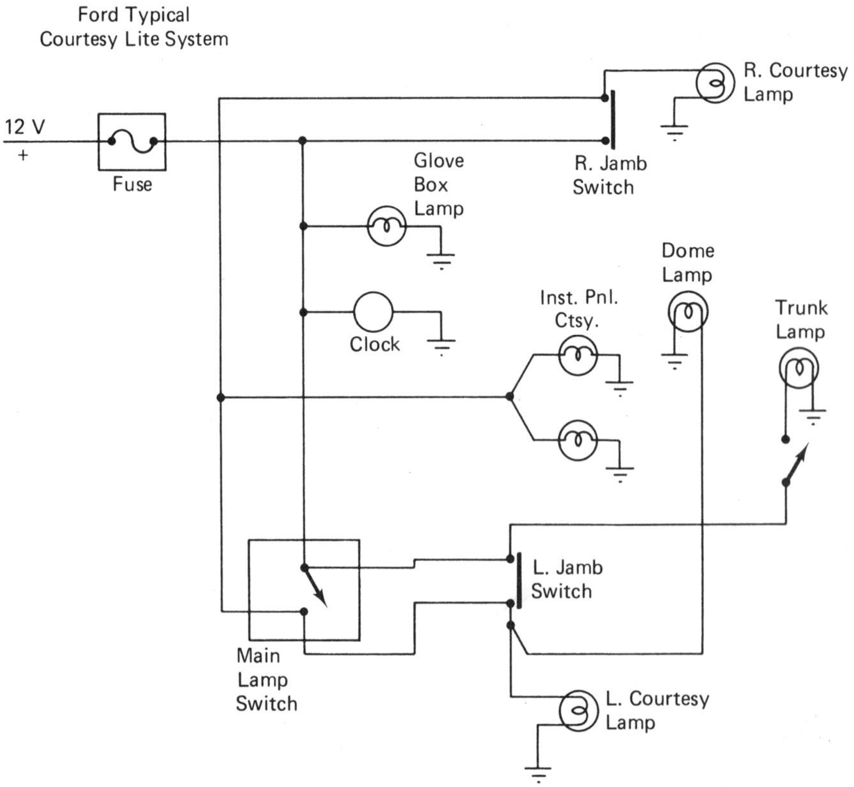

Ford Typical
Courtesy Lite System

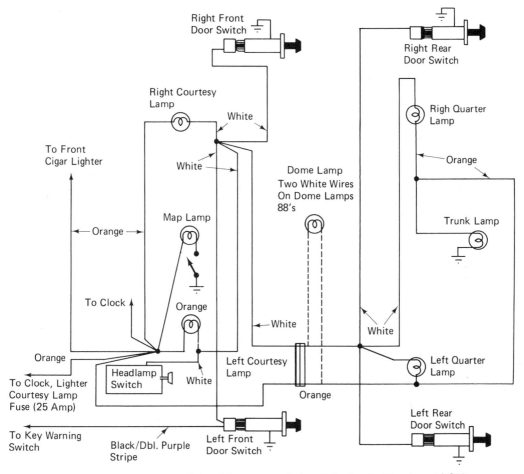

Fig. 8.40. Typical dome light wiring—grounded switch circuit. *(Courtesy of Olds-mobile Division of General Motors Corp.)*

same fuse for power and circuit protection. Additional items that can be found on the same fuse hook-up are power feeds to the clock and cigar lighter.

There are two types of courtesy light circuits. A good way to remember them is to call them the "hot switch circuit" and the "ground switch circuit." In the hot switch circuit, the switches are all insulated and are used as the power relay to the lights. In the ground switch circuit, the switches serve as the grounding media for the lights. These circuit types are shown in Figs. 8-39 and 8-40. Generally, Ford Motor Company vehicles use a hot switch circuit, and American Motors, Chrysler, and General Motors use a ground switch circuit.

BACKUP LIGHTS

Backup lights illuminate the road to the rear of the vehicle and provide a warning signal to pedestrians and other drivers when the vehicle is backing up or about to back up.

In the backup light circuit illustrated in Fig. 8-41, power from the fuse block is continued to the neutral safety switch. When the driver puts the car into reverse, this closes the backup light switch contacts within the neutral safety switch, and completes circuit to the backup lights.

Backup light switches are usually found under the dash on the steering column or on the left side of the transmission. The ignition key must be on for circuit power.

Fig. 8.41. *Courtesy of Buick Division of General Motors Corp.*

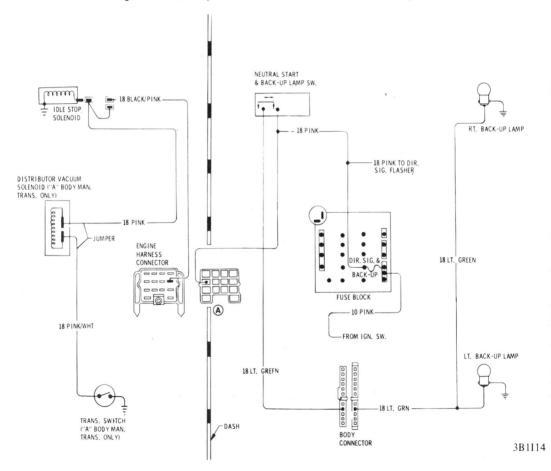

3B1114

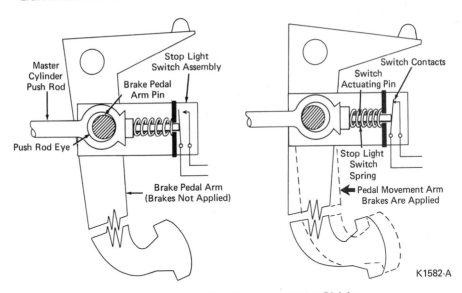

Fig. 8.42.   *Courtesy of Ford Customer Service Division.*
67966 Ford-Mercury
67970 Comet-Falcon-etc.

STOPLIGHTS

The stoplight was probably the first signaling device used on the automobile. It provides a steady bright light to the rear of the vehicle to indicate that the operator intends to stop the vehicle or slow the speed by braking.

Present stoplight circuits employ at least two lights. The stoplights are controlled by a mechanical switch mounted on the brake pedal bracket (Fig. 8-42). When the switch is activated by the brake pedal, the circuit is completed through the turn signal switch and high-current filament in the taillight bulbs (Fig. 8-43); dual filament bulbs with trade numbers 1157 or 1034 are used. The same high-current filaments in the taillight bulbs are also employed as the light source for the turn signal and hazard warning circuits. How these three circuits work together will be discussed in detail, later in this chapter, in the sections "Turn Signals" and "Hazard Warning Lights."

On older vehicles the brake light switch is generally located in the brake line at the master cylinder and is activated by hydraulic pressure build-up when the brakes are applied.

TURN SIGNALS

The turn signal circuit consists of the switch and flasher, two signal indicator bulbs on the instrument panel, the stoplight filaments in the

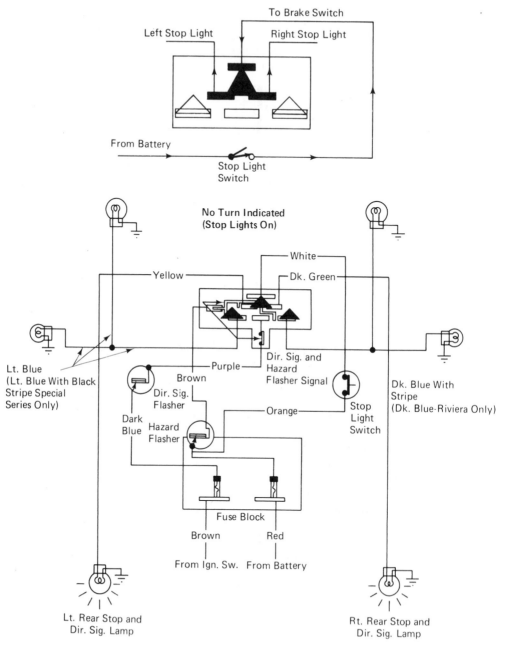

To Brake Switch

Left Stop Light   Right Stop Light

From Battery

Stop Light
Switch

No Turn Indicated
(Stop Lights On)

White

Yellow   Dk. Green

Dir. Sig. and
Hazard
Purple   Flasher Signal

Lt. Blue
(Lt. Blue With Black   Brown
Stripe Special   Dir. Sig.   Dk. Blue With
Series Only)   Flasher   Stripe
(Dk. Blue-Riviera Only)
Dark   Orange   Stop
Blue   Hazard   Light
Flasher   Switch

Fuse Block

Brown   Red

From Ign. Sw.   From Battery

Lt. Rear Stop and   Rt. Rear Stop and
Dir. Sig. Lamp   Dir. Sig. Lamp

Fig. 8.43.   Brake lights *(Courtesy of Buick Division of General Motors Corp.)*

rear lighting, and the turn signal filaments in the parking light bulbs and front side marker lights.

The circuit is controlled by the turn signal switch, which is mounted in a housing at the upper end of the steering column just below the steering wheel (Fig. 8-44). When the turn signal switch is operated to indicate a turn or a lane change, the front and rear signal lights and the front side marker lights flash on and off on the left or right side of the car, as chosen by the driver. A turn indicator bulb on the instrument panel also flashes with the turn signal lights.

After a turn is completed, the return of the steering wheel to a straight-ahead position cancels the signal circuit. On slight turns such as those used in a lane change, the return of the steering wheel to a straight-ahead position will not cancel the circuit. This is normal and

Fig. 8.44.   *Courtesy of The Chrysler Corporation.*

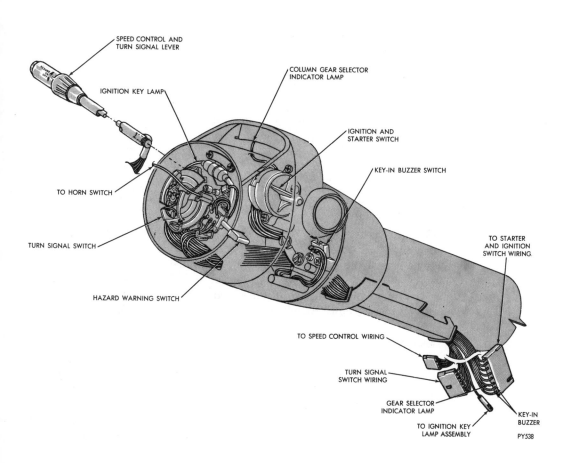

No Turn Indicated

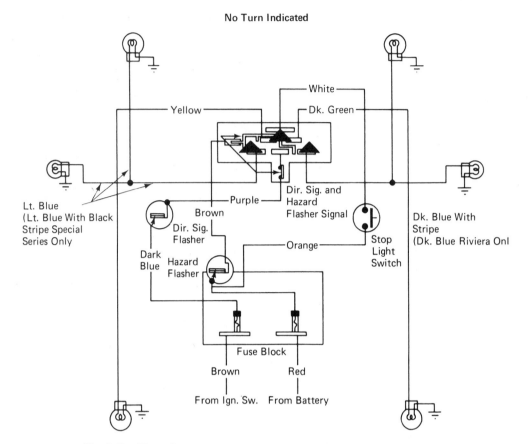

Fig. 8.45.   Neutral. *(Courtesy of Buick Division of General Motors Corp.)*

the turn signal switch must be returned to its neutral position by the driver.

   The turn-signal circuit operation is illustrated in Figs. 8-45, 8-46, and 8-47. A study of the turn signal switch shows that the switch receives power from two different sources—the stoplight circuit and the flasher circuit. Here's how the two circuits work together.

Neutral

In the neutral position, Fig. 8-45, battery voltage from the ignition switch is available to the fuse block, and through the fuse, to the turn signal flasher. Voltage continues through the flasher to the center terminal of the turn signal switch. The voltage is always at the center terminal waiting for a turn to be selected to complete the circuit.

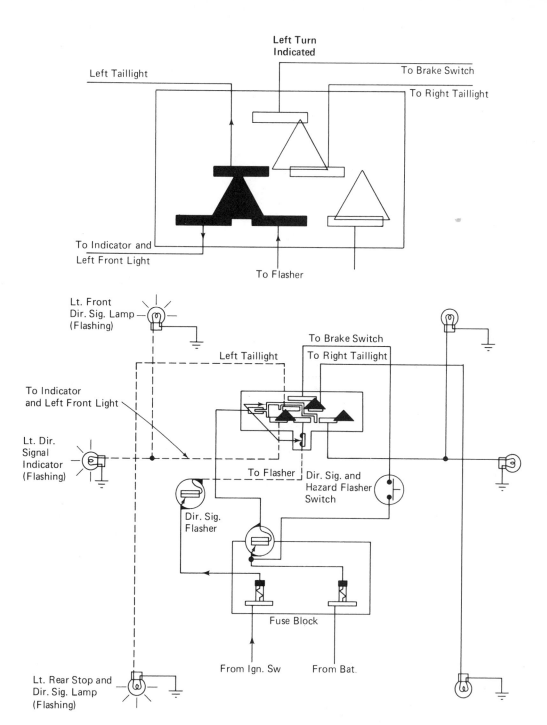

Left Turn
Indicated

Left Taillight

To Brake Switch

To Right Taillight

To Indicator and
Left Front Light

To Flasher

Lt. Front
Dir. Sig. Lamp
(Flashing)

To Brake Switch

Left Taillight

To Right Taillight

To Indicator
and Left Front Light

Lt. Dir.
Signal
Indicator
(Flashing)

To Flasher

Dir. Sig. and
Hazard Flasher
Switch

Dir. Sig.
Flasher

Fuse Block

From Ign. Sw

From Bat.

Lt. Rear Stop and
Dir. Sig. Lamp
(Flashing)

Fig. 8.46.   Left turn. *(Courtesy of Buick Division of General Motors Corp.)*

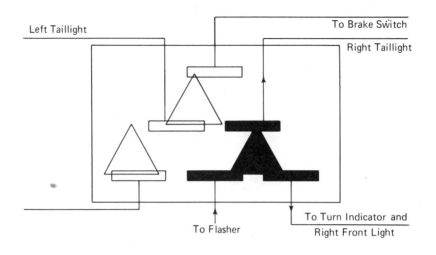

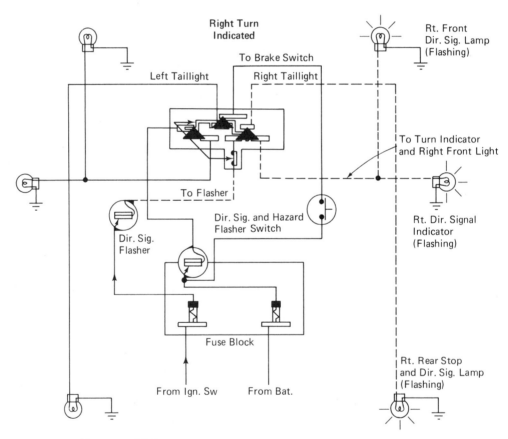

Fig. 8.47. Right turn. *(Courtesy of Buick Division of General Motors Corp.)*

208

When the stoplight switch is closed the circuit is completed through the turn signal switch to the high-current filaments in the taillight bulbs. During left and right turns the stoplights and turn signal lights will share these same filaments.

Left Turn

When a left turn is signalled, Fig. 8-46, the turn signal switch makes contact with the center terminal, the left rear light terminal, and the left front terminal to complete the circuit. The flasher is now sensitive to the current flow and will heat up and break the circuit. When the flasher cools, contact will be made again and the cycle repeated.

During a left turn, the turn signal switch cuts off the stoplight circuit from the left rear lights, and only the right side will provide a steady glow.

Right Turn

When a right turn is signalled, Fig. 8-47, the turn signal switch makes contact with the center terminal, the right rear light terminal, and right front terminal to complete the circuit. The flasher is now sensitive to the current flow and will heat up and break the circuit. When the flasher cools, contact will be made again and the cycle repeated.

During a right turn, the turn signal switch cuts off the stoplight circuit from the right lights, and only the left side will provide a steady glow.

Turn Signal Flashers

The flasher is a very simple thermally actuated circuit breaker. Its normal flash rate varies between 60 and 120 flashes per minute. Should a front or rear bulb burn out, the reduced current in the circuit will cause the remaining signal on the side of the car to glow steadily.

The flasher is mounted in a variety of locations; fuse block, safety panel above the glove box, taped on the wiring harness under the dash and next to the steering column, etc. The flasher unit can be a very difficult item to find without the aid of a service manual.

The flasher unit is made up of a stationary contact and a movable contact mounted on an expansion strip (Fig. 8-48). In their normal at-rest position, the contacts are closed. When a turn is selected, current flows through the expansion strip and the contacts to feed the rest of the circuit. The expansion strip, sensitive to the current flow, heats up and opens the points (Fig. 8-49). With the circuit open, the

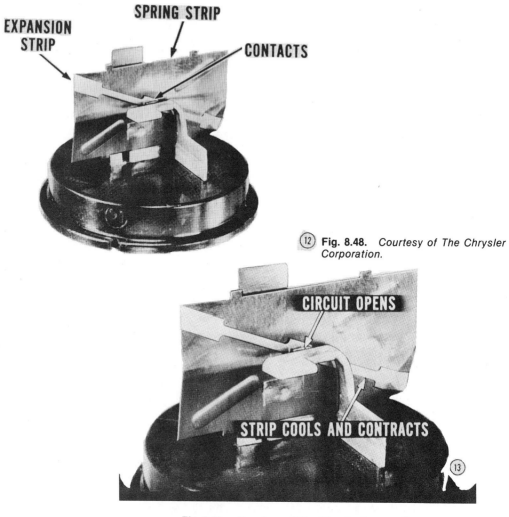

EXPANSION STRIP

SPRING STRIP

CONTACTS

Fig. 8.48.   *Courtesy of The Chrysler Corporation.*

CIRCUIT OPENS

STRIP COOLS AND CONTRACTS

Fig. 8.49.   *Courtesy of The Chrysler Corporation.*

expansion strip cools and snaps back to its normal position. The contacts are closed again and the cycle is ready to repeat itself.

The thermal cycling of the expansion strip produces an audible metallic clicking noise which serves as an additional indicator that the turn signal system is working.

Flashers are designed and calibrated to flash a definite number of bulbs; this number varies in different car models and body styles. The correct flash rate of any turn signal system can be upset by a simple misapplication of a flasher unit. Flasher units may have different calibrations, but they all can plug into any turn signal circuit. Therefore, when you replace a flasher, make sure that it matches the lamp load (Fig. 8-50). Another factor that can upset the flash rate is the misapplication of turn signal bulbs. Turn signal systems are designed to use either 1034 or 1157 bulbs. Both bulbs produce the same candlepower, and can plug into the same socket holders, but the 1157 bulb draws more current. The use of 1034 bulbs in place of 1157 bulbs will slow the flash rate or even stop it completely; the use of 1157 bulbs in place of 1034 bulbs will speed up the flash rate and shorten flasher life.

A heavy-duty flasher (variable-load type) is available to flash any number of bulbs. It will always flash at the same rate, even if a bulb burns out. Heavy-duty flashers are used when the car has a trailer-towing package; otherwise, the standard flasher would not be able to withstand the extra current load. The disadvantage of a heavy duty flasher is that it gives no indication to the driver that a bulb is burned out.

The operation of the variable-load type flasher is discussed in more detail under "Hazard Warning Lights." A hazard-warning-light flasher can be used in the turn signals for heavy-duty service.

Circuit Problems

The turn signal system does not usually present complicated problems. In most cases, system failures are caused by burned-out bulbs. Now that you understand the turn signal system and some electrical fundamentals, let's look at some common problems (other than burned-out bulbs) and their causes.

Dead circuit

1. Blown fuse.
2. Defective flasher.

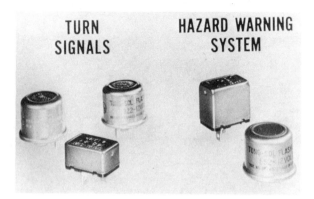

TURN SIGNALS

HAZARD WARNING SYSTEM

Fig. 8.50. *Courtesy of The Chrysler Corporation.*

Flash rate too slow

1. Defective flasher.
2. Wrong flasher application; a three-signal-light flasher in place of a two-signal-light flasher, etc.
3. Wrong light bulb application; a 1034 bulb in place of a 1157 bulb. The flasher action may even stop.
4. Poor ground at one of the lamps.

Flash rate too fast

Although this problem is not objectionable to most car owners, it does cause short flasher life.

1. Wrong flasher application; a two-signal-light flasher in place of a three-signal-light flasher, etc.
2. Wrong light bulb application; a 1157 bulb in place of a 1034 bulb.
3. Extra lights in the circuit, such as trailer lights.
4. High voltage.

Live circuit, no flasher action

1. Burned-out light bulb.
2. Wrong light bulb application; a 1034 bulb in place of a 1157 bulb.
3. Defective flasher; both sides not flashing.

Fig. 8.51.   Turn-signal bulb not grounded. *(Courtesy of Chrysler Corp.)*

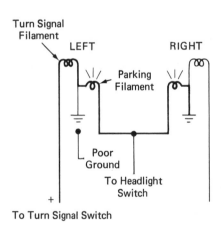

4. Poor light-bulb grounds.

Once in awhile a park lamp will lose its ground because of corrosion on a loose connection, and produces a dim glow from both front bulbs when a turn is signalled through the ungrounded bulb. Since the turn signal current could not find a normal path to ground at the bulb base, it found a new path to ground through the park filament on the opposite side (Fig. 8-51). If you run into this condition, turn off the signal and turn on the parking lights. If the suspected bulb doesn't light, you can be sure that there is a lost ground.

HAZARD WARNING LIGHTS

All cars manufactured in production year 1967 or later are equipped with a system of warning lights to signal any unusual or dangerous condition, such as a disabled car stopped by the side of the road, or some other emergency situation. The hazard warning feature, when turned on, causes all turn signal lights plus the indicator lights to flash simultaneously.

This system is integrated into the turn signal circuit and makes use of the regular turn signal wiring and lights, but has a separate power supply, flasher unit, and on-off switch. The switch is usually located just below the steering wheel on the right side of the steering column, or it may be found on the instrument panel.

In Fig. 8-52, a typical hazard warning system is shown in its power "on" position. The switch controls the flow of power in the circuit as it parallels the left and right sides of the turn signals when closed. Also note that the circuit is energized directly from the battery through the fuse block and can operate with the ignition switch either on or off.

Hazard Warning Flasher

Unlike the standard turn signal flasher, the hazard warning flasher is a variable-load unit and will operate regardless of the number of bulbs that are burned out. It also continues to flash reliably as the battery voltage decreases during a long disablement. Common practice is to locate the flasher on the fuse block or on the safety panel above the glove box as found on some vehicles. In outward appearance, the flasher is identical to the turn signal flasher.

The variable-load flasher action starts with its contact points normally open. This means that when the hazard warning switch is turned on, there is a slight delay before the lights come on and begin to flash.

The flasher is a thermally actuated unit made up of a stationary contact, a movable contact mounted on an expansion strip, and a heating coil (Fig. 8-53). When the switch is closed, the coil is in series with the bulbs. The high resistance of the coil, however, prevents the bulbs from lighting. The coil heats up and the thermal action on the expansion strip closes the contacts (Fig. 8-54). With the contacts together, there is a parallel circuit in the flasher. Since current prefers to follow the path of least resistance, it flows through the contacts to light the bulbs. At this time there is very little current flow through the coil, and the expansion strip is allowed to cool and contract, opening the points. The current again flows through the coil to start the cycle over.

Circuit Problems

There aren't very many things that can go wrong in the hazard warning system. The most likely failures will be burned-out bulbs.

Fig. 8.52.   Hazard warning system—power "on." *(Courtesy Buick Division of General Motors Corp.)*

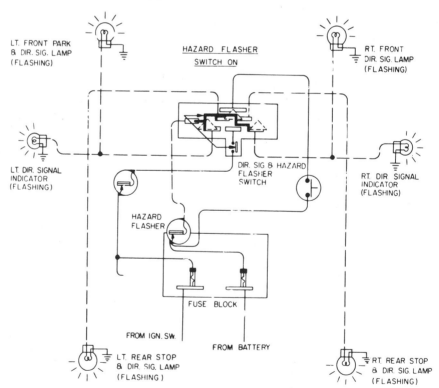

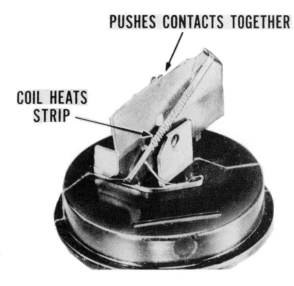

PUSHES CONTACTS TOGETHER

COIL HEATS STRIP

Fig. 8.53. *Courtesy of The Chrysler Corporation.*

Path of Least Resistance

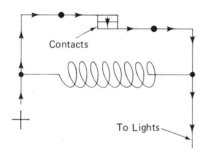

Contacts

To Lights

Fig. 8.54. Parallel circuit inside flasher.

Usually, you can check the bulbs by trying the turn signals in both directions, with the hazard warning switch turned off. Remember, a burned-out bulb will not be noticeable when the hazard lights are on, since the hazard flasher will operate at a constant speed, even with a bulb out. A burned-out bulb *will* stop the turn signal flasher action. But, to be really sure, especially on cars with two or three stoplights on each side, turn on the hazard switch and walk around the car.

If it is necessary to replace either a turn signal flasher or a hazard warning flasher, don't interchange them (except, as already noted, on cars with a trailer-towing package). A turn signal flasher installed in a warning light system will operate at a much faster rate than the variable-load hazard flasher, and it won't last very long. On the other hand, if a variable-load flasher is installed in the turn signal system, the rate of flash will not change, even when a bulb burns out. Therefore, the driver has no warning that there is anything wrong.

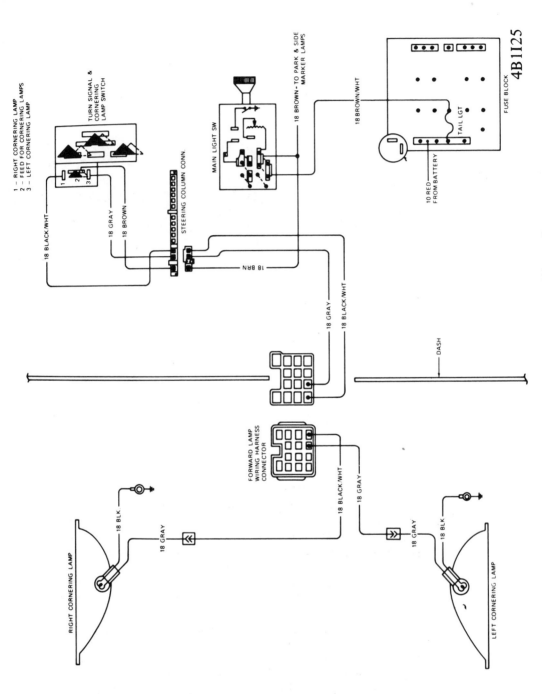

1 – RIGHT CORNERING LAMP
2 – FEED FOR CORNERING LAMPS
3 – LEFT CORNERING LAMP

TURN SIGNAL &
CORNERING
LAMP SWITCH

18 BLACK/WHT

18 GRAY

18 BROWN

STEERING COLUMN CONN.

MAIN LIGHT SW

18 BRN

18 BROWN – TO PARK & SIDE
MARKER LAMPS

18 BROWN/WHT

TAIL LGT

FUSE BLOCK

4B1125

10 RED
FROM BATTERY

18 GRAY

18 BLACK/WHT

DASH

FORWARD LAMP
WIRING HARNESS
CONNECTOR

18 BLACK/WHT

18 GRAY

18 GRAY

18 BLK

18 BLK

18 GRAY

RIGHT CORNERING LAMP

LEFT CORNERING LAMP

Fig. 8.55. *Buick Motor Division of General Motors Corp.*

216

CORNERING LAMPS

Cornering lamps are steadily burning lamps used in conjunction with the turn signal system to supplement the headlamps by providing additional illumination in the direction of turn. They make the car more visible to other drivers approaching from the side and also improve the visibility of nearby objects not illuminated by the headlights during the turn. These lamps are mounted, one on each side, in the forward position of the front fenders.

Cars with cornering lamps require a different turn signal switch which provides an additional set of switching contacts for the cornering circuit only. When either the parking lights or the headlights are on, moving the turn signal level for a left or right turn also causes a cornering light to come on in the direction of the turn. Since there is no circuit flasher, the light does not blink and remains on until the turn is cancelled.

The cornering light circuit shares a common point with the taillight circuit and is protected by the taillight circuit fuse (Fig. 8-55). Cornering lights are usually an optional equipment item on large-size cars.

"CRAZY LIGHTS"

The modern automobile has many lights and electrical interconnections that can cause electrical lights and accessories to operate when they are not supposed to by a process called *feedback*. If a fuse blows open in a circuit, electricity will find another path to follow; this, in turn, will light or operate the electrical accessory connected in that path.

Fuses and Feedback

Once in awhile, electricity plays some pretty fancy tricks on us. But there is always an explanation for any phenomenon, if you know where to look and what to look for. Here are some unusual "crazy light" situations that you might run into. Let's examine a specific situation where the dome light, taillight, and stoplight fuse (a single fuse for all three) and the cigar lighter fuse are located in the main fuse block and connected to the same bus bar on the hot side (Fig. 8-56).

Blown dome light, taillight, and stoplight fuse

When the headlight switch is turned on, Fig. 8-57, the courtesy light, dome light, taillight, parking lights, and instrument lights will

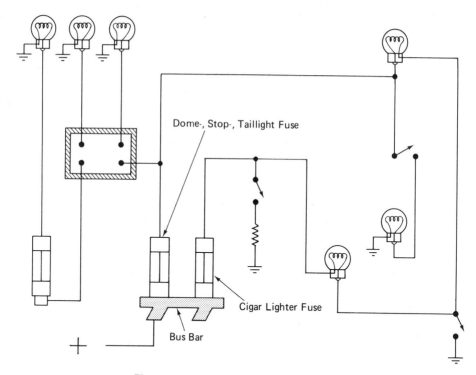

Dome-, Stop-, Taillight Fuse

Cigar Lighter Fuse

Bus Bar

Fig. 8.56. *Courtesy of The Chrysler Corporation.*

Fig. 8.57. *Courtesy of The Chrysler Corporation.*

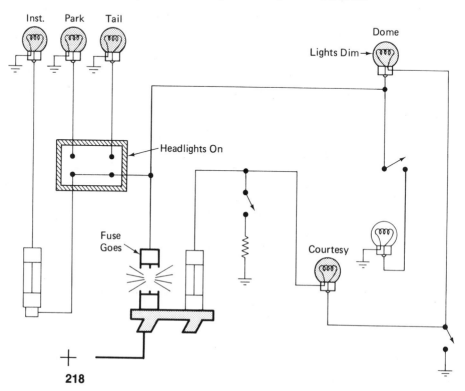

Inst. Park Tail

Dome

Lights Dim →

Headlights On

Fuse Goes

Courtesy

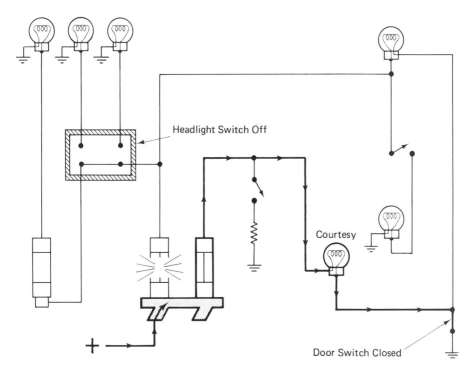

Fig. 8.58.   *Courtesy of The Chrysler Corporation.*

be on, but very dim. The current goes through the cigar lighter fuse to the courtesy light and on to the dome light switch in the door. The door switch is also connected to the dome light, so the current goes through the dome light and back to the headlight switch. Since the headlight switch is closed, the instrument panel lights are also in the circuit.

If the headlight switch is turned off, then all the lights will go out (Fig. 8-58). But with the headlight switch off and the car door open, the courtesy light will glow. The dome light will not light.

Another "crazy light" situation caused by the same blown fuse is illustrated in Fig. 8-59. Closing the stoplight switch will cause the dome light and courtesy light to turn on. But they will be very dim, because all the bulbs are in series.

Blown cigar lighter fuse

Another feedback condition occurs when the cigar lighter fuse burns out (Fig. 8-60). The current to the dome light, stoplight, and taillight creates the feedback. If the cigar lighter is pushed in, current will flow through the dome light, stoplight, and taillight fuse to the dome light, door switch, and courtesy light, and through the lighter to

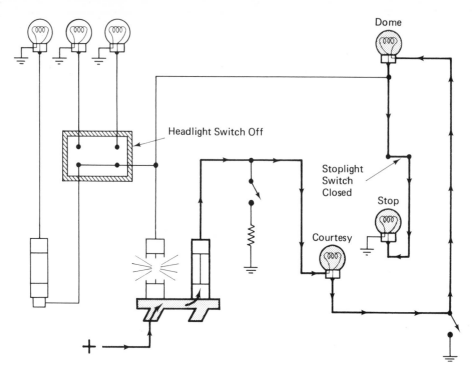

Fig. 8.59. *Courtesy of The Chrysler Corporation.*

Fig. 8.60. *Courtesy of the Chrysler Corporation.*

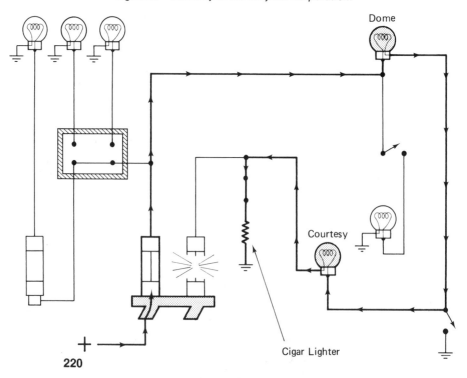

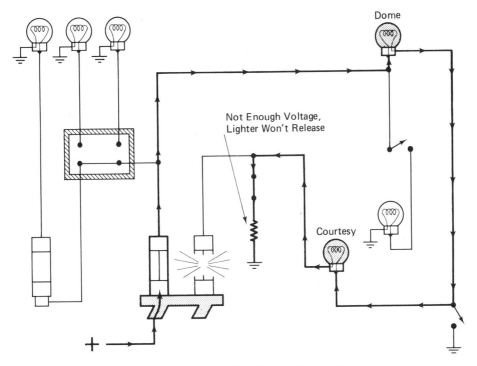

Fig. 8.61. *Courtesy of The Chrysler Corporation.*

ground. The lights will be on, but dim. If the lighter is left pushed in, the battery will run down. There will not be enough voltage available to heat and release the lighter (Fig. 8-61).

You can spot this condition when you open the door (Fig. 8-62). If the dome light gets brighter and the courtesy lights go out, you will know that the cigar lighter fuse has burned out. The dome light will be grounded at the door switch allowing the dome light to operate normally. In the same situation, with the lighter pushed in and the stoplight switch closed, the dome and courtesy lights will turn off (Fig. 8-63). The stoplights will provide a ground before the current gets to the other bulbs.

Glowing alternator signal light

If the signal light glows with the engine running, and an ammeter test indicates that the alternator is charging, check for a blown fuse in the instrument light panel or a loose connection at the fuse block. It is not unusual to find that a blown fuse has caused a feedback problem and has prevented the light from going out.

Troubleshooting Tips

With a systematic approach, "crazy light" problems can become simple problems. First, don't panic and start tearing a wiring harness apart or replacing unnecessary circuit components. Keep in mind that whatever caused the problem, a feedback was created and electricity picked out a new path (an easier way to go). Fouled-up or crossed wiring is the least of your worries.

Start your procedure with the simple checks first. The following four-step procedure should solve most crazy light problems.

Step 1   Check for a blown or missing fuse in the fuse block.

Step 2   Turn all the lights on and walk around the car. If a light is out, replace it. Should one light be too bright (two filaments touching each other) or too dim (wrong bulb application or bad ground), solve these obvious problems first before proceeding.

Step 3   Check the car body ground to the chassis and back to the battery.

Step 4   Check for clean and tight electrical connections in the suspect circuit.

Fig. 8.62. *Courtesy of The Chrysler Corporation.*

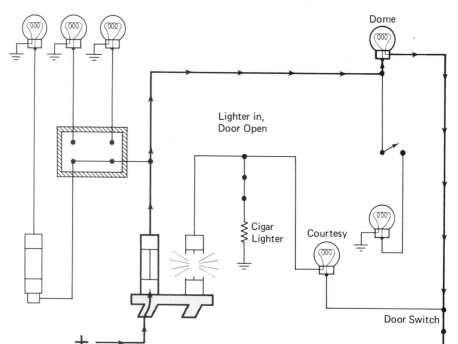

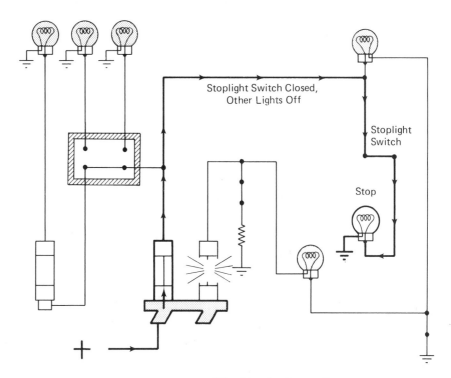

Stoplight Switch Closed,
Other Lights Off

Stoplight
Switch

Stop

Fig. 8.63. *Courtesy of The Chrysler Corporation.*

Review questions

1. All of the headlights in a four-lamp sealed-beam headlight system are connected in _____.
2. In a four-lamp sealed-beam headlight system, two sealed beams have a _____ and _____ filament.
3. Rectangular headlights are designed to _____.
4. A circuit breaker in the headlight system may be located in the _____.
5. The parking lights are controlled by the _____.
6. The stoplights are connected through the brake switch and the _____ switch.
7. What causes the turn signal flasher to flash at different rates?
8. The hazard flasher differs from the turn signal flasher because _____.
9. What can cause feedback problems?
10. Fiber optics are used to _____.

11. Excessive line voltage will shorten the life of a light bulb. If the line voltage is 6 per cent higher than normal, it will reduce the life of the bulb _____ per cent.

12. An incorrect light bulb application can cause two complaints. What are they?

13. The Type-2 sealed beam has two filaments. Which filament carries the higher candlepower?

14. Why does a headlight switch incorporate a thermal circuit breaker instead of a fuse?

15. The brightness of the instrument panel lights is controlled by a _____.

16. The courtesy lights are operated by two switches. What are they?

17. As a general rule, there are two types of courtesy light circuits. Name them.

18. The turn signal switch receives power from two different sources. Name them.

19. What is the difference between a standard flasher and a heavy-duty flasher?

20. If a standard flasher is used, and more bulbs are added to the circuit, will the flash rate increase or decrease?

9

Magnets, Magnetism, and Small Motors

Electricity and magnetism are very closely related. If it weren't for magnetism, electrical energy would have a limited use in practical automotive applications. Magnetism is essential to the operation of the ignition, charging, starting system, and various electrical circuits that use relays, buzzers, and small motors.

PERMANENT MAGNETS

Although magnetism is an invisible force, we can understand it by examining the effects it produces. The simplest type of magnet is the bar magnet. The space affected by a magnet is called a *field of force*, with a designated north pole *N* and a south pole *S* (Fig. 9-1).

A strong magnet produces many lines of force; a weak one produces fewer lines of force. The concentration of the magnetic lines of force is called the *magnetic flux density* (Fig. 9-2). The stronger magnet has the greater flux density. Invisible lines of force leave the magnet at the north pole and enter again at the south pole. Inside the magnet, the lines of force travel from the south pole to the north pole (Fig. 9-3). Each line of magnetic force is, therefore, a continuous line. The *magnetic field*, or the *field of force*, is all the space, outside of the magnet, that contains lines of magnetic force.

Permanent magnets are made of hardened steel alloys that can retain their magnetic properties for a long time. The original magnetism is induced by exposing the magnet to a strong

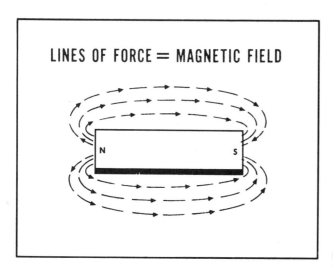

Fig. 9.1.

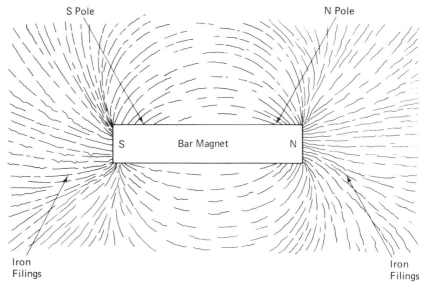

Fig. 9.2. Iron filings illustrate the concentration of the invisible magnetic lines of force that surround a magnet. *(Courtesy of General Motors Corp.)*

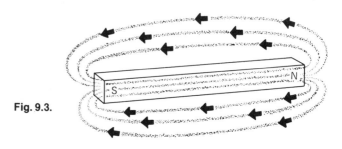

Fig. 9.3.

226

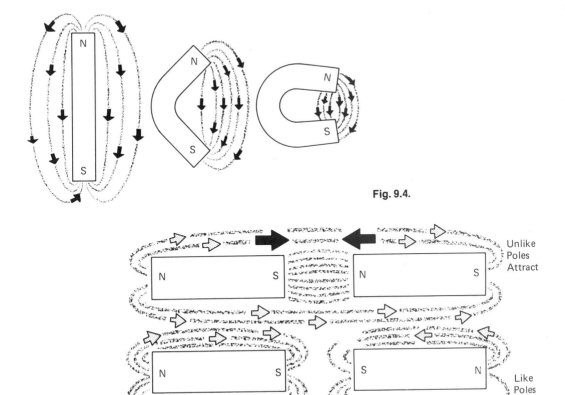

Fig. 9.4.

Fig. 9.5.

electromagnetic field. The magnetic strength stored in the magnetic material after the magnetizing field has been removed is called *residual magnetism.*

Soft iron and soft low-alloy steels store or retain only a small amount of magnetic strength. For this reason they are commonly used in electromagnets where residual magnetism is undesirable.

A permanent bar magnet can be made stronger by bending it into a horseshoe shape and shortening the air gap between the north and south poles (Fig. 9-4). The smaller air gap allows a greater concentration of the magnetic lines of force.

When the poles of two permanent magnets are exposed to each other, they follow a definite behavior pattern (Fig. 9-5). When the poles are close together, the unlike poles attract each other and the like poles repel each other.

Most materials are *nonmagnetic* and have no effect on a

magnetic field, whereas materials such as iron, nickel, cobalt, or their alloy mixtures will magnify or concentrate the magnetic field. These latter substances are called *magnetic* materials.

Magnetic lines of force penetrate all substances. They are deflected or distorted only by other magnetic materials or by another magnetic field. There is no known insulator against magnetic lines of force.

ELECTROMAGNETISM

Another form of magnetism is *electromagnetism*. When an electrical current flows through a conductor, a magnetic field is set up around the conductor (Fig. 9-6). These magnetic lines of force are concentric circles formed around the length of a straight conductor; they have no north or south poles, i.e., no polarity.

The number of lines of force and the strength of the magnetic

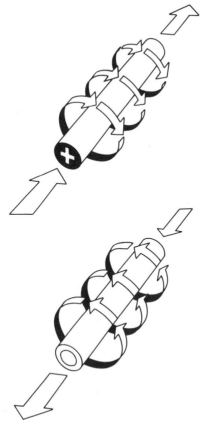

Fig. 9.6.

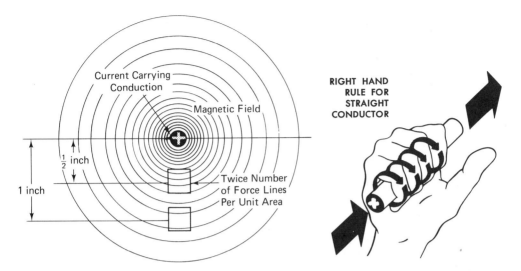

Fig. 9.7. *Courtesy of Delco-Remy Division of General Motors Corp.*

Fig. 9.8. *Courtesy of Delco-Remy Division of General Motors Corp.*

field produced increases in direct proportion to increased current flow. The lines of force (as expanding circles) are more dense at the surface of the conductor and increasingly less dense as the distance increases from the conductor (Fig. 9-7).

The direction of the lines of force around a conductor can be determined by a simple rule known as the *right-hand rule*. This rule assumes that current flows from positive to negative terminals. To apply the rule, the right hand is used to grasp the connector, with the thumb pointed in the direction of the current flow. The fingers now point in the direction in which the lines of force surround the conductor (Fig. 9-8).

ELECTROMAGNETIC FIELDS

If a current-carrying conductor is formed into a loop, the lines of force around the conductor will all pass through the center of the loop. This creates a weak electromagnet with a north and south pole (Fig. 9-9). The magnetic lines leave the inside of the loop at the north pole, then flow around the outside of the loop and enter at the south pole. This produces the same field pattern as a bar magnet.

If more loops are added to form a coil, the magnetic effect of the conductor is greatly increased because the magnetic lines of force become more concentrated (Fig. 9-10). This field force, however, is still not strong enough for use in most electrical equipment. It is, therefore, necessary to add an iron core to an electromagnet, which greatly increases its magnetic strength (Fig. 9-11). The iron core offers very little "magnetic resistance" (*reluctance*), as compared to an air core.

The magnetic pull at the core of an electromagnet will depend upon the following:

1. The amount of current flowing in the coil.
2. The size, length, and type of core material.
3. The number of turns in the coil.

Often the strength of an electromagnet is talked about in terms of ampere-turns.

$$\text{Ampere Turns} = \text{Amps} \times \text{Number of Turns}$$

By using the formula, we can compare electromagnets. For example, in Fig. 9-12, an electromagnet having 1,000 turns of fine wire carrying

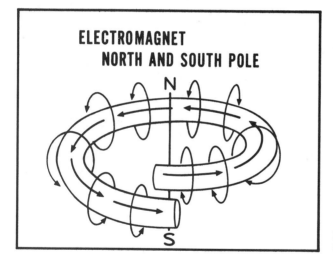

Fig. 9.9. *Courtesy of The Chrysler Corporation.*

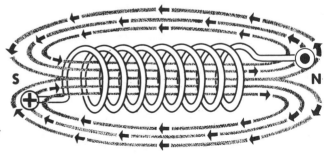

Fig. 9.10. *Courtesy of Delco-Remy Division of General Motors Corp.*

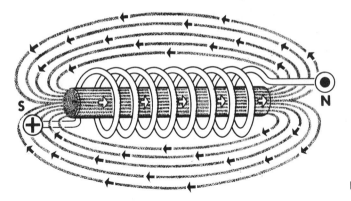

Fig. 9.11.

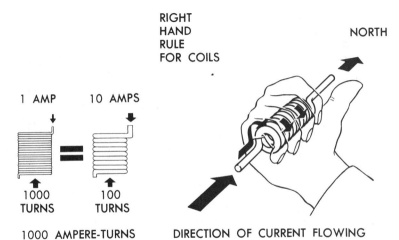

RIGHT
HAND
RULE
FOR COILS

NORTH

1 AMP   10 AMPS

1000   100
TURNS   TURNS

1000 AMPERE-TURNS

DIRECTION OF CURRENT FLOWING

Fig. 9.12. *Courtesy of Delco-Remy Division of General Motors Corporation.*

Fig. 9.13. *Courtesy of Delco-Remy Division of General Motors Corporation.*

one ampere should have the same magnetizing force as an electromagnet having 100 turns of heavy wire carrying ten amperes.

To determine the polarity of an electromagnet, the right-hand rule can again be applied. Simply grasp the coil with the right hand so that the fingers follow the direction of both the current flow and the coil loops (Fig. 9-13). The thumb will then point to the north pole of the electromagnet. The polarity can be changed by reversing the current flow or the direction of the coil loops.

Since electromagnets are like permanent magnets, they behave in the same manner—that is, unlike magnetic poles attract each other and like magnetic poles repel each other.

In automotive chassis and accessory circuits, electromagnets are used in the design of horns, circuit relays, buzzers, and small motors.

SMALL DIRECT-CURRENT MOTORS

The small direct-current motors used in accessory circuits such as power windows, power seats, and windshield wipers work on the same principle of operation as the starter motor—electromagnetism and current-carrying conductors are utilized to change electrical energy into mechanical energy. The motor, in operation, also acts as a generator. We must understand how this motor and generator action works so that we can understand, for example, how speed is controlled in a three-speed wiper or a four-speed blower motor.

Electromagnetic Induction

A magnetic field can be used to make electrons move through a conductor. This generating of electricity by magnetism is called *magnetic induction*.

To induce a voltage potential in a conductor, magnetic lines of force must cut the conductor; therefore, it is necessary to have relative motion between the magnetic field and conductor. Current will then flow when an external circuit is completed. As can be observed in Fig. 9-14, magnetic lines of force cut across the conductor by moving the field (conductor stationary), or by moving the conductor (field stationary).

Alternating current (A.C.) generators used in automotive applications produce voltage by having a rotating magnetic field

Fig. 9.14.   *Courtesy of The Chrysler Corporation.*

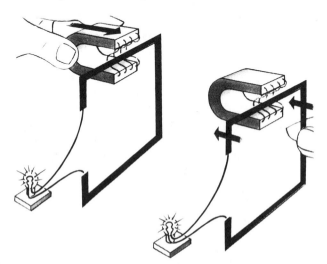

**MOVING CONDUCTOR;
STATIONARY FIELD**

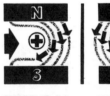

CURRENT IN   CURRENT OUT

**MOVING FIELD WITH
STATIONARY CONDUCTOR**

FIELD
MOVING
TO RIGHT
REVERSES
CURRENT

Fig. 9.15. *Courtesy of Delco-Remy
Division of General Motors Corp.*

CURRENT IN   CURRENT OUT

inside a stationary conductor. Direct current (D.C.) generators have a rotating conductor inside a stationary magnetic field. This D.C. generating action also occurs within an electric motor, and limits the motor current draw.

The direction in which electromagnetic induction moves the current flow in a closed circuit is determined by the movement of the conductor or magnetic field (Fig. 9-15).

Principles of Small Motor Operation

A magnetic field can also be used to produce a force on a conductor. When a current-carrying conductor is placed in a magnetic field (permanent or electromagnet), the concentric lines of force around the conductor act on the lines of force in the magnetic field. Note in Fig. 9-16 that on one side of the conductor the concentric lines of force reenforce the lines of force from the magnetic field. On the other side of the conductor, the concentric lines of force oppose the magnetic field's lines of force. This unbalanced field condition produces a thrust or push on the conductor from the strong side to the weak side. The direction of thrust on the conductor can be changed by reversing the current flow *or* by changing the polarity of the magnetic field. Reversing the current flow together with changing magnetic field polarity, however, will not change the direction of the force acting on the conductor.

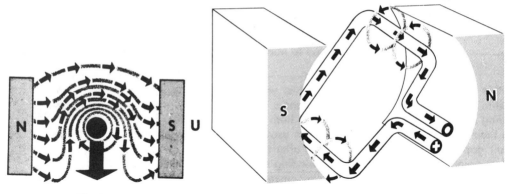

Fig. 9.16.

Fig. 9.17. *Courtesy of Delco-Remy Division of General Motors Corp.*

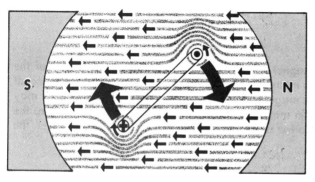

INTERACTING MAGNETIC FORCES ON A CURRENT CARRYING LOOP IN A MAGNETIC FIELD TEND TO PRODUCE ROTATIONAL MOVEMENT OF THE CONDUCTOR

Fig. 9.18. *Courtesy of Delco-Remy Division of General Motors Corp.*

In small motor circuits where a reversing motor action is required, the motor design will provide for a change in either field polarity or armature polarity (change in conductor-current direction).

To produce a rotating motor action, the conductor is formed into a loop and placed in a magnetic field (Fig. 9-17). The current flowing in the loop causes an unbalanced field condition at both the north and the south pole ends of the field (Fig. 9-18). The unbalanced conditions cause the loop to rotate.

After the conductor loop rotates one-quarter turn, it is in the weakest part of the field and ceases to rotate (Fig. 9-19). The conductor loop is trapped in neutral position. The unbalanced field condition at each side of the loop cannot produce a twisting effort on the conductor. The force on the conductor is outward or away from the field.

If another loop is added at right angles to the first then a continuous turning effort is maintained. No matter how many conductor loops are in a motor, each loop must maintain a continuous turning effort in the same direction. Therefore, at the neutral point, which is always halfway between the pole shoes, the direction of the current flow in the loops must be changed. This switching of the current flow in the conductor loops at the neutral point takes place through a split ring called a *commutator* (Fig. 9-20).

The conductor loops and commutator make up that part of the rotating motor assembly called the *armature* (Fig. 9-21). The commutator is made of a number of copper segments (slip rings) to which conductor loops are connected. The conductor loops and commutator are connected in series, which makes it possible for

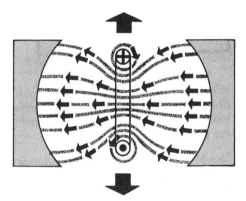

NEUTRAL POSITION: FORCES BALANCED

Fig. 9.19. *Courtesy of Delco-Remy Division of General Motors Corp.*

Fig. 9.20. *Courtesy of Delco-Remy Division of General Motors Corp.*

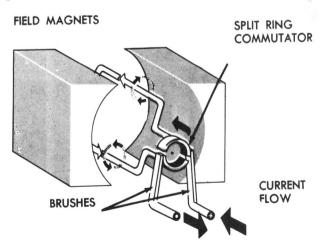

FIELD MAGNETS

SPLIT RING
COMMUTATOR

BRUSHES

CURRENT
FLOW

Fig. 9.21.   Small motor armature.

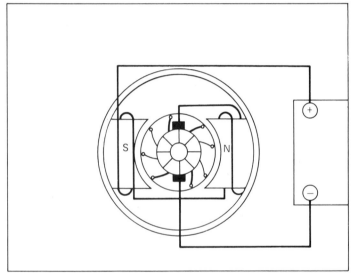

Fig. 9.22.   *Courtesy of The Chrysler Corporation.*

current to flow in all the armature conductors when brushes are placed on the commutator and a source of power is connected to the brushes.

Figure 9-22 is a small, two-brush motor that illustrates the principles of electromagnetism just discussed.

Counter Electromotive Force

When a motor rotates it also produces a generating action; the conductor loops are cutting magnetic lines of force. This induced voltage opposes the voltage that is applied to the motor, and is called a *back voltage* or *counter electromotive force* (counter e.m.f.).

The counter e.m.f. limits the current draw of the motor

(armature). As the speed of the armature increases, so does the counter e.m.f. The actual effective voltage forcing current through the armature is the difference between the applied voltage and counter e.m.f. This can be illustrated by using Ohm's law; the figures given are typical of a small motor.

$$I = \frac{E}{R} \qquad\qquad I_a = \text{armature current}$$

$$I_a = \frac{E_t - E_c}{R_a} \qquad\qquad E_t = \text{total applied voltage}$$

$$I_a = \frac{12 \text{ v} - 11 \text{ v}}{0.05} \qquad\qquad E_c = \text{counter e.m.f.}$$

$$I_a = \frac{1 \text{ v}}{0.05} = 20 \text{ amps} \qquad R_a = \text{armature resistance}$$

A motor will draw only enough current to do its job, no more or no less. If the job assigned to the motor exceeds its capacity, the armature will fail to rotate, but the motor will continue to draw current from the battery in excess of its design capabilities, in an attempt to do a job it cannot do. Since the motor has very low conductor resistance and there is no counter e.m.f. generated, the current draw can get quite high, and the motor will burn out.

$$I_a = \frac{E_t - E_c}{R_a} = \frac{12v - 0v}{0.05\,\Omega} = \frac{12v}{0.05\,\Omega} = 240 \text{ amps}$$

It should be evident that for a motor to work within its design limitations it must produce a certain amount of counter e.m.f.

Motor Speed and Torque

The torque developed by a motor is dependent on two factors:

1. The amount of current flowing in the armature conductors.
2. The magnetic density or flux density of the fields.

In effect, motor torque varies with the load on the motor. As the load increases, motor speed decreases and there is a corresponding decrease in counter e.m.f. As a result, the armature takes on more current and develops more thrust. In motors where the electromagnetic fields are connected in series to the armature, extremely high torque is developed.

Like torque, motor speed varies with the load. For any given load, a motor will operate at a specific speed. With heavy loads, armature speeds are relatively low and with light loads, the speeds are higher.

An armature operates at a speed such that the voltage used in overcoming its load (resistance to armature rotation) plus the counter e.m.f. is equal to the voltage source at the motor. When the load is heavy, the voltage consumed for the high current draw requirement is large. The armature, therefore, does not need to rotate at a high speed to produce the required counter e.m.f. When the used voltage plus the counter e.m.f. equals the source voltage, armature speed is established. Under light loads, the motor uses less of the applied voltage source, and therefore, armature speeds are increased to produce the necessary counter e.m.f.; as the counter e.m.f. becomes higher, the current draw of the motor drops. The number of turns in the armature windings and the magnetic field strength have a direct bearing on the motor speed.

SMALL MOTOR TYPES

Small motors used for accessory drives have varied designs and use various circuit controls to regulate their operation. Depending on application the motors are required to run at different speeds and may also be required to provide a reversing action.

Permanent-Magnet Motors

A permanent-magnet motor simply means that the field poles are permanent magnets. They are made of a hard ceramic material; there are no field windings. The motor has a wound armature and brushes (Figs. 9-23 and 9-24).

Fig. 9.23.   Permanent magnet. Motor field and armature.

(A)   (B)

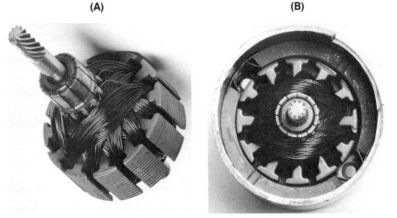

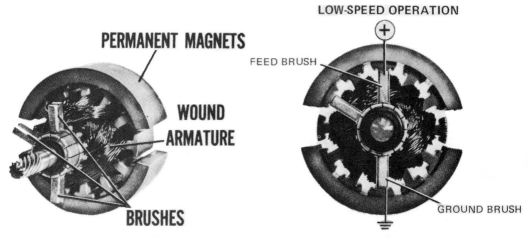

PERMANENT MAGNETS

WOUND
ARMATURE

BRUSHES

Fig. 9.24. Permanent magnet motor—typical two speed. *(Courtesy of The Chrysler Corporation)*

LOW-SPEED OPERATION

FEED BRUSH

GROUND BRUSH

Fig. 9.25.

FEWER
WINDINGS...

SPEED
HIGH

MORE
WINDINGS...

SPEED
LOW

Fig. 9.26.

Figure 9-24 is a typical permanent-magnet two-speed motor used for windshield wiper operation. In the low-speed range, Fig. 9-25, the armature feed comes from the top brush through the armature to the ground brush. When the armature feed is through the low-speed brush, the maximum number of armature windings are in use, so that the motor speed is slow (Fig. 9-26).

For high-speed operation, the circuit feed is switched to the offset brush located 60 degrees from the ground brush. This arrangement uses fewer armature windings, causing the motor speed to increase (Fig. 9-27).

To reverse the motor rotation of a permanent-magnet motor, the polarity of the armature is changed by reversing the current flow direction in the armature through the motor control switch; the field polarity stays the same. Figure 9-28 shows a simple schematic of the motor circuit arrangement for forward and reverse operation.

HIGH-SPEED OPERATION

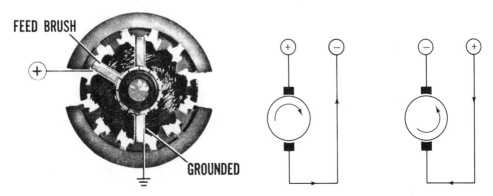

Fig. 9.27.

Fig. 9.28. Reversing permanent-magnet motor rotation.

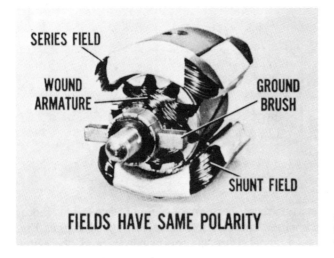

Fig. 9.29. Motor with two wire wound field windings. *(Courtesy of The Chrysler Corporation)*

Wire-Wound Motors

This type of motor uses wire-wound fields. The wire is wrapped around a soft iron core for added field strength when current flows through the wire windings. A wound armature is used with two brushes (Fig. 9-29).

There are several different types of small wire-wound motors: series wound, shunt wound, compound wound, and split series. Basically, they differ in the relationship of the field windings to the armature, so that the motors can meet the requirements of a specific job.

Series wound

The armature and fields are connected in series (Fig. 9-30). This motor has a high-torque characteristic but is subject to high speeds as the motor load decreases. A heavy-duty wire must be used for the field winding.

Shunt wound

The armature and fields are connected in parallel (Fig. 9-31). The shunt field uses a fine wire winding and since it is in parallel to the armature its current draw and field strength remain relatively the same regardless of the armature load. Thus, this motor operates at practically a constant speed, regardless of load.

Compound wound

This motor design uses a combination of series and shunt fields (Figs. 9-32 and 9-33). The motor has a high starting torque and operates at a relatively constant speed. It is easy, however, to use a circuit design to control the current in the shunt winding and consequently vary the motor speeds. This is usually done with step-type resistors in the motor control switch. Increasing the resistance in the shunt field reduces the strength of the magnetic field and increases motor speed.

Motor rotation can be reserved in a series-shunt motor by

Fig. 9.30.

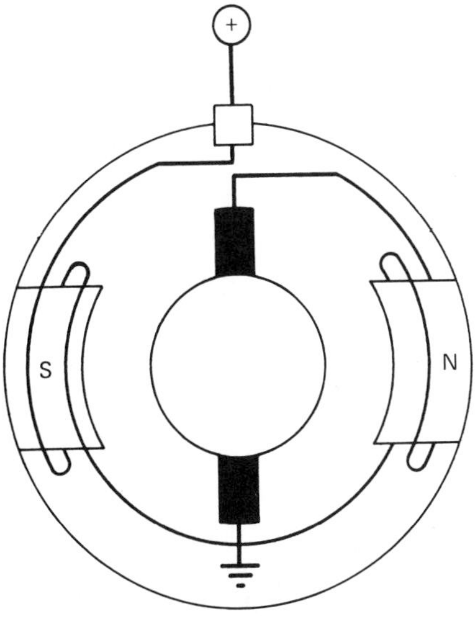

Fig. 9.31.   Shunt wound motor.

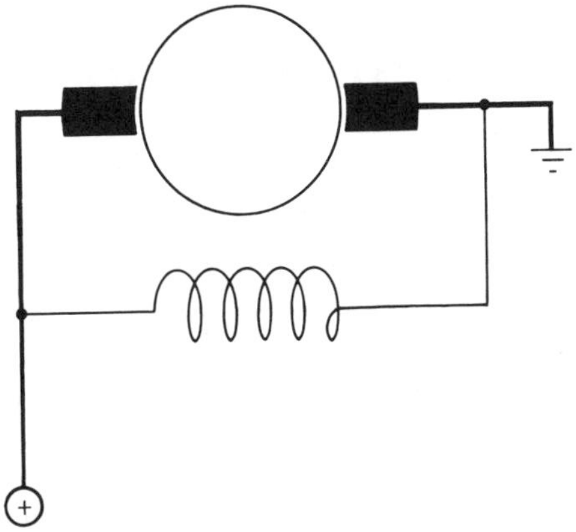

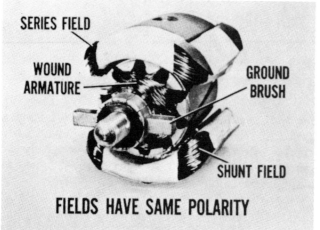

SERIES FIELD

WOUND ARMATURE

GROUND BRUSH

SHUNT FIELD

FIELDS HAVE SAME POLARITY

Fig. 9.32. Compound motorfield assembly. *(Courtesy of The Chrysler Corporation)*

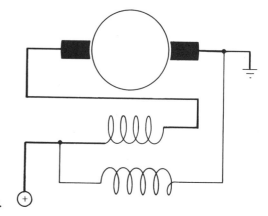

Fig. 9.33.   Compound (series-shunt) motor.

changing the direction of current flow in the field windings; armature polarity remains the same.

Split series

This motor features two field windings, each connected in series to the armature (Fig. 9-34). The field coils have opposite polarity, and only one is used at a time. Therefore, the direction of motor rotation depends on the selection made at the motor circuit control switch.

Blower Motor Speed Control

Motor speed can also be controlled by the use of external circuit resistors to decrease or increase the applied voltage to the motor (Fig. 9-35); in a wire-wound motor, this includes voltage applied to both the

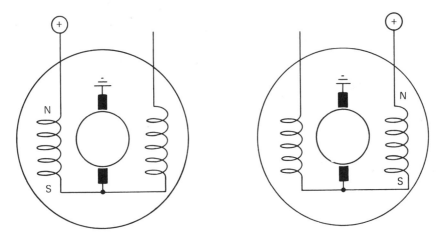

Fig. 9.34. Reversing rotation in split series wound motor.

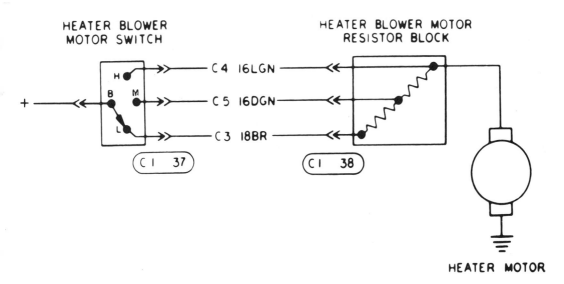

Fig. 9.35. Blower motor circuit. *(Courtesy of The Chrysler Corporation)*

armature and the field windings. The speed of the blower motor used in the heater and air-conditioning systems is controlled in this way.

The blower motor is designed to run on a 12-volt source and a specific amperage draw for proper maximum speed. When resistors are added in series to the external circuit to drop the applied voltage, motor efficiency or blower speed decreases.

In Fig. 9-35, the resistor block provides for low and medium blower-speed operation. For high speed, the blower speed switch connects to a by-pass that feeds 12 volts directly to the motor. The motor now draws its maximum current for best efficiency.

Note that this blower motor switch does not have an "off" position, as is the practice on some automobile models.

Review Questions

1. What is meant by magnetic flux density?
2. How would you define a magnetic field?
3. What are some characteristics peculiar to magnetic lines of force?
4. What is a permanent magnet?
5. Why is a horseshoe-shaped magnet stronger than a bar magnet?
6. How does a material such as iron affect a magnetic field?
7. How do *like* and *unlike* magnetic poles behave when they are exposed to each other? Is this behavior capable of doing work?
8. What causes an electromagnetic field?
9. Indicate with an arrow the direction of the current flow and magnetic field in the illustrated wire connector.

10. Indicate the north and south poles of the illustrated electromagnet.

11. What are the factors that determine the strength of an electromagnetic field?
12. Explain this statement: Electromagnets and permanent magnets behave in the same manner.
13. What is electromagnetic induction?
14. Briefly describe the two methods used in producing electromagnetic induction. Where are these methods used in automotive applications?

15. What happens to a current-carrying conductor when it is exposed to a magnetic field?

16. When does an armature loop reach its neutral position?

17. What is the reference made to the rotating part of the motor assembly?

18. What is the function of the motor commutator?

19. Explain why reversing the current flow in both the starter field and the armature does not reverse motor rotation.

20. What two methods are employed in reversing motor rotation for automotive accessory drives?

21. Explain why a rotating motor also acts as a generator.

22. Explain why the slower a motor rotates, the more current it draws.

23. What are the two factors that determine motor torque?

24. When the load increases, what happens to the motor torque and speed?

25. How does the motor generating action (counter e.m.f.) control motor speed?

26. How is the armature rotation reversed in a permanent-magnet motor?

27. How do you identify the shunt winding in compound-wound motor fields?

28. How is armature rotation reversed in compound-wound motors?

29. How is armature rotation reversed in a split-series field-wound motor?

10

Horns and Buzzer Warning Systems

There are many types of warning systems in the modern automobile; those in common use are covered in this chapter. They may be manually operated, such as the horn; or automatic, such as the buzzer which reminds the driver that the key has been left in the ignition switch.

Another automatic device is the light or buzzer that tells the passengers and/or driver to fasten their seat belts. In some cases the seat belt warning system will prevent the driver from starting the engine until the belt is fastened.

HORNS

Automotive electrical horns have vibrating-type power plants that operate on a magnetic principle to produce sound used as a warning signal (Fig. 10-1). Current flows through the field windings within the horn power plant whenever the horn circuit is completed. The resulting magnetic field attracts the movable armature "A" toward the pole. A diaphragm is connected to the armature, and movement of the armature thus causes similar movement of the diaphragm. The contact points, "B," which are normally closed are connected in series with the horn winding and are opened mechanically as the armature moves toward the pole. When the current is interrupted, the armature returns because of the spring-back action of the diaphragm. The return movement of the armature allows the contact points to close,

246

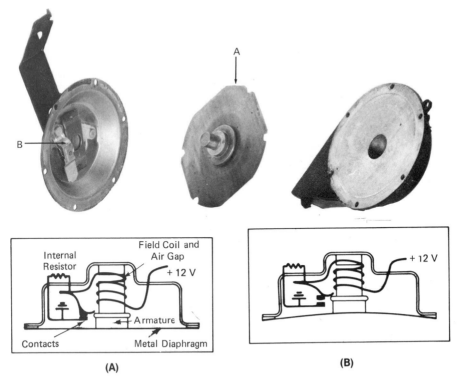

Fig. 10.1.

again completing the circuit. This cycle is repeated many times per second, resulting in a rapid vibration of the diaphragm that produces sound. The number of vibrations produced per second determines the pitch of the sound. The greater the number of vibrations, the higher the pitch.

The horns, which are located in the engine compartment, are controlled by a horn switch at the top of the steering column. One, two, three, or four horns may be used (Fig. 10-2), to produce a blended tone that gives a pleasing effect. Most cars are equipped with a matched pair of horns, one having a slightly lower musical pitch than the other, Fig. 10-3.

Some horn systems incorporate a horn relay, and other horn systems use no relay. This chapter will explain both systems.

Horn Circuit With Relay

The horn(s) is (are) operated by a horn relay located in the engine compartment, under the instrument panel, or mounted on the fuse

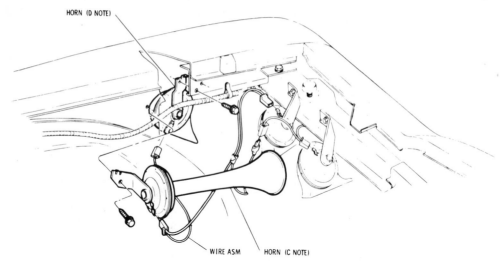

HORN (D NOTE)

WIRE ASM   HORN (C NOTE)

Fig.10.2

Fig. 10.3.

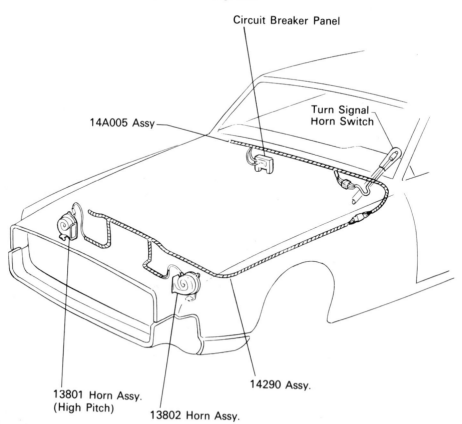

Circuit Breaker Panel

Turn Signal
Horn Switch

14A005 Assy

13801 Horn Assy.
(High Pitch)

13802 Horn Assy.

14290 Assy.

block. The relay is controlled by the horn switch at the top of the steering column, which closes the circuit between the battery and the horns when the horn button is depressed. The horn relay permits control of the horns with a small amount of current passing through the horn switch (Fig. 10-4).

When the horn button is depressed, current flows from the battery through the relay windings to ground at the horn button. This

Fig. 10.4. *Courtesy of Ford Customer Service Division.*

Horn Circuit with Relay

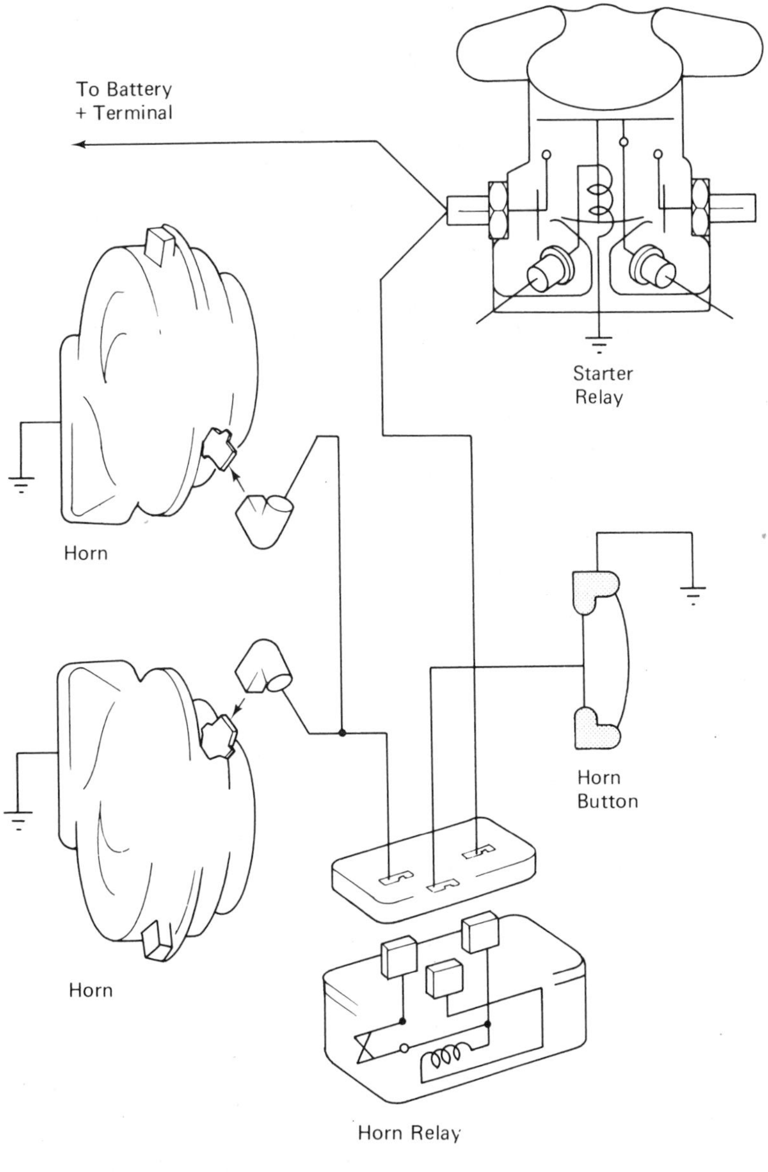

To Battery + Terminal

Starter Relay

Horn

Horn Button

Horn

Horn Relay

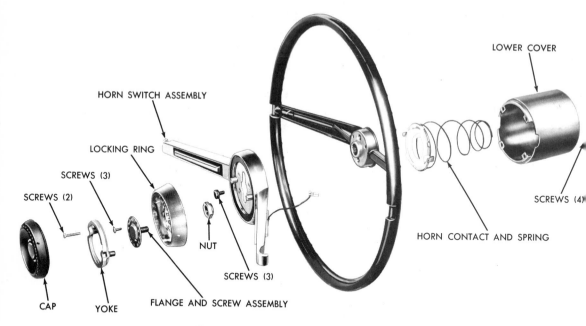

Fig. 10.5. *Courtesy of The Chrysler Corporation.*

magnetizes the relay core and attracts the flat steel relay armature. The armature closes and contacts the stationary point, completing the horn circuit.

An actuator bar is mounted across the steering wheel. Fastened to the actuator bar, but insulated from it, is a contact plate which is hot at all times. When the bar is depressed, it touches the ground plates to provide a ground for the horn-relay winding. When the horn button is released, springs move the bar away from the ground plate (Fig. 10-5).

Horn Circuit without Relay

In this circuit design, the horns must be of low amperage since the horn-button switch must carry the total amperage of the horns. Depressing the horn button completes the hot circuit from the source of power to the horn (Fig. 10-6).

New York City-Country Horns

All new vehicles sold in New York after 1974 must be equipped with a two-level horn called the city-country horn system. Under normal

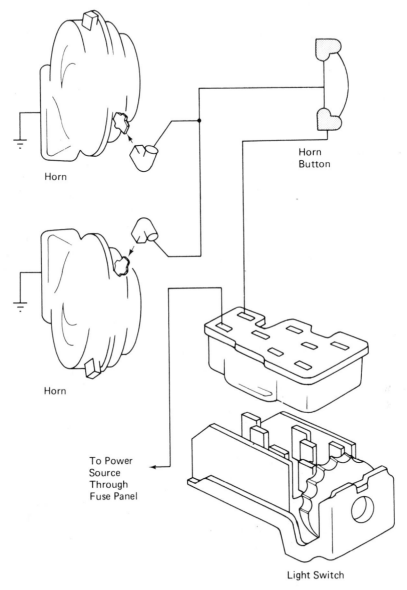

Horn

Horn
Button

Horn

To Power
Source
Through
Fuse Panel

Light Switch

Fig. 10.6. *Courtesy of Ford Customer Service Division.*

driving conditions, at speeds over approximately 15 miles per hour, the louder "country" level is automatically selected. Below 15 miles per hour, only the softer "city" level will sound. With the ignition on, a manual override switch located on the underside of the instrument panel can be used to select the country level at any speed.

Speed sensor

The speed sensor is the same sensor used in the speed control system. It is connected to the speedometer cable and produces a signal frequency proportional to the speed of the vehicle.

Electronic control module

The electronic control module is sensitive to the signal frequency of the speed sensor. Power for the control module is supplied by the ignition circuit. When power is not supplied (key off), only the city horn will sound. When the ignition switch is on and the vehicle attains the specified speed, the signal from the speed sensor triggers the electronic control module and provides a ground for the holding coil of the horn-selector relay. This causes the horn-selector relay to switch to the country horn.

Two sets of relay switch contacts determine which horn system is in operation. The normally-closed contacts (holding coil not energized) provide power for the city horn. When the holding coil is energized, the open contacts are closed and provide power for the country horn.

SERVICING & TROUBLESHOOTING THE HORN

To adjust the horn:

1. Disconnect the horns, one at a time, to determine which horn is not operating.
2. With the proper tool, turn the tone adjuster counter-clockwise, Fig. 10-7, until there is no vibration.
3. Turn the tone adjuster clockwise, one-quarter turn at a time, until the tone has a clear sound. Do not turn the tone adjuster while the horn is sounding.
4. Connect a test ammeter between the positive post of the battery and the horn terminal post. Connect another wire from the negative post of the battery to the horn base. Turn the tone adjuster screw to obtain the proper amperage, usually 3.5 amps and 8 amps, as specified in the service manual. If the

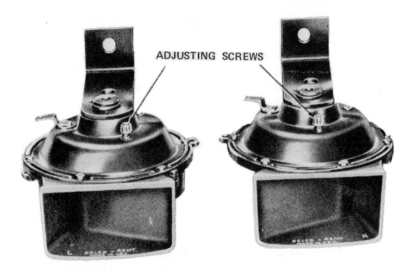

ADJUSTING SCREWS

Fig. 10.7. *Courtesy of Buick Division of General Motors Corp.*

Fig. 10.8. *Courtesy of Ford Customer Service Division.*

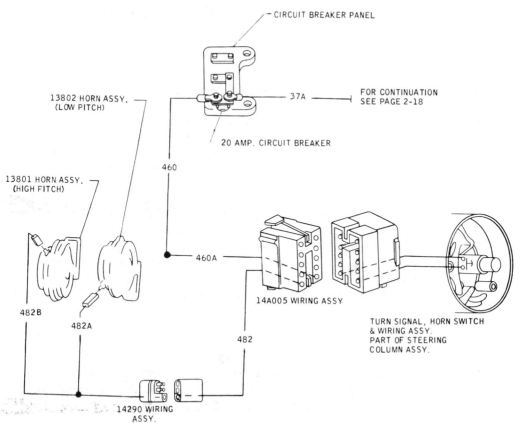

CIRCUIT BREAKER PANEL

13802 HORN ASSY.
(LOW PITCH)

37A

FOR CONTINUATION
SEE PAGE 2-18

20 AMP. CIRCUIT BREAKER

460

13801 HORN ASSY.
(HIGH PITCH)

460A

14A005 WIRING ASSY.

482B

482A

482

TURN SIGNAL, HORN SWITCH
& WIRING ASSY.
PART OF STEERING
COLUMN ASSY.

14290 WIRING
ASSY.

253

horn does not work after these adjustments, the horn should be replaced. Some horns are protected by a circuit breaker (Fig. 10-8), and others are protected by a fuse in fuse block or by a fusible link.

Horn Voltage Test

You can test for improper horn operation by connecting a voltmeter between the horn terminal and the ground and observing the voltage while the horn is blowing.

1. No voltage indicates trouble in relay, horn button, wires or ground.
2. Voltage less than 9 volts could be caused by resistance in the wiring or by excessive current draw due to a short circuit in the horn.
3. Voltage of 9-11 volts indicates that the wiring is OK. Look for sticking or improper adjustment of horn.
4. Voltage above 11 volts indicates improper adjustment or open circuit in horn due to broken coil lead.

HORN RELAY AND IGNITION KEY-IN BUZZER— CHRYSLER, GENERAL MOTORS, AMERICAN MOTORS

In Chrysler, General Motors, and American Motors cars, the horn relay includes both the horn relay and the ignition key-in buzzer. The buzzer operates when either front door is opened to remind the driver that the ignition key has been left in the ignition switch (Fig. 10-9). Buzzer operation is shown in Fig. 10-10. With the key in the off position but fully inserted into the ignition switch, current will flow from the battery to #1 terminal energizing the coil, then through the upper contacts to #4 terminal to the key switch and door switch to ground. The energized coil causes the upper contacts to open, which deenergizes the coil, and the upper contacts reclose. This cycle repeats many times per second to give a buzzing sound. The lower contacts do not close because the key buzzer takes a small amount of current.

Horn Operation

When the horn switch is closed, the coil is energized and the lower contact moves toward the coil to close the horn relay contact. The horns are then connected to the battery. The horns demand more

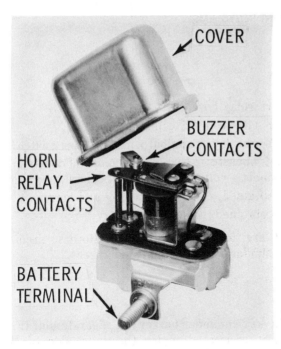

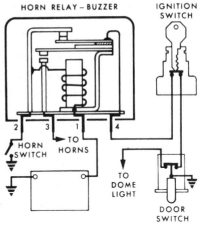

1. Red - "Bat."
2. Black
3. Black - Green Tracer
4. Pink - Black Tracer

Fig. 10.9. *Courtesy of the Oldsmobile Division of General Motors Corp.*

Fig. 10.10 *Courtesy of Oldsmobile Division of General Motors Corp.*

current to operate, which makes the coil stronger, and keeps the contacts closed. The buzzer contacts (upper points) remain open.

Key Buzzer Checks

Refer to Fig. 10-10.

1. Make sure that the key is fully inserted into the ignition switch and in the off position.
2. Open the driver's door and check the dome lights.
3. If the buzzer and dome lights are off, check the door switch.
4. If the dome light is on, and the buzzer fails to operate, remove buzzer.
5. Connect a jumper wire from #4 terminal to ground.
6. If the buzzer operates, check the ignition switch wiring and ignition switch.
7. If the buzzer does not operate, connect a voltmeter from #1 terminal to ground.
8. If the reading is zero, the circuit is open to the battery.
9. If a voltage reading is obtained, replace the key buzzer.

Horn Relay Checks

Refer to Fig. 10-10.

1. Remove the horn relay buzzer.
2. Connect jumper wire from #2 terminal to ground.
3. If horn operates, check #2 terminal wire and horn switch.
4. If horns do not operate, leave #2 terminal connected to ground, and connect a voltmeter from #3 terminal to ground.
5. If a reading is obtained, check horn wiring and horns.
6. If no reading is obtained, replace horn relay.

The above tests are for typical General Motors circuits. Numbers might not be similar with other manufacturers.

FORD IGNITION KEY-IN BUZZER

On Ford automobiles the key-reminder buzzer is a separate unit (Fig. 10-11). On small cars, it is located under the right side of the instrument panel. In the other models, the buzzer is located either in the relay panel under the dash or on the fuse panel.

Current flows from the fuse block to the door jamb switch; when the door is open, the current energizes the coil in the buzzer, and continues on to the key-reminder switch and then to ground. The buzzer vibrates to remind the driver that the key is still in the ignition switch. The diode located in the buzzer prevents feedback and point arcing.

Fig. 10.11.   *Courtesy of Ford Customer Service Division.*

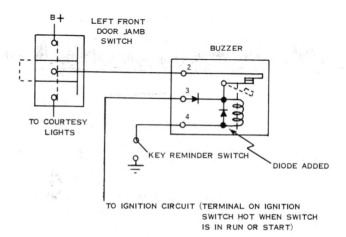

Fig. 10.12. *Courtesy of Gordon Bechelli—FSC.*

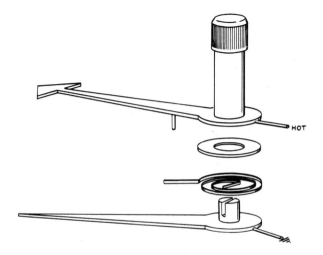

HOT

Fig. 10.13. *Courtesy of Gordon Bechelli—FSC.*

SPEEDOMETER BUZZER

The speedometer buzzer is a buzzer that may be adjusted by the driver to sound at any speed between 30 and 120 miles per hour by turning a knob at the speedometer face (Fig. 10-12). The speed at which the buzzer is set is indicated by a special pointer in the speedometer face.

The speed-alert electrical circuit starts at the battery and feeds through the fusible links to the starter solenoid to the buzzer contacts. After passing through the buzzer contacts, a very small amount of current goes through a resistor to ground and the rest of the current passes through a wire to the connector located on the speedometer case (Fig. 10-13).

In the speedometer, current is conducted from the separate buzzer connector through a wire to an insulated pin in the lower end of the buzzer pointer. As the speedometer pointer moves up to coincide with the buzzer pointer, a grounded hair spring on the lower end of the speedometer pointer makes contact with the hot insulated pin on the speed pointer.

This grounds the circuit, causing the buzzer to buzz. If the car speed is increased beyond the buzzer setting, the insulated pin on the safety buzzer pointer "picks up" the hair spring as the speedometer pointer and the hair spring winds up slightly. This will keep the buzzer pointer grounded as the speedometer pointer passes the buzzer pointer.

HEADLIGHTS-ON WARNING BUZZER

The headlights-on warning buzzer is a separate unit (Fig. 10-14a). When the headlights are on and the driver's door is open, the circuit is energized and the buzzer sounds. The buzzer contains a resistor to prevent point arcing when the points open.

To make the buzzer operate, power is applied to the buzzer when the left front door is opened and the door jamb switch is closed. The buzzer is grounded through the normally-open contacts of the headlights on relay.

Fig. 10.14(A).   *Courtesy of Ford Customer Service Division.*

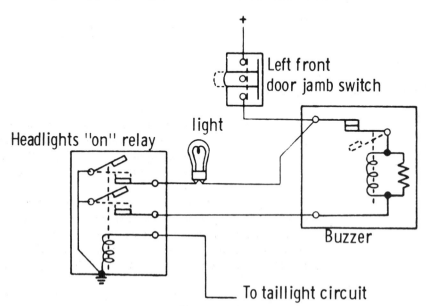

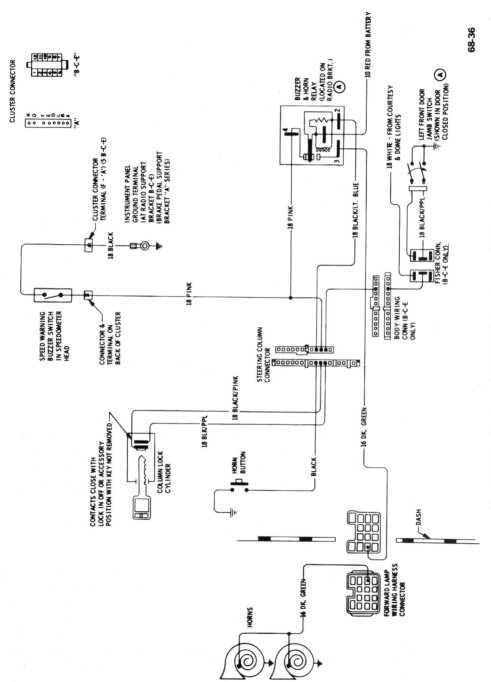

CLUSTER CONNECTOR

"B-C-E"

"A"

CLUSTER CONNECTOR TERMINAL (F - 'A') 15 B-C-E

INSTRUMENT PANEL GROUND TERMINAL (AT RADIO SUPPORT BRACKET B-C-E) (BRAKE PEDAL SUPPORT BRACKET "A" SERIES)

18 BLACK

SPEED WARNING BUZZER SWITCH IN SPEEDOMETER HEAD

CONNECTOR & TERMINAL ON BACK OF CLUSTER

18 PINK

18 PINK

STEERING COLUMN CONNECTOR

CONTACTS CLOSE WITH LOCK IN OFF OR ACCESSORY POSITION WITH KEY NOT REMOVED

COLUMN LOCK CYLINDER

18 BLK/PPL

18 BLACK/PINK

HORN BUTTON

BLACK

16 DK. GREEN

BODY WIRING CONN (B-C-E ONLY)

18 BLACK/LT. BLUE

18 PINK

BUZZER & HORN RELAY (LOCATED ON RADIO BRKT.)

10 RED FROM BATTERY

18 WHITE - FROM COURTESY & DOME LIGHTS

18 BLACK/PPL

FISHER CONN. (B-C-E ONLY)

LEFT FRONT DOOR JAMB SWITCH (SHOWN IN DOOR CLOSED POSITION)

FORWARD LAMP WIRING HARNESS CONNECTOR

DASH

HORNS

16 DK. GREEN

68-36

Fig. 10.14(B) *Courtesy of Buick Division of General Motors Corp.*

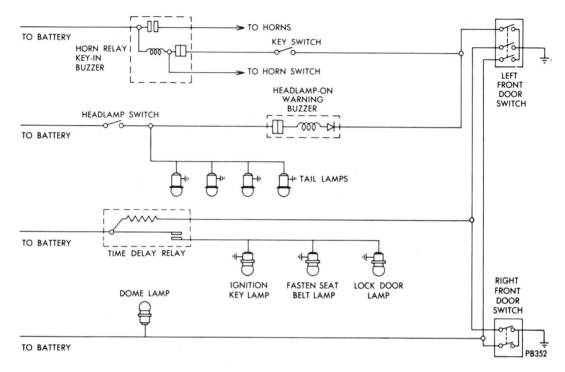

Fig. 10.14(C). **Typical Chrysler buzzer and horn relay system.** *(Courtesy of The Chrysler Corporation.)*

The headlights-on relay is self-grounding and receives its power from the taillight circuit. Whenever the headlight switch is in park or "on" position, it applies power to, and energizes the headlights-on relay, thereby providing a ground path for the headlights-on buzzer.

The second set of contacts in the headlights-on relay grounds one side of the headlights-on indicator light. The other side of the light is wired back to the buzzer.

INTEGRATED BUZZER-HORN RELAY SYSTEMS

Figures 10-14b and 10-14c typically illustrate how warning buzzer and horn relay systems are tied-in together to operate off the door jam switches. It is the practice of AMC, Chrysler, and GM to use grounding door switches and of Ford to use insulated door jam switches.

In Figure 10-14c, note how a time delay relay turns on the ignition key lamp, the seat-belt lamp, and the door-lock lamp when the door is opened. The current through the heating coil heats up the points, and the points close. After the door is closed, the lights remain on for approximately 30 seconds to remind the driver to fasten his seat belt and lock the doors. When the points cool off, they open and the lights go out. A diode in the "Headlights On" buzzer circuit prevents an electrical feedback.

SEAT-BELT WARNING SYSTEM

In compliance with Federal Motor Vehicle Safety Standards all American vehicles built after January 1, 1972 have a seat-belt warning system designed to alert the driver and the right-front-seat passenger to fasten their seat belts.

The belt warning system can be considered in two parts:

1. The signal circuit that determines if the seats are occupied and the belts are fastened.
2. The warning devices of the dash panel (light and buzzer).

1972-73 Ford Seat-Belt Warning System (Fig. 10-15)

A warning light and loud buzzer command the driver and the front-seat passenger to fasten their seat belts when the following conditions exist:

1. Ignition switch is on.
2. Belts are not fastened in the front seat by the driver and/or passenger.
3. Automatic transmission is in an operating range. (Manual transmission park brake light switch is released.)

The warning system will not turn off until the belts are fastened.

All cars use essentially the same arrangement: a switch built into each outboard front seat-belt anchor is closed to complete a ground circuit when the belts are retracted. While they are closed, the switches activate the alarm system much as a horn button blows the horn by completing the ground system. When a belt is pulled 5 to 10 inches out of the retractor, its grounding switch is open and the warning light and buzzer turn off.

The passenger seat has a pressure switch wired in series with its belt retractor switch. With about 50 pounds on the seat, this switch closes, so that it is necessary to extend that belt to turn the warning system off.

Chrysler Seat-Belt Warning System (Fig. 10-16)

This warning system includes a buzzer and light, two lap belt retractor switches, a front passenger seat switch and a relay. The circuit is also tied into the neutral safety switch.

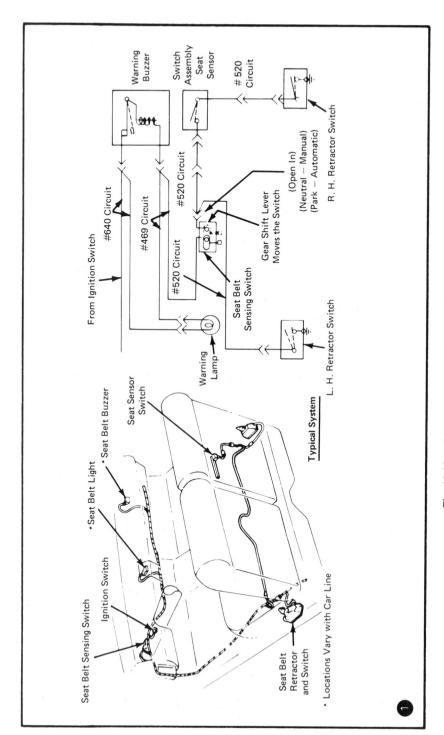

Fig. 10.15. *Courtesy of Ford Customer Service Division.*

Warning Buzzer

Switch Assembly Seat Sensor

#520 Circuit

#640 Circuit

#469 Circuit

#520 Circuit

#520 Circuit

(Open In)
(Neutral — Manual)
(Park — Automatic)

R. H. Retractor Switch

From Ignition Switch

Gear Shift Lever Moves the Switch

Warning Lamp

Seat Belt Sensing Switch

L. H. Retractor Switch

<u>Typical System</u>

Seat Belt Sensing Switch

Ignition Switch

*Seat Belt Light

*Seat Belt Buzzer

Seat Sensor Switch

Seat Belt Retractor and Switch

• Locations Vary with Car Line

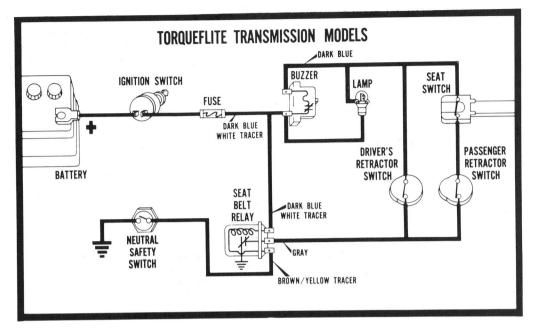

Fig. 10.16. *Courtesy of The Chrysler Corporation.*

The current starts at the ignition switch and flows through a fuse to the relay. It continues through the relay and is grounded at the neutral safety switch. The neutral safety switch is closed in park and neutral. The current flowing through the relay creates a magnetic field, opens the points, and breaks the ground circuit for the seat-belt warning system. When the vehicle is shifted into any forward gear, the neutral safety switch opens and the current can no longer flow through the relay. The contact points in the relay close, creating a ground for the warning system. Current now flows through the buzzer and warning light through the left-hand seat-belt switch (unless it is pulled out 5 to 10 inches) to the relay to ground.

General Motors Seat-Belt Warning System (Fig. 10-17)

This seat-belt warning system uses two fuses in the circuit. One fuse marked "gauges" supplies power to the warning light. The other fuse marked "back up" supplies power to the buzzer. The neutral safety switch is a multiple switch that contains contacts which will allow the driver to start the vehicle in park or neutral, and it will also feed current to the seat-belt warning switch if the driver shifts the vehicle in any forward gear without the seat belt fastened. The neutral safety switch will also complete the electrical connection to the backup lights when the vehicle is shifted to reverse.

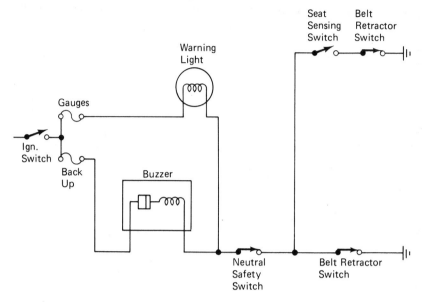

Fig. 10.17.

If the ignition is on and the neutral switch is closed (by putting the gear shift in any forward position), the warning light and buzzer will operate. To shut off the warning light and buzzer, the seat belt must be pulled out 5 to 10 inches. When the belt is pulled out of the retractor, it opens the ground circuit and the warning system will not operate.

SEAT-BELT-STARTER INTERLOCK SYSTEM

The seat-belt-starter interlock system is designed to prevent engine start when the right-front passenger seat and/or the driver's seat are occupied and the seat belts are not fastened.

Seat-Belt-Starter Interlock Legislation

The seat-belt-starter interlock system is required by Federal law (Motor Vehicle Safety Standard #208) in vehicles built after 1973.

This law permits silencing of the continuous buzzer and bypassing of the interlock, but it does not allow extinguishing of the seat-belt warning light. Therefore, reaching under the seat and pulling apart the connector to the seat sensor is prohibited, for the light also would be affected.

An amendment to the Federal Motor Vehicle Safety Standard #208 stipulates that passenger vehicles produced on or after February

24, 1975, must be equipped with a nonsequential 4-8 second seat-belt warning light and buzzer system that is activated from the driver's seat only. The new system has an instrument panel warning light that lights up every time the ignition switch is turned on, whether or not the driver's seat is buckled, but which automatically goes off after 4-8 seconds. The buzzer also is controlled by the 4-8 second timer but operates only if the driver has not buckled up. If the driver does not buckle up after turning on the ignition, the buzzer also shuts off automatically after 4-8 seconds.

In this chapter, we will describe the operation of seat-belt-starter interlock systems used in 1974 automobiles.

Seat-Belt-Interlock System—Operation

Three waffle-type seat sensors are located under the seat cushion of the front seat (Fig. 10-18, #10). Each of the three belt buckles in the front seat has a built-in switch.

Figure 10-18 shows other components of the system: an

Fig. 10.18. **System components and location.** *Courtesy of General Motors Corp.*

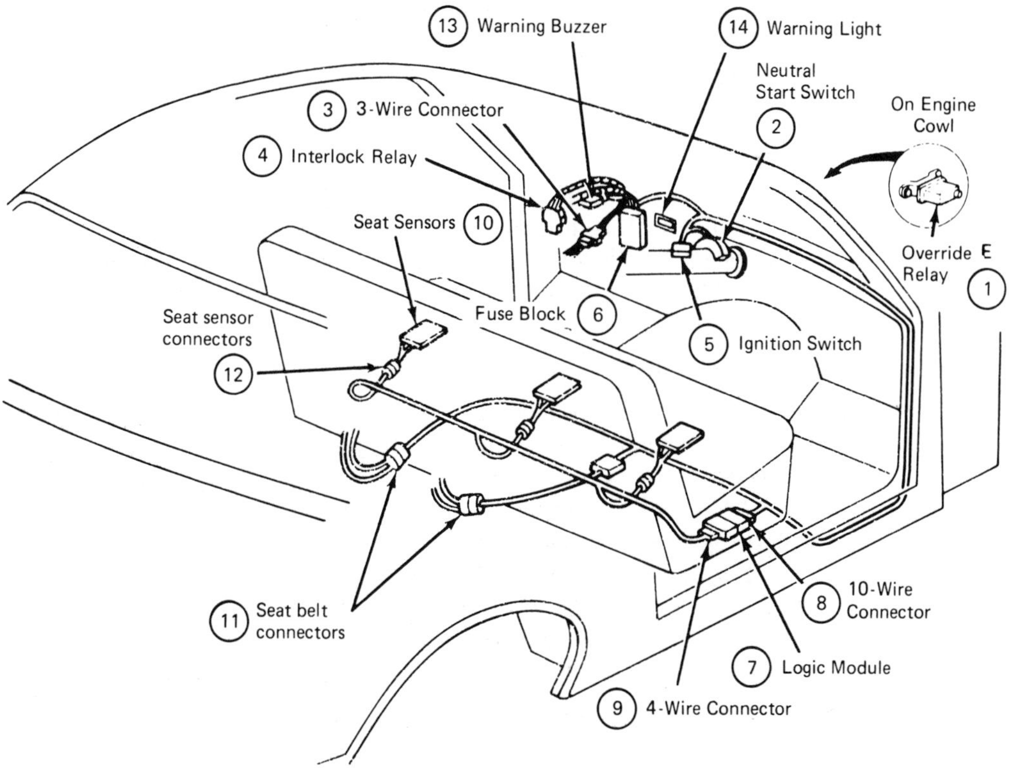

electronic logic module located under the front seat (#7); an interlock relay mounted close to the fuse block (#4); a buzzer that plugs into a connector (#13); a warning light located in the instrument cluster (#14); and an override relay located on the driver's side under the hood (#1).

Remember that (1) the interlock relay points are normally closed and (2) current is continually fed to the electronic logic module through the clock fuse. To start the engine:

1. Sit on the seat.
2. Fasten the seat belt.
3. Start the engine.

If the right-front seat is occupied before the engine is started, the seat belt must also be buckled before the engine can be started.

As the driver's seat and the right front outboard seat are occupied, the respective seat sensors inform the logic module and the interlock relay contacts are opened.

When the seat belts are fastened, the buckle switches inform the logic module and the interlock relay contacts are again closed. With the shift lever in park or neutral and the ignition turned to start, current is fed through the backup lamp and the seat-belt warning switch to the interlock relay and then to the solenoid.

General Motors, Chrysler, and AMC have the belt sensors in the buckle. Ford places the sensors in the belt retractor.

Override relay

The override relay permits you to start the engine in the event of a failure in the interlock system. To activate the override relay, turn the ignition key to "on". Open the hood, press and release the start button on the override relay, and then turn the ignition key to start the engine.

Mechanic's start

A mechanic's start procedure can be used to turn over the engine without first having to occupy the front seat or be concerned about whether the belts are buckled. You can start the engine by reaching into the car and turning the ignition switch to start. The warning system will not operate *unless* the car is placed in a drive mode.

Figures 10-19, 10-20, 10-21, 10-22, and 10-23 are wiring diagrams with some of the main wiring shown in boldface to make it somewhat easier to understand and to determine some quick check points for troubleshooting. If the starter does not operate, check these points:

1. Check the clock fuse and backup light fuse.

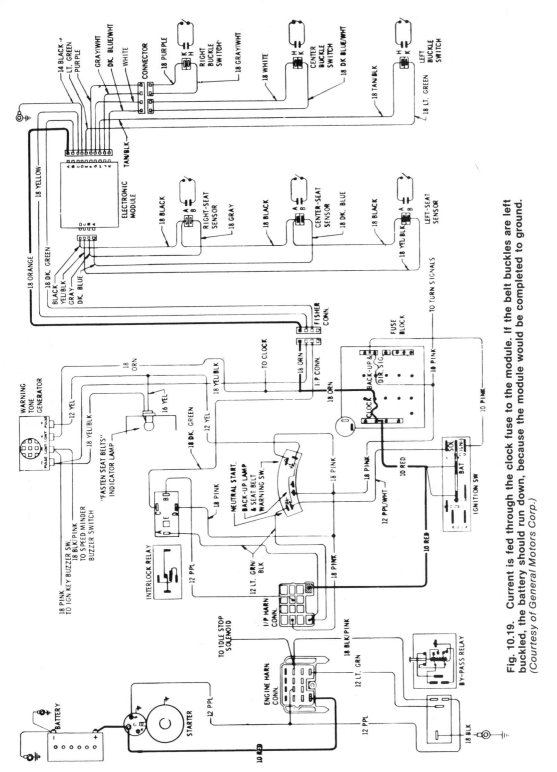

Fig. 10.19. Current is fed through the clock fuse to the module. If the belt buckles are left buckled, the battery should run down, because the module would be completed to ground. *(Courtesy of General Motors Corp.)*

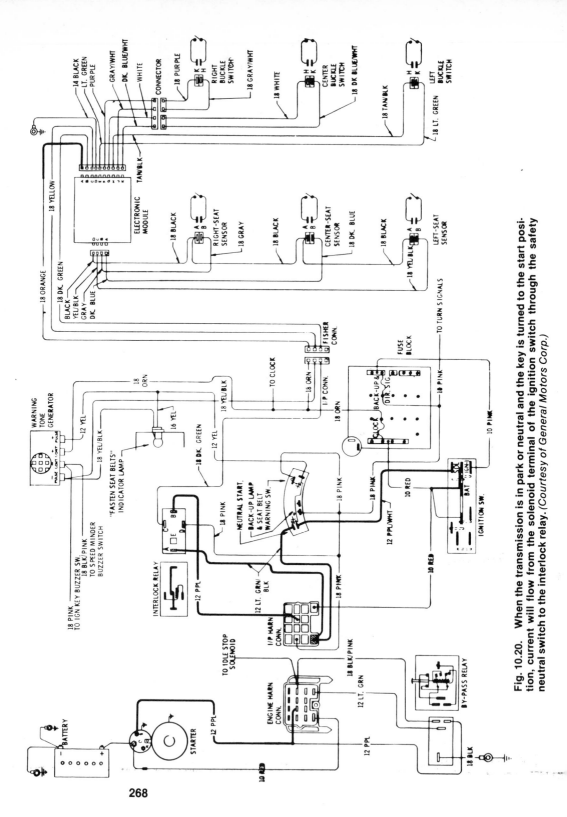

Fig. 10.20. When the transmission is in park or neutral and the key is turned to the start position, current will flow from the solenoid terminal of the ignition switch through the safety neutral switch to the interlock relay. (Courtesy of General Motors Corp.)

268

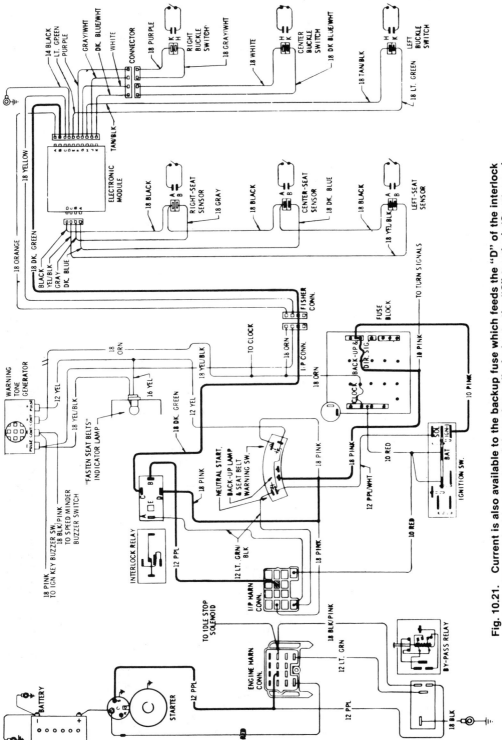

Fig. 10.21. Current is also available to the backup fuse which feeds the "D" of the interlock relay. The "D" terminal is connected through a coil of wire to the "C" terminal. *(Courtesy of General Motors Corp.)*

269

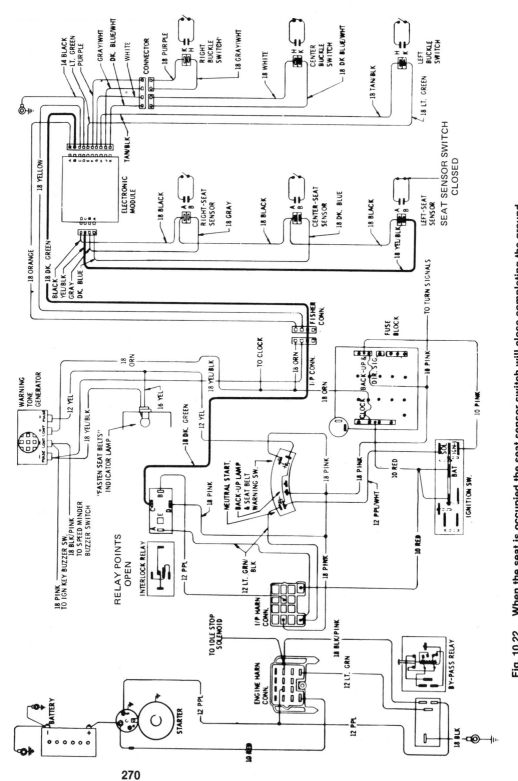

Fig. 10.22. When the seat is occupied the seat sensor switch will close completing the ground circuit for the interlock relay and the points will open interrupting the current flow to the starter solenoid. The seat belt is not buckled. (*Courtesy of General Motors Corp.*)

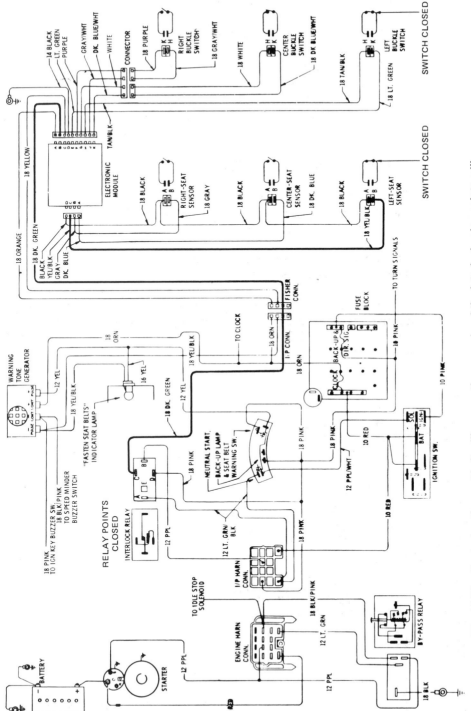

Fig. 10.23. Fastening the seat belt will remove the ground and the interlock relay points will be closed by spring tension completing the circuit to the starter solenoid. *(Courtesy of General Motors Corp.)*

271

2. There should be battery voltage at the "A" terminal of module.

3. With the key in start position and the transmission in park or neutral, there should be battery voltage at interlock relay "A" terminal. Seat sensor closed and seat buckles closed.

4. With the key in start position, there should be battery voltage to the "S" terminal of the starter solenoid.

1974 Ford Starter Interlock System

The starter interlock system has a seat-belt warning light and buzzer, sensors in the seat, electrical switches in the outboard belt retractors, and an electronic logic module. The passenger cars that have three front seating positions also have a switch in the center buckle. This switch is part of the warning light and buzzer system but *not* part of the starter interlock system.

Before starting the car the driver must sit in the seat and pull out his seat belt. The belts cannot be pulled out permanently or buckled on the seat behind the passenger, or the car will not start. The seat belt switch in the retractor must be cycled before the starter will engage.

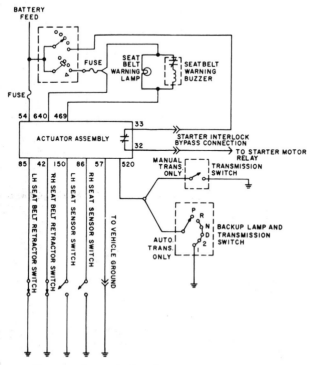

Fig. 10.24. *Courtesy of Ford Customer Service Division)*

The system is energized at all times. Leaving a package on the seats or one or more belts fastened can drain the battery. For detailed troubleshooting, a service dealer should have the wiring diagrams either from the car makers or a Chilton Manual.

SEAT BELT INTERLOCK

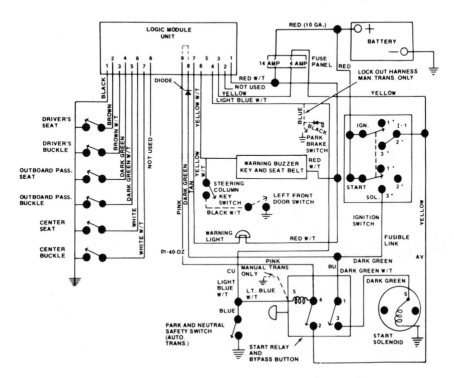

Fig. 10.25. *Courtesy of American Motors Corporation.*

If the driver fails to follow the proper sequence, the warning light and buzzer will operate when the key is turned on. The warning light and buzzer will also function if the belts of any occupied front seating position are not kept extended after the engine has been started and the transmission put into gear.

This system has a starter bypass switch located in the engine compartment in case of a malfunction in the interlock system.

The wiring diagram is shown in Fig. 10-24 to help you understand and troubleshoot the interlock system.

1974 A.M.C. Seat-Belt-Interlock System

The seat-belt-interlock system (Fig. 10-25 prevents starting of the car's engine unless all front-seat occupants buckle their seat belts *after* being seated.

The following sequence will allow the engine to start:

1. Sit down and close the doors. This activates the seat sensor switch which sends a signal to the logic module.
2. Fasten seat belts. This completes the circuit and sends another signal to the logic module.
3. Start the car. In case of a malfunction in the interlock

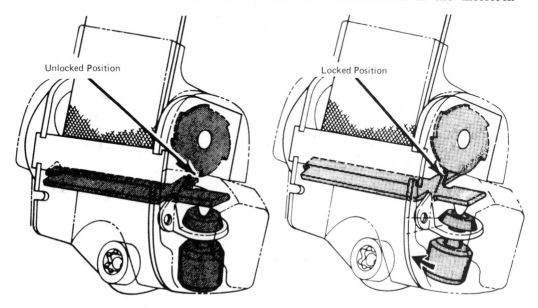

Fig. 10.26.

Fig. 10.27.   *Courtesy of The Chrysler Corporation.*

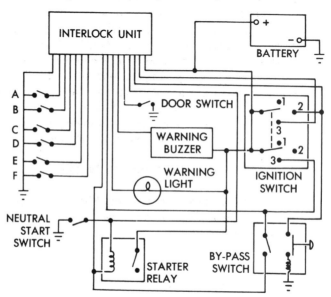

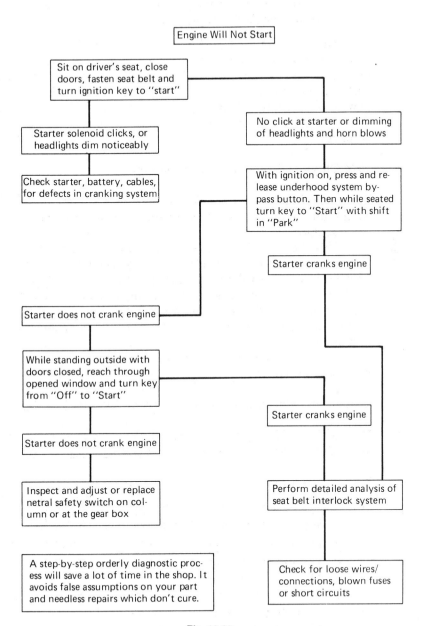

Fig. 10.28.

system, a starter relay is located in the engine compartment. It is identified with a decal.

The shoulder belt retractors, Fig. 10-26, will lock when the vehicle is braked or stopped suddenly. Any such abrupt change in vehicle speed causes a quick movement of a pendulum suspended within the retractor device. When the pendulum swings, it causes a pawl to engage a ratchet attached to the end of the retractor reel. With the pawl engaged, the reel cannot turn, and belt travel is stopped.

1974 Chrysler Starter Interlock System

The seat-belt starter interlock system prevents cranking of the car's engine unless all front-seat occupants buckle their seat belts after being seated.

This belt reminder system provides an audible and visual indication that a front seat belt is not being used by an occupant. If the ignition key is turned to the start position when a front-seat occupant's seat belt is not buckled or an occupant has buckled the seat belt before being seated, the engine will not crank, the seat-belt reminder system will buzz, and the indicator light on the dash board will be illuminated.

Figure 10-27 is a wiring diagram of the 1974 Chrysler starter interlock system.

Diagnostic Procedure—Starter Interlock System

Figure 10-28 is a step-by-step procedure that will help you efficiently and quickly diagnose problems in the starter interlock system.

Review questions

1. The horn relay completes the circuit between what two units?
2. Why is a horn relay used to complete the circuit?
3. In a system without a horn relay, what completes the circuit?
4. The key-in-ignition buzzer and the headlights-on buzzer are operated by what switch?
5. In seat-belt warning systems built before 1974, what is the location of the switch that operates the buzzer?
6. The seat-belt interlock system is designed to do a specific job. What is it?
7. What is the purpose of the override relay?
8. What is a mechanic's start?

11

Instrument Panel Gauges and Indicator Lights

Instrument gauges and indicator lights monitor various vehicle operating systems and keep the driver informed of their correct operation. The more essential instruments are concerned with the fuel level, engine-coolant temperature, oil pressure, charging rate, and vehicle speed. Indicator lights sometimes take the place of the engine-temperature and oil-pressure gauges and the charging-system ammeter. It is not unusual for a car manufacturer to mix indicator lights with gauges in a variety of combinations.

Back in the old days, a shiny, nickle-plated motometer on the radiator cap was the last word in temperature gauges. The fuel level in the gas tank was indicated by the height of a red-colored liquid in a vertical glass tube on the instrument panel. The gauge worked on the hydraulic head principle and required a tubing link between the tank and gauge unit.

Today's gauges and indicator systems are more sophisticated and do a better job. Although they are slightly more complicated, they are not impossible to understand and service. As you study the various gauge and indicator systems, you'll find that they are only simple electrical systems.

THERMOELECTRIC GAUGES

Thermoelectric gauges are currently used in American Motors, Chrysler, and Ford vehicles. They are simple dial-and-pointer

277

indicators that transform the heating effect of electricity into a mechanical movement. The same basic mechanism is used in the fuel, temperature, and oil-pressure gauges; only the dials are different. Thermal gauge pointer movement is relatively slow and smooth, and therefore, avoids responding to sudden changes that might cause a flickering pointer. For example, there's no flickering pointer to distract the driver when fuel sloshes around in a partly filled tank. Another important advantage is that accuracy is not affected by changes in the charging-system voltage because gauge input voltage is closely regulated. To understand how the thermoelectric gauge works, the complete gauge circuit must be considered—gauge, sending unit, voltage limiter, and circuit wiring (Fig. 11-1).

The construction of a thermal gauge is very simple. It features an indicating pointer that is linked to the free arm of a U-shaped bimetal strip. The free arm has a resistance wire winding (heater coil) that is connected to the gauge terminal posts (Fig. 11-2).

The bimetal arm with its heater is the heart of the thermoelectric gauge—it is the "motor" that moves the pointer. When current flows through the resistance coil, it heats the bimetal arm, causes the arm to bend, and moves the pointer across the gauge dial.

Fig. 11.1.   Complete thermal electric gauge circuit. *(Courtesy of Ford Customer Service Division)*

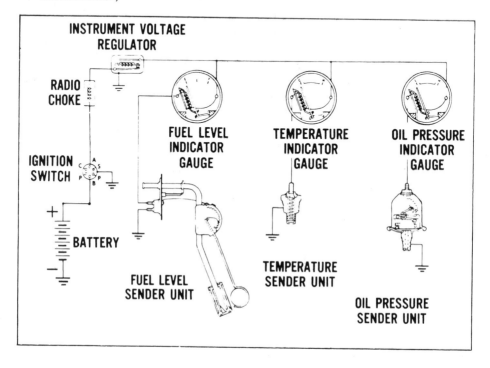

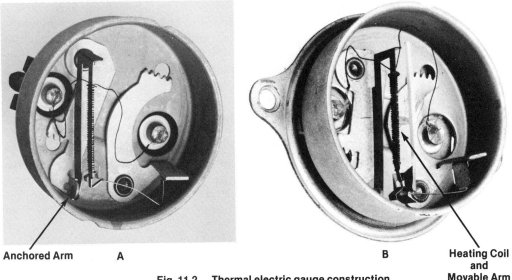

Anchored Arm   **A**   **B**   **Heating Coil
and
Movable Arm**

Fig. 11.2.   Thermal electric gauge construction.

The amount that the bimetal strip bends is proportional to the heat produced by the current flow through the resistance coil. When the current is small, the heating effect and pointer movement are slight. With increased current, additional heating occurs and causes further deflection of the bimetal arm and movement of the pointer. When the gauge input current is terminated by turning off the ignition switch, the bimetal strip returns to its neutral position and moves the pointer off scale, below the first dial marking at the extreme left.

Since the bimetal arm reacts to heat, what about the effect of outside or ambient temperature on gauge accuracy? That is, ambient high or low temperatures could add or subtract heat from the heating coil and affect normal pointer movement if there were no provision for temperature compensation.

Thermoelectric gauge compensation is simple. The "U" shape of the bimetal element does the trick. When the outside temperature bends the free arm, it also equally affects the fixed arm. However, the fixed arm bends in the opposite direction and cancels the effect of outside temperature; see Fig. 11-2.

Thermoelectric Sending Units

The fuel, temperature, and oil-pressure gauges each have a sending unit designed to suit the needs of each system. Each sending unit is nothing more than a variable resistance linked to a sensing mechanism. The sensing mechanism measures the changes that occur in the system being monitored by varying the electrical resistance of the sender. The varying resistance of the sending unit changes the current flow in the heating coil, which controls the gauge pointer movement; refer to Fig. 11-1.

Fuel-Tank Sending Unit

A typical fuel-tank sending unit, Fig. 11-3, has a fuel intake tube designed with an intake filter for fuel pick-up, a fuel level float and arm that varies the electrical resistance in the sender, and float stops which limit the up-and-down movement of the float. Extreme float travel up or down can cause the float to stick or get damaged should it rub on the tank. Float arm stops are also used for setting the minimum and maximum resistance of the unit at the ends of the float travel range.

The variable resistance part of the tank sender has an insulated resistance strip with one end connected to the gauge, and a grounded moving contact attached to the float arm (Figs. 11-4 and 11-5). It is essential that the sending unit has a good ground for the gauge system to work properly.

When the float moves upward, the float arm moves the grounded contact toward the low resistance end of the strip. This gives the extra current flow needed to heat the gauge and move the pointer toward the full mark (Fig. 11-4). As the float drops with the

Fig. 11.3.   Fuel tank gauge unit. *(Courtesy of The Chrysler Corporation)*

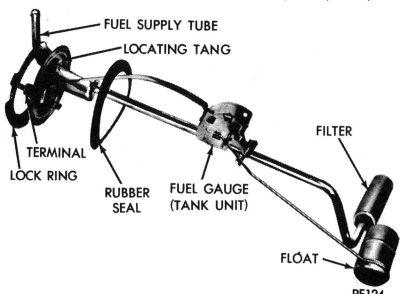

FUEL SUPPLY TUBE

LOCATING TANG

FILTER

TERMINAL

LOCK RING

RUBBER
SEAL

FUEL GAUGE
(TANK UNIT)

FLOAT

PF124

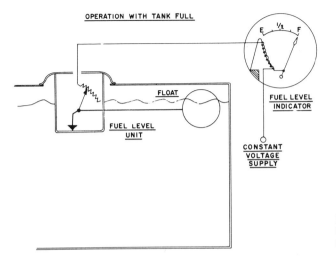

OPERATION WITH TANK FULL

FLOAT

FUEL LEVEL
UNIT

FUEL LEVEL
INDICATOR

CONSTANT
VOLTAGE
SUPPLY

Fig. 11.4. Operation with the tank full. *(Courtesy of The Chrysler Corporation)*

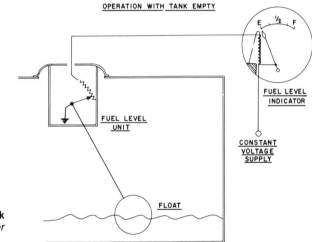

OPERATION WITH TANK EMPTY

FUEL LEVEL
INDICATOR

CONSTANT
VOLTAGE
SUPPLY

FUEL LEVEL
UNIT

FLOAT

Fig. 11.5. Operation with the tank empty. *(Courtesy of The Chrysler Corporation)*

fuel level, the grounded contact increases circuit resistance and the gauge pointer moves toward "Empty" (Fig. 11-5).

Movement within the sending unit variable resistor does produce arcing. However, the fuel vapor does not ignite because of the over-rich mixture—the fuel vapor purges air from the tank leaving no oxygen for combustion.

Temperature Sending Unit

The temperature sending unit is a sealed unit located in the car's cooling system where it can sense changes in coolant temperatures. It is usually threaded in the engine block or in a cylinder head. Within

Resistor Element

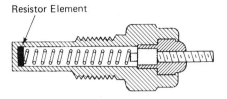

Heat Decreases Element Resistance

Fig. 11.6. Heat decreases element resistance.

TEMPERATURE UNIT OPERATION
WITH LOW TEMPERATURE

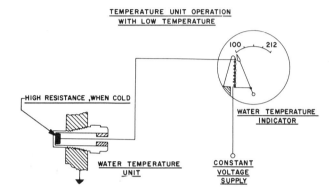

HIGH RESISTANCE, WHEN COLD

WATER TEMPERATURE
INDICATOR

Fig. 11.7. Operation at low temperature. *(Courtesy of The Chrysler Corporation)*

WATER TEMPERATURE
UNIT

CONSTANT
VOLTAGE
SUPPLY

TEMPERATURE UNIT OPERATION
WITH HIGH TEMPERATURE

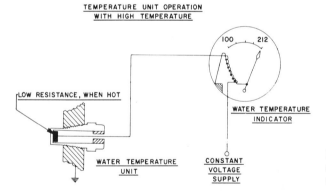

LOW RESISTANCE, WHEN HOT

WATER TEMPERATURE
INDICATOR

WATER TEMPERATURE
UNIT

CONSTANT
VOLTAGE
SUPPLY

Fig. 11.8. Operation at high temperature. *(Courtesy of The Chrysler Corporation)*

the sealed metal bulb of the sending unit is a special temperature-sensitive resistor called a thermistor. One side of the thermistor connects to the gauge and the other is grounded through the sender bulb (Fig. 11-6). The thermistor element reacts to temperature changes. When the engine is cool, the element's resistance is high; this means that current flow in the gauge circuit is low and the gauge pointer stays on the "cold" side of the dial (Fig. 11-7). As the engine heats, the sender's resistance decreases and the gauge pointer moves toward the "hot" side of the dial (Fig. 11-8).

Oil-Pressure Sender

The oil-pressure sender is a self-contained unit that taps into the engine's oil-pressure system where it will react to pressure changes. It is usually threaded into the engine block (Fig. 11-9).

The sender has a built-in resistor strip with one end connected to the gauge and the other connected to ground by a moving contact. The ground contact is moved by an oil-pressure diaphragm.

When engine oil pressure increases, the diaphragm moves the grounded contact to the low resistance end of the resistance strip. The gauge current increases and the gauge pointer moves toward "high." As pressure decreases, the sensing mechanism movement gives a reverse effect and the gauge pointer moves toward "low" (Fig. 11-10).

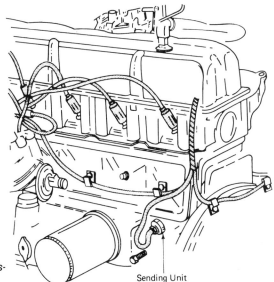

Sending Unit

Fig. 11.9. *Courtesy of Ford Customer Service Division.*

Fig. 11.10. **Oil pressure sending unit.** *(Courtesy of The Chrysler Corporation)*

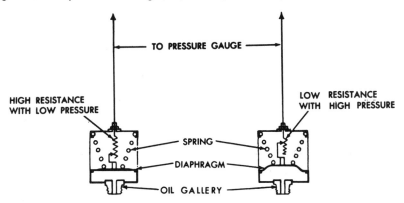

Voltage Limiter

All thermal gauge systems employ a voltage limiter to insure that a constant voltage rate is applied so that gauge accuracy is maintained regardless of voltage values in the charging system. Figure 11-11 is an illustration of a typical voltage limiter. It consists of a bimetallic arm surrounded by a heating coil and a pair of point contacts. Like the gauges, a voltage limiter works on the thermoelectric principle, and it stabilizes the input voltage to the gauge system by its vibrating action (Fig. 11-12).

The limiter contact points are normally closed. When the source voltage is applied, current flows through the contacts to the gauge systems and limiter heating coil. The bimetallic arm responds to the heating effect of the coil and bends. This bending movement opens the contacts and stops the current flow through both the gauges and heating coil.

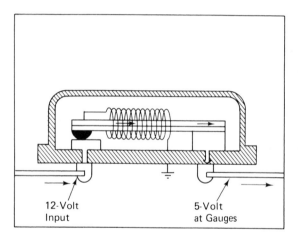

12-Volt Input   5-Volt at Gauges

Fig. 11.11. Cycling produces pulsating current.

Fig. 11.12. Cycling produces pulsating current.

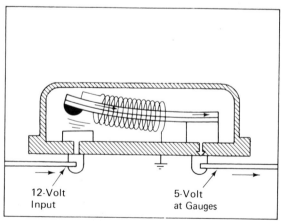

12-Volt Input   5-Volt at Gauges

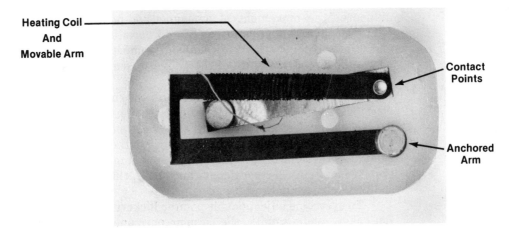

Heating Coil And Movable Arm

Contact Points

Anchored Arm

Fig. 11.13.   Top view of "U"-shaped bimetal element-voltage limiter.

When the heating coil cools, the bimetal arm straightens and closes the contacts to begin the cycle again. This cycling action causes a pulsating or intermittent current flow which produces an average heating effect on the gauges equivalent to five volts at a steady current.

The voltage limiter's opening-closing action does not actually decrease the gauge input voltage—this will always be at the source voltage. The heating effect of the current flow at the gauges is basically controlled by the length of time the contacts stay closed. The limiter contacts open and close faster when input voltage is high and slower when the voltage is low.

The bimetal element in the voltage limiter is affected by outside temperatures and, therefore, temperature compensation must be provided. This is accomplished in the same manner as described for the gauges. The familiar U-shaped bimetal element is used, with the fixed arm designed to cancel out the effect of external temperature variations on the free arm (Fig. 11-13). Voltage limiters are usually plugged-in or mounted on the backside of the instrument panel. In some cases the limiter is built into one of the gauges. Only one limiter is needed for all the gauges.

ELECTROMAGNETIC GAUGES

Electromagnetic gauges, built by their AC-Delco Division, are popularly used in General Motors vehicles. This type of gauge uses the resultant or effective strength of a magnetic field produced by the interaction of three electromagnetic coils. The magnetic field in turn influences the movement of a magnet-and-pointer assembly. The electromagnetic gauge is insensitive to variations in voltage supply and is affected very little by ambient temperatures. Figure 11-14 shows the circuit made up of the gauge, a sending unit, and circuit wiring.

Figures 11-15, 11-16, and 11-17 show the construction of a typical electromagnetic gauge. The three coils of fine wire are wound on a square plastic frame. A bearing sleeve extending from the frame supports a needle shaft which attaches to the gauge pointer. The shaft links the pointer to a circular permanent magnet enclosed within the plastic frame. The permanent magnet is, thus, surrounded by the coil windings around the frame.

To overcome objectionable pointer flickering from road shock on the gauge sending units, the circular permanent magnet rides in a

Fig. 11.14.   Typical electromagnetic gauge circuit. *(Courtesy of Buick Division of General Motors Corp.)*

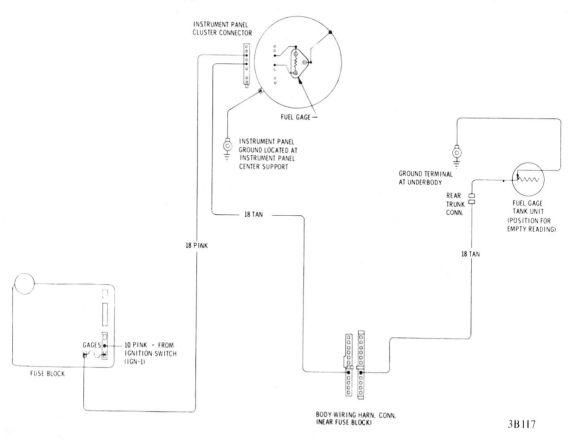

3B117

Fig. 11.15. Fuel gauge facings. Electro-magnetic gauge.

Fig. 11.16A. Plastic frame with needle shaft.

Fig. 11.16B. Plastic frame and needle shaft surrounded by three coil windings.

Fig. 11.16C. Plastic frame assembly mounted in housing gauge pointer attached to needle shaft.

high-viscosity silicone dampening fluid. The dampening fluid also affects the gauge needle movement when the ignition switch is turned off. Typically the gauge needle stays at its indicated reading and then gradually falls toward the high or low end of the dial. If the needle is at its balance point, it may not move. These gauge characteristics are normal and are simply caused by the silicone dampening fluid.

To compensate for production tolerances in the coil winding assembly and to maintain gauge accuracy, a selective production shunt resistor is attached to the insulated terminals on the back side of the gauge housing (Fig. 11-18).

287

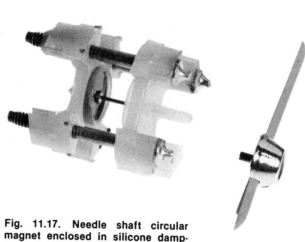

Fig. 11.17. Needle shaft circular magnet enclosed in silicone dampening fluid.

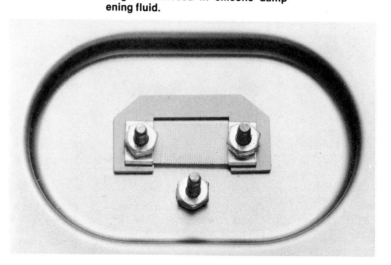

Fig. 11.18.

Electromagnetic Fuel Gauge System

Figure 11-19 shows a simplified schematic of an electromagnetic fuel gauge system. The gauge dash unit is located in the instrument cluster and a float-type tank sending unit is located in the gasoline tank.

The gauge pointer responds to the changing balance between the magnetic pull of three coils designed into the gauge. This balance is controlled by the tank sending unit, which acts as a variable resistor. Although the tank sending unit is similar in construction and operation to the sensor assembly used in the thermoelectric gauge system, the fuel tank sensor is at its maximum resistance at full and minimum resistance at empty—the exact opposite action of its thermoelectric counterpart.

In Fig. 11-19, the gauge coils are designated as the E (empty), F (full), and B (bucking) coils. The E and F coils have their poles at right angles and will both produce a magnetic pull on the circular armature. The B coil has a polarity opposite to the E coil, and therefore, opposes the E coil magnetic field. The variable resistance of the fuel tank sensor is shunted across the B and F coils and will essentially control the amount of current flow in these coils.

For proper operation of the system, the dash gauge and fuel-tank sending unit must be provided with good grounds (Figs. 11-14 and 11-19). When the fuel tank is full, the variable resistance of the sensor is at its maximum. This condition also produces a maximum current and magnetic field in the B and F coils. Since the B coil opposes the E coil, the F coil has the stronger magnetic pull and the gauge pointer is pulled to the "Full" position.

Fig. 11.19   *Courtesy of AC-Delco Division of General Motors Corp.*

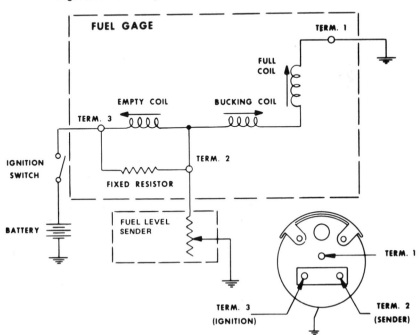

As the fuel level drops, the fuel-tank sensor resistance increases and reduces the current flow in the B and F coils. The greater influence of the F coil pulls the pointer away from the "Full" mark. When the tank float is at "Empty," the current flow is almost entirely through the E coil and variable resistor.

In summary, the interaction of the magnetic field of the three coils produces an effective (resultant) magnetic field which controls the rotation and position of the armature and pointer assembly.

Electromagnetic Oil-Pressure Gauge System

The basic gauge movement in this system is identical to the fuel gauge just discussed. The same type of oil-pressure sensor unit employed with thermoelectric gauges is used in the electromagnetic system, with one slight variation. The electromagnetic oil-pressure sensor increases its variable resistance value with higher pressures and decreases its variable resistance value with lower pressures, the exact opposite of the action of the thermoelectric oil-pressure sensor.

Electromagnetic Water-Temperature Gauge System

The basic gauge movement in this system is identical to the fuel gauge just discussed. However, the thermistor action employed in the temperature sending unit (same as the one used in thermoelectric systems) requires a slight modification of the gauge wiring (Fig. 11-20).

The gauge coils are designated as the H (hot), C (cold), and B (bucking coil) coils. The H and C coils have their poles at right angles and will both produce a magnetic pull on the gauge pointer circular armature. The B coil has an opposite polarity to the H coil, and therefore, opposes the H coil magnetic field.

When the ignition switch is closed, the circuit current flows through the B and C coils and the fixed production resistor to ground, and through the H coil and the variable-resistance temperature sender to ground.

With coolant liquid temperature at 100°F the resistance of the temperature sender is high. This results in a very low current flow through the H coil and a negligible magnetic field. The pointer and armature assembly, therefore, aligns itself with the effective magnetic field produced by the C and B coils at the 100°F position. As the temperature of the coolant liquid increases, the resistance of the sender decreases since the thermistor has a negative temperature coefficient—resistance decreases with increasing temperature. This permits an increase in the current flowing in the H coil with the

TEMPERATURE GAGE CIRCUIT DIAGRAM

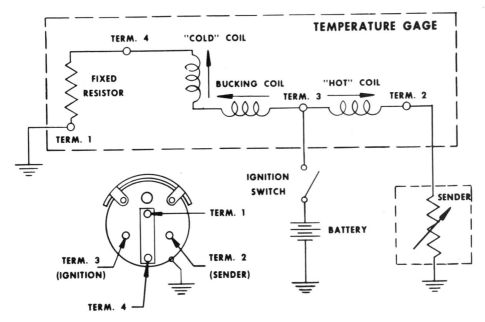

Fig. 11.20.   *Courtesy of AC-Delco Division of General Motors Corp.*

pointer and armature assembly aligning itself with the effective magnetic field produced by the three coils. Maximum current in the H coil will produce a full scale reading.

INDICATOR LIGHT SYSTEMS

Indicator lights began to be used in automobiles in the early 1950s. Tabbed as "idiot lights" by car owners and mechanics, indicator lights replaced the normal complement of dash gauges other than the fuel gauge. But dash gauges did not fade away entirely. Mixed car owner reaction over accepting the lights has resulted in a compromise between the use of indicator lights and dash gauges.

Today light indicator systems are used as a check on charging system operation, coolant temperature, oil pressure, brake system, and fuel level. These signal systems are essentially on-off indicators that are much simplier than gauge units in both design and servicing requirements. An indicator light bulb is used instead of a gauge, and a sensing switch replaces the variable-resistance sending unit. The indicator bulb normally remains unlit as long as its system operates within the proper range. The bulb lights as a warning signal when a critical point is reached.

Indicator lights can burn out, and therefore it is necessary to design the indicator circuits with an automatic bulb checkout. The indicator bulbs light for proof-testing when the ignition switch is turned to the "on" or "start" position. If the bulb is in working order, it will burn brightly until its system reaches proper operating level, and then it will go out.

Some typical indicator-light-cluster circuitry is illustrated in Figs. 11-21, 11-22, and 11-23.

Oil-Pressure Warning Light

This system includes only an indicator light bulb, a pressure switch threaded into the engine block oiling system, and circuit wires (Figs. 11-21, 11-22, and 11-23).

The pressure switch contacts, linked to a diaphragm, are

Fig. 11.21.   Indicator lights. *(Courtesy of Buick Division of General Motors Corp.)*

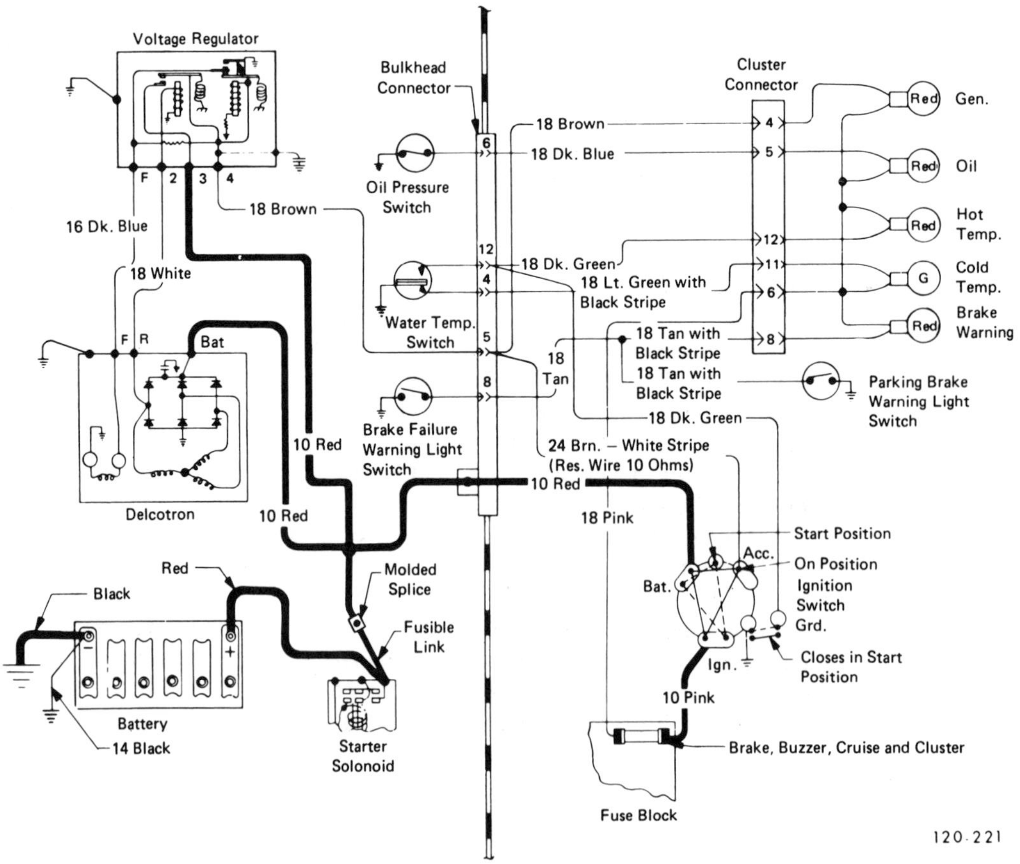

120-221

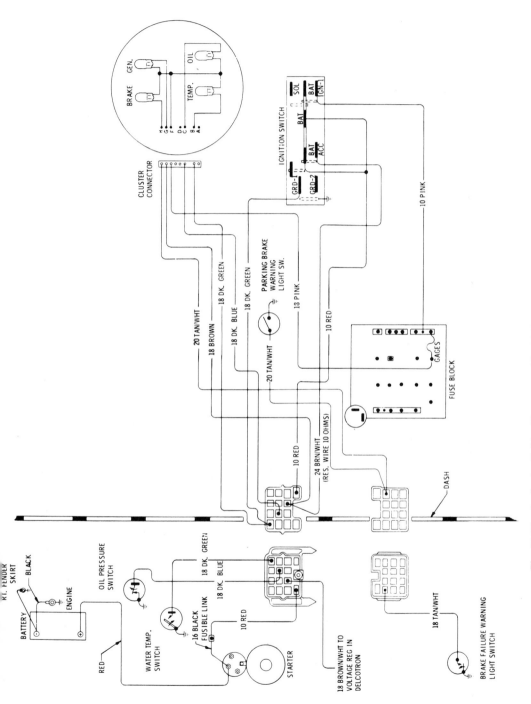

Fig. 11.22. Indicator lights. *(Courtesy of Buick Division of General Motors Corp.)*

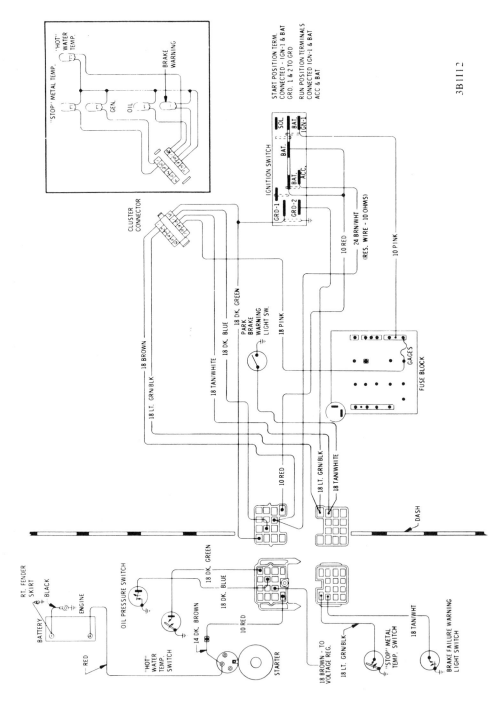

Fig. 11.23. Indicator lights. *(Courtesy of Buick Division of General Motors Corp.)*

294

normally closed when oil pressure is below a safe value or when the engine is not running. When the ignition switch is turned on, the red indicator bulb lights and is proof-tested before the engine starts. As soon as engine oil pressure reaches a safe operating level, the pressure switch diaphragm flexes and opens the contacts. With switch contacts open, the warning light goes out.

Temperature Light

Figure 11-24 shows several temperature-indicating systems currently used in passenger cars and trucks.

In the standard "Hot" coolant-temperature indicator systems, Figs. 11-21, 11-22, and 11-23, a bimetallic sensing switch is threaded

Fig. 11.24. Temperature indicator systems.

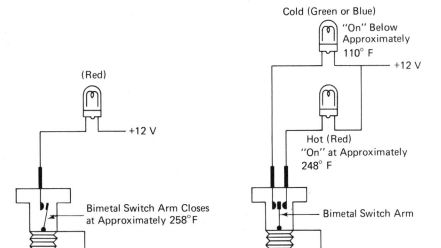

(a) Coolant Hot Temperature Indicator   (b) Coolant Cold/Hot Temperature Indicator

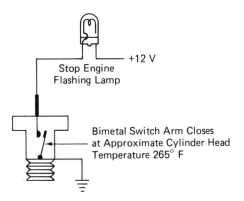

into the engine block coolant system. This switch controls the red or "Hot" indicator light in the instrument cluster. Under normal temperature operating ranges the contacts in the sensing switch remain open and the light is off. If the coolant temperature rises above normal (approximately 258° F), the bimetal arm in the sensing switch closes the contacts and the "Hot" light is turned on.

To proof-test the "Hot" light, a circuit wire leads to a ground (GND) terminal in the ignition switch. During engine crank or when the ignition is in the "start" position, the "Hot" light circuit is grounded inside the ignition switch and the light comes on. After the engine starts and the ignition switch is returned to ignition "Run," the proof-test circuit is opened and the indicator light control returns to the temperature sensing switch.

In a Hot/Cold engine temperature indicator light system, two lights, red and green or red and blue, are used to indicate cooling system conditions. Both lights are connected to a bimetallic temperature sensitive switch with dual contacts (Figs. 11-21 and 11-24). When the switch is cool, the bimetal arm closes the contacts in the green light circuit. This makes the green signal light come on when the ignition switch is turned on and keeps it on until the coolant warms up (approximately 160°F). The green cold light indicates to the driver that the car should not be subject to heavy acceleration.

After the bimetallic arm moves away from the cold contact it stays in a neutral position between the hot and cold contacts and both lights are unlit over the normal temperature range.

If the coolant temperature rises above normal, the bimetallic arm bends and makes contact with the red light or hot circuit and lights the signal to warn of overheating. The red light in the hot circuit is proof-tested as previously discussed under "Hot" light coolant temperature system.

In high-performance engines it is not uncommon to find a metal temperature switch located in the rear of the left cylinder head. Its function is to sense cylinder-head temperature. This warning system is provided in addition to the normal coolant temperature monitoring (Figs. 11-23 and 11-24).

The sensing switch contacts remain open until the temperature danger point is reached (265°F) and then the bimetal arm moves to close the contacts and complete the "STOP ENGINE" circuit. A breaker in the light provides a flashing light action in the instrument cluster. Thus, any sudden malfunction such as starved oiling in the upper engine will be quickly detected and the message will be flashed to the driver.

The indicator bulb has a separate proof-test circuit connected to ground when the ignition switch is cranking; see Fig. 11-23.

Brake System Warning Light

In recent years, the brake warning light has been added to the cluster of warning lights on the instrument panel. It functions to keep track of the park brake position and master cylinder pressure.

The brake system warning light circuit appears in Figs. 11-21, 11-22, and 11-23. Note that the indicator light is connected in series with two parallel grounding switches.

The park brake switch is mechanically operated by the parking brake mechanism. When the park brake is applied, the switch is closed and the light circuit is completed to ground. The light will then glow when the ignition switch is turned to the "on" position and the driver forgets to release the park brake.

The second switch is a hydraulic-pressure-actuated switch mounted in the disc brake combination or distributor valve (Fig. 11-25). The switch is sensitive to the pressures from the two hydraulic lines connected to both sections of the master cylinder when the brake pedal is depressed. Should the switch sense a pressure differential of 150-250 psi between the two hydraulic lines, the switch contacts close and the warning light comes on. The driver is alerted to the fact that his hydraulic brake system needs immediate attention.

Combination Gauges and Warning Lights

These are illustrated in Figs. 11-26 and 11-27. The operation of the gauges and lights is the same as those discussed previously.

Fig. 11.25.   Brake switch located in disc brake combination valve. *(Courtesy of Buick Division of General Motors Corp.)*

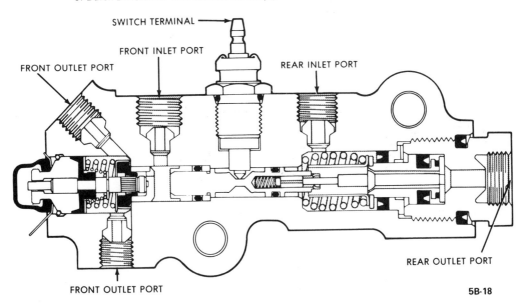

SWITCH TERMINAL

FRONT INLET PORT

FRONT OUTLET PORT

REAR INLET PORT

REAR OUTLET PORT

FRONT OUTLET PORT

5B-18

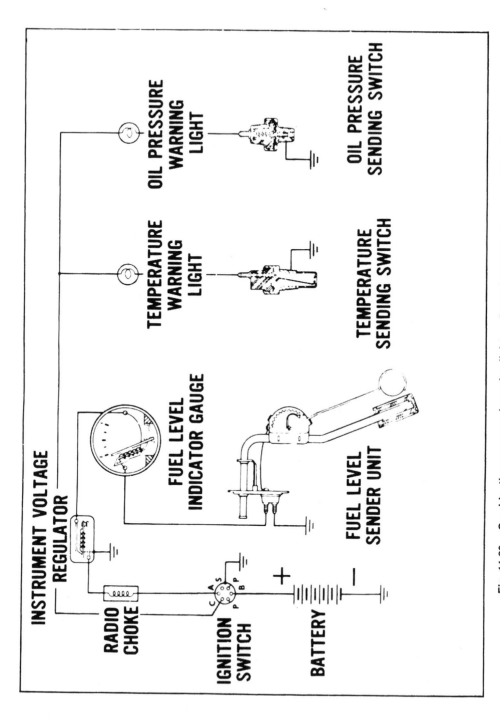

Fig. 11.26. Combination gauge and warning lights—thermal electric. *(Courtesy of Ford Customer Service Division)*

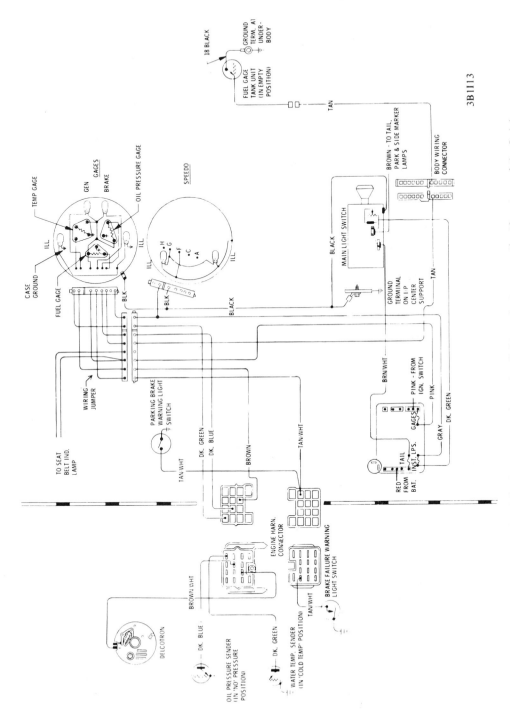

Fig. 11.27. Combination gauge and warning lights—electromagnetic. (Courtesy of the Buick Division of General Motors Corp.)

Engine Warning Indicator Light

On some cars, the coolant temperature and oil-pressure sensing switches are paralleled and are connected in series to a red engine warning light (Fig. 11-28).

Thus, when the indicator light comes on it signals the driver of an unsafe engine condition with respect to coolant temperature or oil pressure.

Low-Fuel Warning Light

Primarily used in Chrysler and Ford cars as an optional addition, the low-fuel warning system supplements the reading of the regular fuel gauge. When the fuel tank is less than one-quarter full, a red low-fuel indicator light is turned on.

Figure 11-29 shows a low-fuel warning system used by Ford Motor Company. It consists of a low-fuel relay and a low-fuel indicator

Fig. 11.28.   *Courtesy of Ford Customer Service Division.*

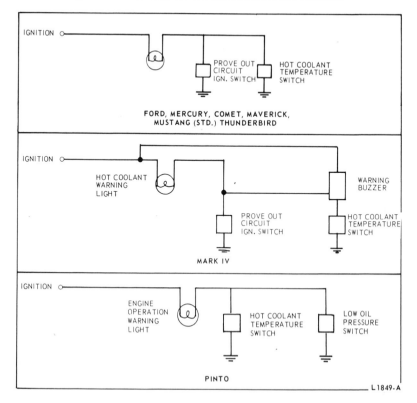

L 1849-A

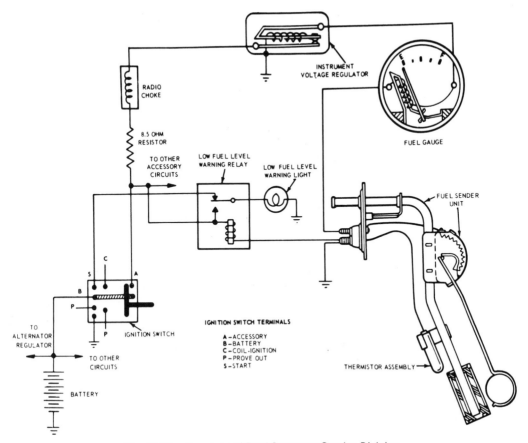

Fig. 11.29. *Courtesy of Ford Customer Service Division.*

light located on the instrument panel, and a thermistor attached to the fuel sender outlet tube located in the fuel tank.

The system in Fig. 11-29 is shown in its neutral condition. Note that the warning light proof-test circuit is completed through the low-fuel relay upper contacts when the ignition switch is in the "start" position. The main circuit itself works very simply. The thermistor attached to the fuel sender outlet tube is kept cool when it is covered with gasoline, and therefore only a slight current flow is applied in the thermistor circuit—not enough to excite the relay coil. The gasoline acts as a heat sink, absorbing the heat from the thermistor created by the current flow. Thermistor resistance remains at a relatively constant high valve as long as it remains in contact with the gasoline. When the fuel level drops and the thermistor is no longer in contact with the fuel, the exposure to air causes the thermistor to heat up. The thermistor resistance decreases and allows sufficient current flow to excite the relay coil and activate the warning light.

Fuel Pacer Light

Offered as an option on 1975 Chrysler vehicles, the fuel pacer system is a driver mileage-control aid. As illustrated in Fig. 11-30, the system is keyed to the directional signal monitor light mounted on the left front fender facing the driver. Should the driver push too hard on the accelerator, the vacuum switch will close and activates the relay. Power from the headlight switch can then turn on the signal light to warn the driver that he is not driving economically. The vacuum switch sensitivity is adjustable by rotating a set screw.

EGR Maintenance Reminder Light

1975 Chrysler vehicles equipped with a catalytic converter have an instrument panel light reminder that signals the driver that the engine's exaust gas recirculation (EGR) system is in need of maintenance (Fig. 11-31). This occurs at 15,000-mile intervals, when the words "CHECK EGR" light up.

    The switch that controls the reminder light is actually a counter

Fig. 11.30.   Fuel pacer light. *(Courtesy of the Chrysler Corporation)*

INSTRUMENT PANELS—ELECTRICAL-

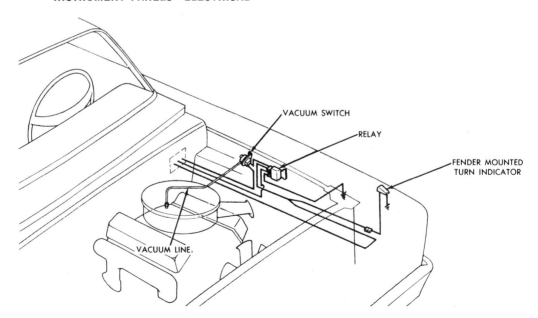

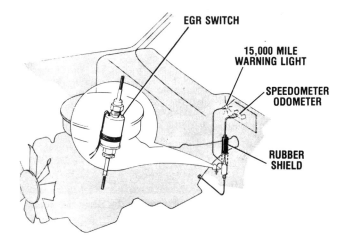

Fig. 11.31. EGR maintenance reminder system. Service is needed when "Check EGR" lights up. *(Courtesy of The Chrysler Corporation)*

Fig. 11.32. EGR switch counts miles by use of small gears, which are zeroed by reset screw to turn EGR lights off. *(Courtesy of The Chrysler Corporation)*

mechanism connected in series with the speedometer cable. It acts like an odometer and counts the miles traveled by the car. When the first 15,000 miles are completed, a set of internal electrical contacts close and the reminder light comes on. This requires about 30 million revolutions of the speedometer cable and means that the car owner must have the EGR system serviced.

Once the EGR maintenance is performed the light can be easily turned off and the switch reset for the next 15,000-mile interval. This is done by rotating the EGR switch reset screw about one-half turn and releasing it (Fig. 11-32).

CHARGING SYSTEM INDICATORS

The red "Gen" warning light and the ammeter are both used in modern passenger cars to indicate the charging system condition— the red light indicator on a "go/no-go" basis and the ammeter on a "charge/discharge" basis.

The Charge Indicator Light

Figure 11-33 shows a typical alternator charging system with a charge indicator or warning light. When the ignition is turned on and before the engine is started, the warning light is proof-tested and should light. The light circuit is completed through the regulator and alternator field. When the engine is started, voltage at the alternator stator terminal closes the regulator field relay. With the field relay closed, the alternator field circuit current passes through the (A) terminal. In effect, this puts equal voltage potential (+) on both sides of the indicator light, causing it to go out. A built-in resistor wire in parallel to the charge indicator light insures that the alternator field circuit current will flow should the light be burned out.

The preceding "Gen" warning light circuit operation is typical of those used with charging systems designed with either electro-mechanical or electronic IC regulators. An IC system is shown in Fig. 11-34.

Fig. 11.33. Charging circuit wiring. *(Courtesy Ford Customer Service Division.)*

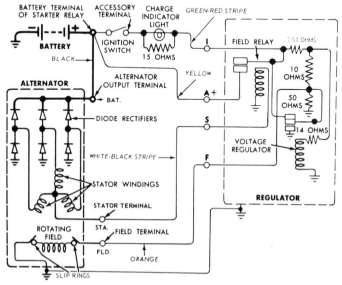

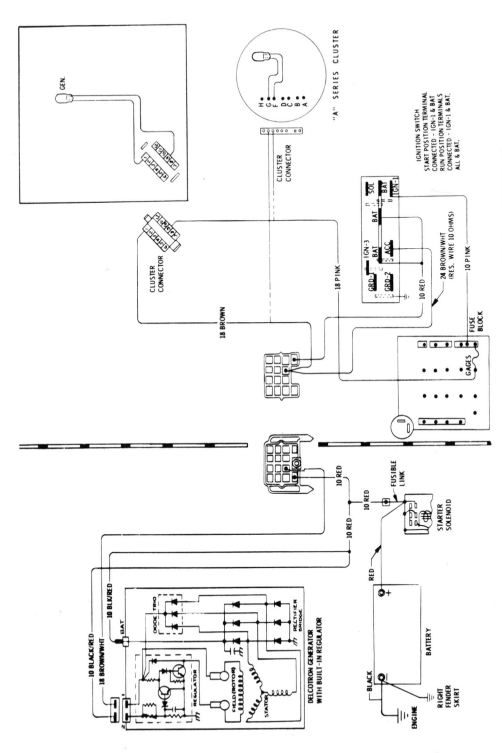

Fig. 11.34. IC regulated charging system. *(Courtesy of Buick Motor Division of General Motors Corp.)*

The Ammeter

Although use of the indicator charge light was strongly established in the 1950s, the ammeter still has its popularity as a dash instrument (Fig. 11-35). Like other dash instrumentation, it is not a precision instrument, but it has sufficient accuracy to serve the purpose for which it was designed—to indicate the current flow into (charge) or out of (discharge) the car battery.

The dash ammeter is very simple in construction: it has a pointer shaft with a steel armature that is influenced by a permanent horseshoe magnet about the armature, and a current-carrying brass plate bridged across the ammeter terminals. The permanent magnet holds the pointer at zero when no current flows (Fig. 11-36).

When the current flows to the battery, a magnetic field is set up proportional in strength to the amount of that current flow (Fig. 11-37). The combined (resultant) effect of the magnetic fields from the permanent horseshoe magnet and the current-carrying brass plate causes the pointer and armature assembly to rotate from the zero position (Fig. 11-38). A charge or discharge will be indicated depending on the direction of current flow.

Fig. 11.35. Ammeter—front face. *(Courtesy of Gordon Bechelli-FSC)*

Fig. 11.36. Ammeter—rear view. *(Courtesy of Gordon Bechelli-FSC)*

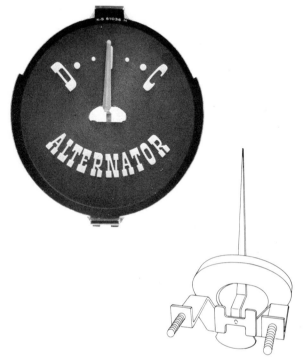

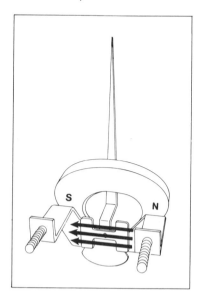

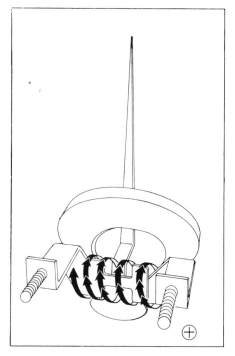

Fig. 11.37. Ammeter—rear view. *(Courtesy of Gordon Bechelli-FSC)*

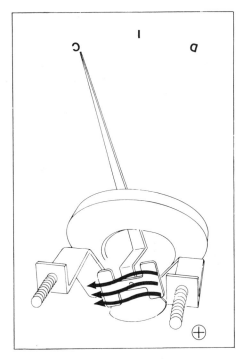

Fig. 11.38. Ammeter—rear view. *(Courtesy of Gordon Bechelli—FSC)*

GAUGE AND INDICATOR LIGHT TROUBLESHOOTING

Like other diagnostic procedures, gauge or indicator light checking should begin with an analysis of the symptoms to pinpoint the trouble as quickly as possible.

Gauge problems are usually simpler to track down than other electrical system troubles because gauge pointer movement, or lack of movement, gives you a direct indication of the cause. Trouble sources can be narrowed down to those that affect all the gauges, or those that affect only one gauge. In addition, the ignition switch proof-test light feature can be used as the first step in checking out a warning light system.

Our objective here is to give you a few tips and simple checks that can help speed up the troubleshooting process. We're going to leave the specifics to the applicable manufacturer's service manual.

Caution: Always disconnect the battery ground cable before removing an instrument cluster or working with tools behind the instrument panel. An accidental short circuit can do costly damage to gauges, circuit boards, or other circuit parts. If the battery is needed for any reason after a gauge cluster is rolled out of the panel, connect a jumper wire between the metal of the cluster housing and a good ground. Be sure that nothing is shorted before the battery ground is reconnected.

Failure to ground the cluster housing while using the battery will "smoke" the gauges in a thermoelectric system, and electromagnetic gauges depend on a solid ground system to the dash for normal operation.

Thermoelectric Gauge Testing—Trouble in All Gauges

When all the thermal gauges are affected with a problem at the same time, it points to problems in the voltage limiter operation since the limiter controls current to the gauge circuits. An understanding of voltage-limiter operation should make it easy to analyze some of the following problems.

Full-scale readings:

All the gauge pointers move beyond their full-scale position when the ignition switch is turned on. This may be caused by an open heating coil which keeps the contacts permanently closed, or the contacts themselves may be stuck closed. Either condition will permit full battery voltage (unregulated) to feed the gauge circuits, which can seriously damage or burn out the gauges.

The heating coil ground circuit through the instrument cluster may be permanently interrupted; this keeps the voltage limiter from operating and is another cause of full-scale deflection. In most cases this can be corrected by tightening the cluster mounting screws.

Erratic scale readings:

The gauge pointers temporarily move down scale or up scale from their normal operating readings.

When all the gauge pointers temporarily move down scale it is usually caused by a voltage drop from dirty or burnt contacts in the voltage limiter.

If all the gauge pointers temporarily move up scale from normal positions, then a poor ground circuit is highly suspect. This is usually eliminated by tightening the cluster mounting screws.

No pointer movement:

This trouble symptom is the complete absence of any gauge pointer movement and is related to the voltage limiter—it is usually caused by open or burnt contacts, or an open in the input side of the limiter circuit.

Voltage limiter testing:

Testing the voltage limiter is easy and can be done on the car with a test light or voltmeter. The test light or voltmeter is connected between the most accessible sending unit terminal (usually the temperature sender) and a good ground (Fig. 11-39). With the ignition switch turned on, give the limiter 10-15 seconds to start its cycling action. A flashing test light or fluctuating voltmeter indicates that the voltage limiter is working correctly. If the light burns steadily or the voltmeter indicates a steady full-system voltage, the limiter is defective or there is a poor limiter ground.

CAUTION. When testing a voltage limiter or gauge circuit, avoid any direct short to ground at the sender terminal or wire. Grounding any thermoelectric gauge sender circuit permits a high circuit current flow that can damage or burn out the gauge.

Some voltage limiters are accessible behind the dash and are easily removed and replaced while others are accessible only after the instrument cluster is rolled out of the dash.

Fig. 11.39.   Testing for voltage limiter action using a test light at the temperature sending unit.

Trouble in One Gauge

When only one gauge is not working properly, the trouble is confined to the gauge itself, the wiring, or the sending unit. The voltage limiter in this case can be considered in operating order.

To isolate single gauge circuit troubles, we follow the same basic pattern regardless of which gauge system has the fault. Using a simple process of elimination, our fact-finding starts at the gauge sending unit and proceeds back through the circuit wire sections to the gauge.

We will use the fuel gauge circuit as an example, but the test procedure techniques can be applied to the oil-pressure and coolant-temperature gauge systems as well.

Fuel gauge circuit tests:

Most fuel gauge troubles are located right at the tank sending unit, especially on older cars. Typically, corrosion has set in from road splash contamination, destroying the tank sending unit ground or wire terminal connection. A visual and ground check at the tank

Fig. 11.40.   *Courtesy of The Chrysler Corporation.*

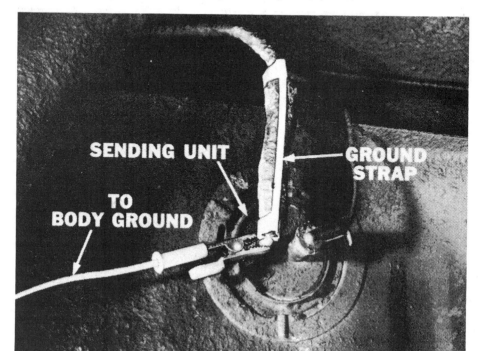

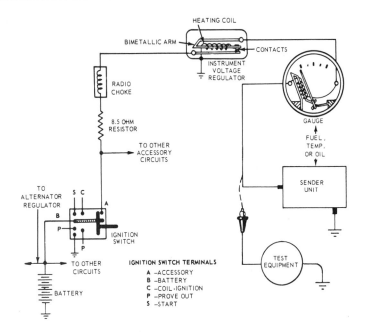

Fig. 11.41. *Courtesy of Ford Customer Service Division.*

sending unit is, therefore, a logical place to start looking for the circuit problem.

First, check the wire end at the tank unit for a disconnect or corrosion and make any necessary repairs. If the gauge still does not indicate properly, proceed with a ground check of the tank sending unit. This is done by connecting a jumper wire between the tank sending unit housing and a good body ground (Fig. 11-40). If the gauge now works properly, check the ground strap connections. The visual and ground check at the tank sending unit will generally solve most gauge complaints, especially where gauge readings stay on "Empty" or fail to indicate a full tank.

In summary, an unwanted ground at the tank sending unit will cause the gauge to read "Full" and an unwanted open will cause the gauge to read "Empty."

Once the sending unit hot wire and ground connections have been checked, isolating the problem to the sending unit or gauge unit is the next step. For accurate results, disconnect the sending unit wire and attach it to a gauge tester or to a known good tank sending unit. Be sure that the substitute test unit is provided with a good ground (Fig. 11-41). If the dash gauge pointer now responds accurately to the Empty, Full, and One-Half scale, the tank sending unit needs replacement.

Where gauge indications are still not accurate, the trouble narrows down to the gauge or the circuit wiring. By connecting the tester to the gauge at the dash, gauge operation can be isolated from the circuit wiring.

Fuel tank damage:

Fuel tank damage can be an unsuspected cause of false fuel gauge readings.

The intake tube filter of the tank sending unit is located at the tank bottom where it can pick up all the fuel (Fig. 11-42). If the tank bottom is caved in, the intake tube will be bent upward and will stop

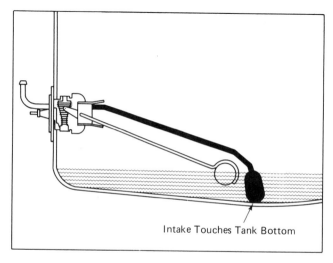

Intake Touches Tank Bottom

Fig. 11.42. *Courtesy of The Chrysler Corporation.*

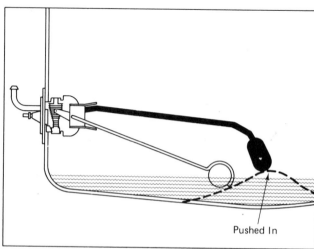

Fig. 11.43. Tank damage bends intake tube. *Courtesy of The Chrysler Corporation.*

Pushed In

drawing fuel short of the tank bottom (Fig. 11-43). The customer complains of running out of fuel even though the gauge shows gasoline in the tank.

The tank cave-in can usually be forced out by using compressed air in the tank, or it may even pop back out from road jars. The intake tube, however, will still remain bent, off the tank bottom, while the fuel gauge shows a normal reading.

On tank senders with the resistance unit and float arm stop assembly mounted on the intake tube, both the tube and the stops are bent out of normal position when there is tank bottom cave-in. In this situation, the car would also run out of gas with a reserve remaining in the tank, but fortunately the **gauge** would read "Empty" before disaster struck. You should suspect this condition when it takes less gasoline than usual to fill the tank, and the **gauge** does not read "Full" (because the float contacts the top of the tank while the resistance unit is still in a part-full position).

Fuel tank repair:

This can be a risky operation and can be fatal if good judgment is not used. *Absolutely do not use a heating flame close to or in direct contact with the leak area for any type of repair such as brazing or soldering.* Fuel tanks are extremely difficult to purge. Even fuel tanks that have been empty for months still contain dangerous fuel vapors and are a serious explosive threat.

Although there are types of liquid bonding metal that can seal minor fuel tank leaks, a fiber glass patch is a very effective and safe method.

Electromagnetic (AC) Gauge Problems

Electromagnetic gauges have troubles similar to thermoelectric gauges, and therefore the test procedures used in isolating an electromagnetic gauge circuit problem follow the same pattern. Test results, however, need to be related to electromagnetic gauge circuit operation.

Review the test procedures in the section on troubleshooting thermoelectric gauges. Our objective, here, will be to highlight some of those key test procedures and talk about how to interpret the test results. Keep in mind that electromagnetic gauge circuits operate from a constant 12 volts and do no use a voltage limiter.

Caution: Always disconnect the battery ground cable before you remove the instrument cluster or work with tools behind the instrument panel.

Start your diagnosis by verifying the complaint and observing the gauge behavior. In most General Motors passenger cars and light trucks the use of indicator lights are highly favored for monitoring the oil pressure and coolant temperature, so in most cases you'll only have the fuel gauge to worry about.

Trouble in All Gauges

No gauge pointer movement:

When the pointer or pointers do not move when the ignition switch is turned on, and the complementary indicator lights fail to light on the proof-test, check for a blown fuse and related circuit short.

"Crazy" gauges:

In a three-gauge cluster, the gauges may all behave in an unusual manner. For example, the fuel and oil-pressure gauge pointers do not move when the ignition switch is turned on, but the temperature gauge pointer reads high. This situation is usually accompanied by "crazy" dash indicator light operation and is most likely caused by a poor instrument-cluster-to-dash ground or by a blown fuse in an unrelated circuit. Sometimes the cause is a missing fuse, so be alert to empty holders in the fuse block.

Where only a fuel gauge is used, and it has a problem and there are "crazy" dash indicator lights, look for the same likely causes.

Trouble in One Gauge

When the problem is confined to a single gauge circuit, the logical way to find the trouble is to start at the gauge sending unit. In most cases it is easily accessible and most problems are solved at this point. Visual inspection alone can quickly pick up a corroded, broken, or disconnected wire lead at the sender.

Fuel gauge:

When the gauge unit continuously reads "Full" it means excessive circuit resistance. To pinpoint the problem, ground the sender unit hot terminal with a jumper wire. The fuel gauge should read "Empty"; this means that either the sender unit ground or the sender itself is at fault. The gauge and circuit wire can be considered OK. The sender unit ground can be quickly checked with a jumper hook-up to a solid ground. If this does not provide a normal gauge reading, then the sender is at fault.

When the gauge unit continuously reads "Empty," it is evident that circuit resistance is too low. Disconnect the circuit wire at the sender unit and observe the gauge; it should read "Full." A "Full" reading means that the gauge and circuit wiring are OK and that the problem is confined to the tank sender unit.

Where gauge inaccuracy exists at part-full positions and the problem isn't a definite "always full" or "always empty" situation, check the gauge and sender unit accuracy by substituting a known good tank sender unit or a manufacturer's tester unit in the circuit at the tank.

Of course, you must always be alert to sender unit tank damage that might cause an inaccurate gauge reading.

If the fuel gauge pointer responds freely from "Empty" to "Full," replace the tank sender unit. Failure of the gauge to respond correctly means trouble in the gauge or circuit wire to the sender unit. To isolate the trouble, connect the circuit tester to the gauge at the dash for a direct checkout of the gauge, or, if it is necessary, remove the gauge and bench test it. If the gauge proves to be in good working order, the wiring between the dash and tank sender is at fault.

Oil-pressure gauge:

The oil-pressure gauge circuit responds in the same way as the fuel gauge circuit—an open circuit reads high and a grounded circuit reads zero.

A manufacturer's tester or a fuel-tank sending unit can be substituted in the circuit to check out the oil gauge and sender unit for accuracy, or to isolate the problem to circuit wiring between the gauge and sender.

When gauge accuracy is in question, it is always a good policy to measure the actual engine oil pressure with a pressure test gauge and compare it to the gauge reading before condemning either the sender unit or the gauge.

Coolant temperature gauge:

Again the test procedures are the same as for the fuel and oil-pressure gauge systems; however, the test responses are not the same. Disconnecting the circuit wire at the engine unit and keeping it from a ground should result in a 100°F (low) gauge reading. Grounding the circuit wire to the engine block should give a full-scale pointer deflection to over 212°F.

Here again, when gauge accuracy is in question, check the gauge reading against the actual coolant temperature before isolating the problem to a sender unit or a gauge.

Indicator Light Testing

Failure of an indicator light to glow during the ignition switch proof-test may be caused by a burnt-out bulb, a defective switch, or an open in the wiring.

An indicator bulb that does not light on the proof-test can easily be checked out with a test light or jumper wire. Disconnect the circuit indicator wire from its switch in the engine compartment and connect it in series with the test light or jumper wire to a good ground (Fig. 11-44). With the ignition switch turned on, the test light should produce a dim glow (it is in series with the indicator bulb) or the jumper wire should light the indicator bulb in the instrument panel.

If the above check out produces the described result, then the signal switch is the trouble source and needs to be replaced. Failure of the test light or indicator light to glow is most likely to be caused by a burnt-out indicator bulb. An open in the circuit itself is a rare occurrence.

When you check for a no-glow condition in the coolant "Hot" light circuit, with the ignition switch on "Start," use the same hook-up as above at the temperature switch—the test light or jumper wire is

Fig. 11.44. Testing coolant temperature light circuit at temperature switch.

hooked in series to the disconnected wire end. If the test light glows dimly or the jumper wire turns on the red light, then the circuit ground in the ignition switch is the probable cause and the ignition switch should be replaced.

Indicator light circuits are subject to "crazy light" situations; therefore, be alert to check for a poor dash ground or a blown fuse in an unrelated circuit.

Review questions

Thermoelectric gauge operation

1. Briefly describe a thermoelectric gauge.
2. What are some desirable operating features of a thermoelectric gauge?
3. Name the car manufacturers that use thermoelectric gauges in their vehicles.
4. Name the three essential parts of a thermoelectric gauge circuit.
5. How do the bimetal arm and heating coil team up and provide a motor action?
6. Why is the bimetal element shaped like a "U"?
7. What is the function of the sending unit?
8. Briefly describe the sending unit operation.
9. Indicate whether the sending unit resistance is *high* or *low* in the following conditions:
   a. fuel tank empty
   b. coolant temperature cold
   c. oil pressure high
10. How does a thermistor element react to temperature changes? Where is it used in the gauge circuits?
11. What is the function of the voltage limiter?
12. How does the cycling action of the voltage limiter produce an average 5.0 volt effect on the gauge circuit regardless of the changes in applied voltage?
13. What parts of the gauge circuit must be provided with an electrical ground?

Electromagnetic gauge operation

1. Briefly describe an electromagnetic gauge.
2. What are some desirable operating features of an electromagnetic gauge?

3. Name the car manufacturer that uses electromagnetic gauges in its vehicles.

4. Name the two essential parts of an electromagnetic gauge circuit.

5. How is objectionable pointer flickering dampened in the gauge?

6. What is the purpose of the selective shunt resistor used on the gauge?

7. What happens to the strength of the gauge bucking field coil as the fuel tank gets filled? How does this cause the gauge needle to be pulled toward the "Full" reading?

8. Compare the operation of the fuel gauge and oil-pressure gauge circuits.

9. What happens to the strength of the gauge bucking field coil as the coolant temperature increases? How does this cause the gauge needle to be pulled toward the "Hot" readings?

10. What parts of the gauge circuit must be provided with an electrical ground?

11. Make a comparison of the fuel, oil-pressure, and temperature sending units used in thermoelectric and electromagnetic gauges.

Indicator light systems

1. What are some typical systems that are monitored by dash indicator lights?

2. How are dash indicator lights proof-tested by the vehicle operator for a burned-out bulb?

3. Name the two essential parts of a dash indicator light circuit.

4. Briefly describe how a dash indicator light circuit works.

5. How are the following dash indicator light circuits grounded for proof-testing?
   a. oil pressure warning
   b. coolant temperature
   c. brake system
   d. engine warning
   e. charging system

6. Briefly describe how a Hot/Cold coolant temperature swtich works.

7. Briefly explain how the charge indicator light is turned off.

8. What is the approximate temperature at which engine coolant is considered to be excessively hot?

9. Briefly explain the action of the tank thermistor in a Ford low-fuel warning system.

10. Briefly explain this statement: "The Chrysler Fuel Pacer Light System is a driver mileage-control aid."

11. What activates the Chrysler EGR maintenance reminder light circuit at the required 15,000 mile intervals? Once the light turns on, how is it turned off?

Ammeter

1. What does a car dash ammeter usually measure?

2. How is the ammeter pointer held in the zero position when no current flows?

Shop safety

1. Give two safety precautions that a technician should observe when working with gauge or indicator light circuits.

2. What would happen in a thermoelectric gauge circuit if a jumper wire or screw driver were used as a direct short to ground at the sender terminal?

3. What safety precaution must be taken when you work under the dash with instrumentation and light circuits?

4. What are the safety precautions to practice when repairing a fuel tank? What is a safe way to repair a fuel tank leak?

Troubleshooting—thermoelectric gauges

1. Explain your answers. How would the gauge readings respond to:
   a. an open heating coil in the voltage limiter?
   b. an interrupted instrument-cluster ground?
   c. dirty voltage-limiter contacts?
   d. intermittent interruption of instrument-cluster ground?

2. Explain: When all the gauges are affected by the same problem, the cause must be the voltage limiter.

3. How can the voltage limiter be tested on the car? Where can the test hook-up be made? What test results indicate a normal operating voltage limiter?

4. When only one gauge is not working properly, why is it best to start your troubleshooting at the gauge sending unit?

5. Explain your answers. How would the following conditions affect individual gauge readings?
   a. a disconnected wire terminal at the sending unit.
   b. a grounded circuit wire at the sending unit.
   c. a corroded circuit wire terminal at the sending unit.
   d. an interrupted sending unit ground such as the tank-sending-unit-to-body ground.

6. Describe a safe technique that can be used to isolate a sending unit problem from the remainder of the gauge circuit.

7. How can unsuspected fuel tank damage cause false gauge readings?

Troubleshooting—electromagnetic gauges

1. How would the following conditions affect individual fuel, oil, and temperature gauge readings? Explain your answers.
   a. a disconnected wire terminal at the sending unit.
   b. a grounded circuit wire at the sending unit.
   c. a corroded circuit wire terminal at the sending unit.
   d. an interrupted sending unit ground such as the tank-sending-unit-to-body ground.
   e. a poor instrument panel ground.

2. Describe a safe technique that can be used to isolate a sending unit problem from the remainder of the gauge circuit.

3. What are two causes of "crazy" gauges?

Indicator light testing

1. Describe a simple procedure you might use to checkout an indicator light circuit, if the bulb fails to light during a proof-test.

2. How would you proceed to isolate the ignition switch ground as the probable cause of a "no glow" condition during the coolant hot light proof-test checkout?

3. What are two causes of "crazy" indicator lights?

12

Power Seats and Power Windows

This chapter covers the electrical portion of the power-seat and power-window systems available in most automobiles. Ford, Chrysler, and American Motors use permanent-magnet motors, which require one type of electrical circuit; General Motors uses split-series wire-wound motors, which require a different type of electrical circuit. Examples of each type of circuit are presented. You must know and understand which system is being used before you can troubleshoot the circuit.

POWER SEATS

There are many types of seats in today's automobiles:

1. Full-width bench seat.
2. 60-40 seat. Individual passenger seat (60% of front seat width) and individual driver seat (40% of front seat width).
3. Bucket seats.
4. Reclining seats.
5. Folding rear seats.
6. Front seat back locks.

Most of the seats can be operated manually or electrically. The electrically operated seats have additional options: two-way, four-way, or six-way seat positions.

This chapter covers electrical operation of the full-width bench seat and all the electrical options.

General Motors Power Seats

The seat adjusters are actuated by a 12-volt reversible motor, with a built-in circuit breaker. The motor is energized by a toggle-type control switch installed in the left seat side panel or in the left door arm rest.

On four-way and six-way power-operated seats, the seat operating mechanism incorporates a transmission assembly which includes solenoids and drive cables to the seat adjusters.

On the four-way seat, one solenoid controls the horizontal movement of the seat and the second solenoid controls the vertical movement of the seat.

On the six-way seat, one solenoid controls the vertical movement of the front of the seat, the second solenoid controls horizontal movement of the seat, and the third solenoid controls the vertical movement of the rear of the seat. When the control switch is actuated, the motor and one of the solenoids are energized simultaneously. The solenoid plunger engages with the driving gear dog. The driving gear rotates the drive cable and operates both adjusters. When the adjusters reach their limit of travel, the drive cables stop their rotating action and the torque is absorbed by the rubber coupler connecting the motor and the transmission. When the control switch is released, a return spring returns the solenoid plunger to its original position disengaging it from the driving gear dog.

Two-way power seat (*Full Width*)

The major components in the two-way power seats (Fig. 12-1) are:

1. the motor (6)
2. drive cables (9)
3. gear nut (10)
4. jack screw (12)

The seat adjusters for the bench seat are actuated by a 12-volt series wound motor and are energized through a control switch installed in the seat side panel or in the door arm rest.

The horizontal seat circuit is protected by a circuit breaker.

As the motor operates, it drives the drive cables, which operate the gear nut, which pulls the seat along the jack screw.

The circuit diagram is shown in Fig. 12-2.

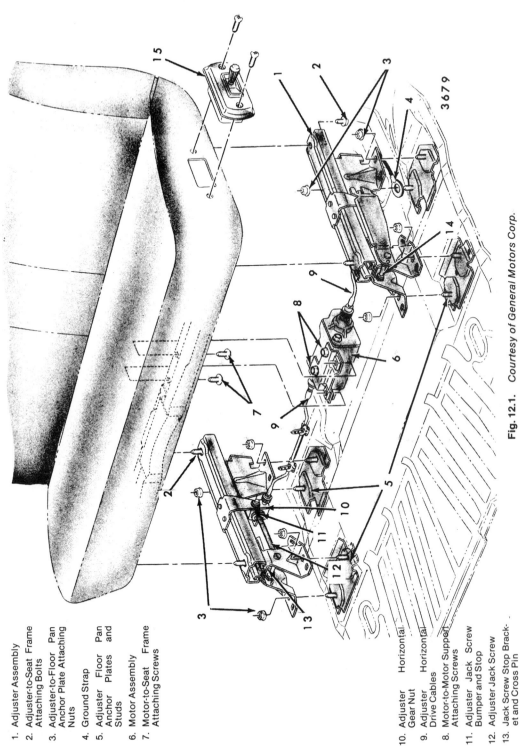

3679

Fig. 12.1. *Courtesy of General Motors Corp.*

1. Adjuster Assembly
2. Adjuster-to-Seat Frame Attaching Bolts
3. Adjuster-to-Floor Pan Anchor Plate Attaching Nuts
4. Ground Strap
5. Adjuster Floor Pan Anchor Plates and Studs
6. Motor Assembly
7. Motor-to-Seat Frame Attaching Screws

10. Adjuster Horizontal Gear Nut
9. Adjuster Horizontal Drive Cables
8. Motor-to-Motor Support Attaching Screws
11. Adjuster Jack Screw Bumper and Stop
12. Adjuster Jack Screw
13. Jack Screw Stop Bracket and Cross Pin

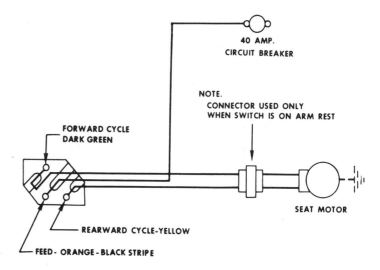

Fig. 12.2.   *Courtesy of General Motors Corp.*

Four-way power seat (Full Width)

The seat adjuster for the bench-type seat is actuated by a 12-volt, reversible, shunt wound motor with a built-in circuit breaker.

The seat motor is energized by a toggle-type control switch installed in the left seat side panel or in the left front door arm rest.

The seat adjuster operating mechanism incorporates a transmission assembly which includes two solenoids and four drive cables leading to the seat adjuster (Fig. 12-3). One solenoid controls the rear vertical movement of the seat, and the other solenoid controls the horizontal movement of the seat. When the control switch is actuated, the motor and one of the solenoids are energized simultaneously. Then the solenoid plunger causes the shaft dog to engage with the large gear dog.

Power is then transmitted through the transmission shaft to drive the actuator cables. When the adjusters reach their limit of travel, the drive cables stop their rotating action and torque is absorbed by the rubber coupler connecting the motor and transmission (Fig. 12-4). When the control switch lever is released, the switch contacts open and a spring returns the shaft dog and the solenoid plunger to their original position, disengaging the shaft dog from the large gear dog. The electrical circuit is shown in Fig. 12-5.

Six-way power seat (Full Width)

The seat adjusters for the six-way power seat are actuated by a 12-volt motor. The motor is energized by a three-button control switch located in the left seat side panel or in the left front door arm rest.

When the control switch is actuated, current flows to the transmission solenoid which controls the desired seat movement (Fig. 12-6). The energizing of the solenoid coil causes the solenoid plunger dog to engage the gear mechanism and rotate the control cable. The same switch action which energized the solenoid produces a current flow through the motor control relay to one of the motor field coils. The current flows through the relay, closes the contacts between the relay power source and the armature motor lead wire, and operates the seat motor. When the control switch lever is released, the switch

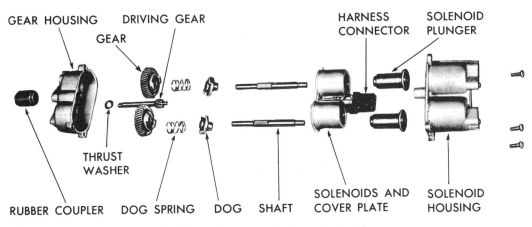

GEAR HOUSING   DRIVING GEAR   GEAR   HARNESS CONNECTOR   SOLENOID PLUNGER

THRUST WASHER

RUBBER COUPLER   DOG SPRING   DOG   SHAFT   SOLENOIDS AND COVER PLATE   SOLENOID HOUSING

Fig. 12.3. *Courtesy of General Motors Corp.*

Fig. 12.4. *Courtesy of General Motors Corp.*

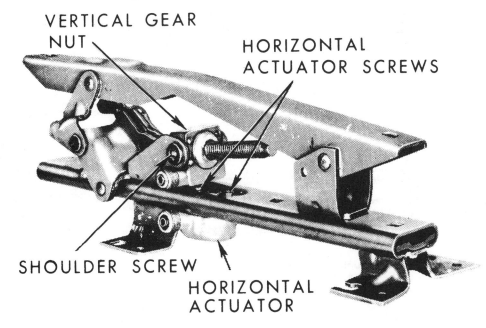

VERTICAL GEAR NUT   HORIZONTAL ACTUATOR SCREWS

SHOULDER SCREW   HORIZONTAL ACTUATOR

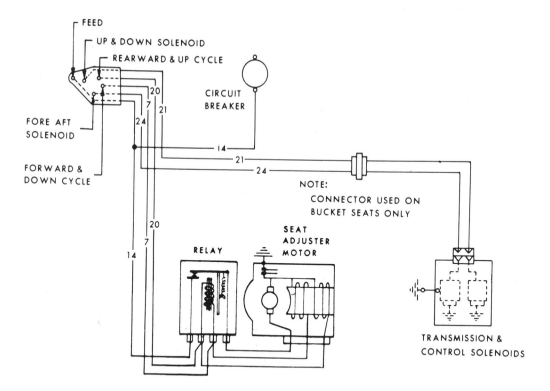

FEED

UP & DOWN SOLENOID

REARWARD & UP CYCLE

20

7

21

24

CIRCUIT
BREAKER

FORE AFT
SOLENOID

FORWARD &
DOWN CYCLE

14

21

24

NOTE:

CONNECTOR USED ON
BUCKET SEATS ONLY

20

7

14

RELAY

SEAT
ADJUSTER
MOTOR

TRANSMISSION &
CONTROL SOLENOIDS

Fig. 12.5. *Courtesy of General Motors Corp.*

Fig. 12.6. *Courtesy of General Motors Corp.*

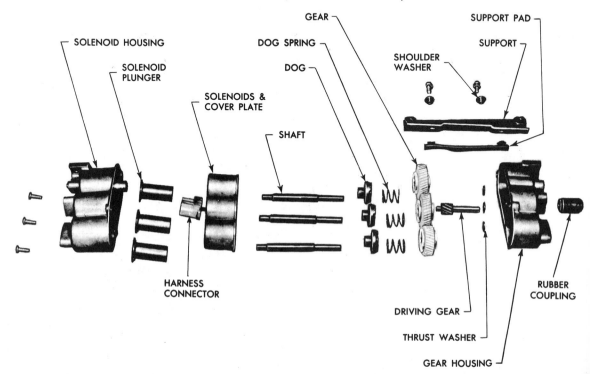

SOLENOID HOUSING

SOLENOID
PLUNGER

SOLENOIDS &
COVER PLATE

SHAFT

DOG

DOG SPRING

GEAR

SHOULDER
WASHER

SUPPORT

SUPPORT PAD

HARNESS
CONNECTOR

DRIVING GEAR

THRUST WASHER

GEAR HOUSING

RUBBER
COUPLING

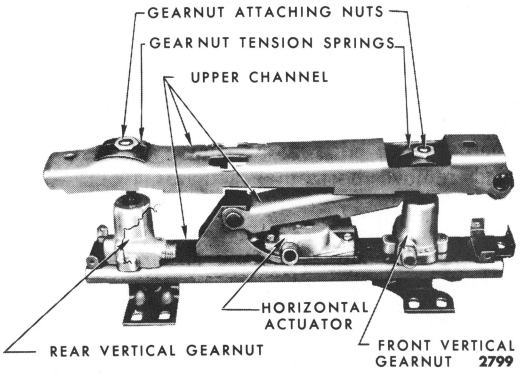

GEARNUT ATTACHING NUTS

GEARNUT TENSION SPRINGS

UPPER CHANNEL

HORIZONTAL ACTUATOR

REAR VERTICAL GEARNUT

FRONT VERTICAL GEARNUT 2799

Fig. 12.7. *Courtesy of General Motors Corp.*

contacts open, and a spring returns the shaft dog and the solenoid plunger to their original position, disengaging them from the gear dog.

The drive cables from the transmission operate the gear nut selected by the driver of the vehicle (Fig. 12-7). The horizontal actuator moves the seat forward and rearward, the rear gearnut moves the rear of the seat up or down, and the front gearnut moves the front of the seat up or down.

The electrical circuit of the six-way seat is shown in Fig. 12-8.

Checking the seat switch

A three-way jumper wire is used to check the operation of the seat switch. To make the jumper wire, obtain two pieces of 12-gauge wire, each 4 1/2 inches long, and join one end of each wire as shown in Fig. 12-9. The joined end can be inserted in the feed location.

To obtain a seat movement using a three-way jumper wire at the switch block, the switch feed location, one of the motor field wire

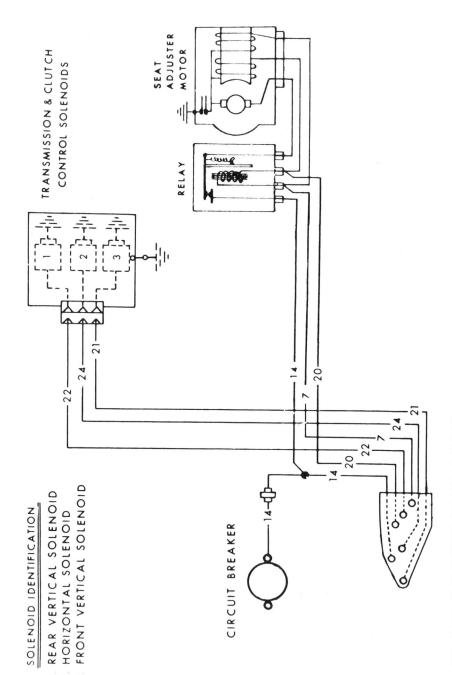

SOLENOID IDENTIFICATION
1. REAR VERTICAL SOLENOID
2. HORIZONTAL SOLENOID
3. FRONT VERTICAL SOLENOID

TRANSMISSION & CLUTCH
CONTROL SOLENOIDS

SEAT
ADJUSTER
MOTOR

RELAY

CIRCUIT BREAKER

SIX - WAY SEAT SWITCH TERMINAL BLOCK

Fig. 12.8.   Courtesy of General Motors Corp.

SIX-WAY SEAT CONTROL SWITCH BLOCK

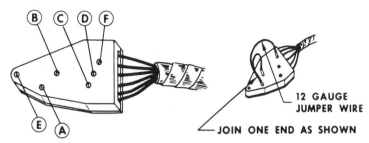

Fig. 12.9. *Courtesy of General Motors Corp.*

locations and one of the solenoid locations must be connected simultaneously.

1. To raise front edge of seat, connect jumper to A, F, and E.
2. To lower front edge of seat, connect jumper to A, C, and E.

A: Switch feed

B: Solenoid—Horizontal movement

C: Field feed—Rearward and down cycle

D: Solenoid—Rear edge vertical cycle

E: Solenoid—Front edge vertical cycle

F: Field feed—Forward and up cycle

Ford Power Seats

Two-way power seats

The two-way power seat is adjusted forward or backward in a horizontal plane by a single electric motor. Flexible drive shafts connect the right and left ends of the motor shaft to a transmission and horizontal rack on the right and left seat tracks.

Electric current is fed to the motor through a toggle switch. The switch controls the direction of seat track travel by controlling the direction of motor shaft rotation.

The electrical system is protected against an overloaded circuit by a 30-amp circuit breaker mounted on the instrument panel in front of the glove box or mounted in the engine compartment at the starter motor relay.

Six-way power seats:

The six-way power seat provides horizontal, vertical, and vertical tilt adjustments. It consists of a reversible, three-armature

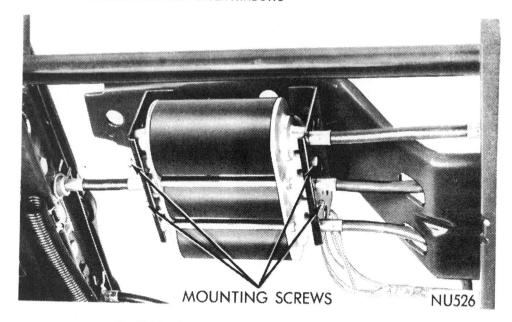

MOUNTING SCREWS   NU526

Fig. 12.10.   *Courtesy of The Chrysler Corporation.*

motor, a switch and housing assembly, vertical worm gear drives, and horizontal rack-and-pinion drives (Fig. 12-10).

The mechanical portion of the seat track in the horizontal drive consists of a rack and pinion on each track. The pinion housing and motor are attached to the movable section of the track. When the switch is actuated, the front armature is energized and the horizontal drive units are activated. The seat is then propelled forward or rearward by the pinion gear traveling in a rack in each lower track section.

In the vertical drive, worm gear mechanisms are utilized. The drive units are located in the rear of the right track and in the front of the left track. When the switch is actuated, the center and rear armatures are energized simultaneously and the vertical drive units are activated. The seat is then propelled up or down by the worm gear.

When the tilt switch is actuated, the center armature drives the front vertical worm gear and moves the seat to the desired position. When the rear tilt switch is actuated, the rear armature drives the rear vertical worm gear and moves the seat to the desired position. The power seat circuit is protected either by a 20-amp or 30-amp circuit breaker located on the starter solenoid or fuse panel. The electrical circuit for the six-way power seat is shown in Fig. 12-11.

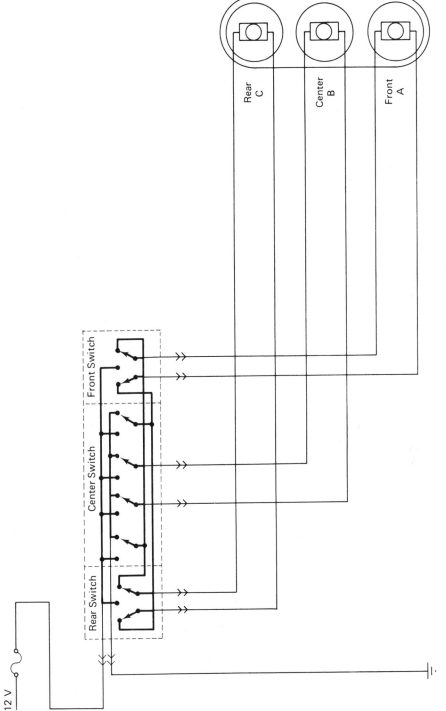

Fig. 12.11. *Typical Ford six-way power seat circuit.*

Chrysler Power Seats

Six-way power seats:

This power seat can be adjusted in six directions: up, down, forward, back, tilt forward, or tilt rearward.

The control switch is located on the lower outboard side of the seat. The front lever on the switch, Fig. 12-12, raises or lowers the front of the seat. The center lever controls the complete seat; when the lever is moved down, it raises or lowers the seat; when it is moved forward or rearward, it moves the seat rearward. The rear lever raises or lowers the back of the seat.

A three-armature permanent-magnet reversible motor is coupled through cables to rack-and-pinion assemblies located in the seat tracks, providing the various seat movements.

The circuit is protected by a 30-amp circuit breaker located on the fuse block; the complete circuit is shown in Fig. 12-13.

Remember: The return path to ground is through the switch on AMC, Ford, and Chrysler products. When one switch is activated, the other switch is spring-loaded to the ground position.

ELECTRICAL TESTING OF POWER SEATS

Before you attempt any electrical testing, make sure that the battery is fully charged and that all electrical connections are clean and tight to insure proper continuity and grounds. With everything connected and the dome light on, apply the switch in the direction of the failure; if the dome light dims, this indicates that the seat motor is trying to work and there is mechanical jamming. If the dome light does not dim, proceed with the following electrical tests:

1. Disconnect hot wire to circuit breaker. Connect test lamp to hot wire and ground. Lamp should light.

Fig. 12.12. *Courtesy of The Chrysler Corporation.*

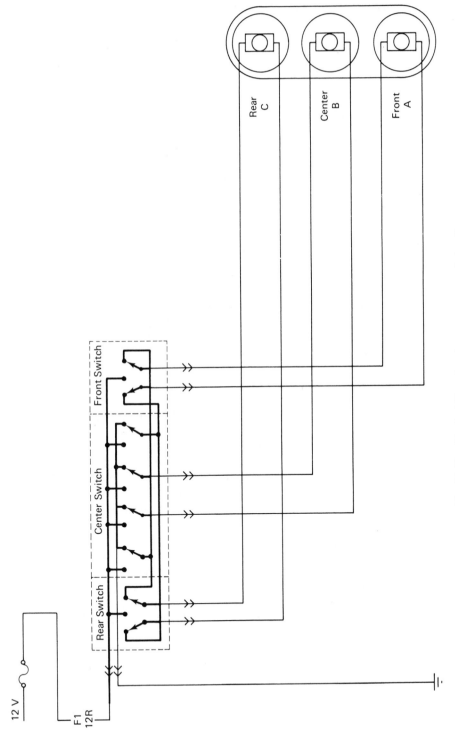

Fig. 12.13. *Typical Chrysler six-way power seat circuit.*

2. Connect hot wire to circuit breaker.

3. Disconnect wire from the other side of circuit breaker. Connect test lamp between circuit breaker terminal and a good ground. If lamp lights circuit, breaker is good. Reconnect wires.

4. Disconnect wiring harness under seat and check for continuity.

5. Using a covered wire, apply current to each of the motor leads under the seat.

POWER WINDOWS

Power windows are operated by a 12-volt reversible motor attached to the window regulator. Two types of motors used by manufacturers—a permanent magnet motor and a split-series, wire-wound motor. Each motor type requires a different wiring system.

All power window systems have a master switch on the driver's door and an individual switch at each window. For safety reasons, some power windows incorporate an ignition relay to prevent window operation unless the ignition switch is turned on.

Ford and Chrysler Windows (Fig. 12-14)

Electric window lift motors are the permanent-magnet type, using polarity of the circuit to change motor rotation.

An individual control switch is provided for each side window. A complete set of control switches on the driver's door enables remote control operation of all side windows. All the power window motors are grounded through the master switch. The power window circuit is protected by a circuit breaker. The window relay is protected by a fuse.

The ignition switch must be in the on or run position to operate window relay, before the power windows can be operated. When the ignition switch is turned to the run position, current flows from the ignition switch to the window relay coil, which creates an electromagnet. The electromagnet pulls the points closed and current flows from the circuit breaker to the master switch and each side window.

American Motors Windows (Fig. 12-15)

The window motors are of the two-wire, permanent magnet design, using polarity of the circuit to change motor rotation. The motor

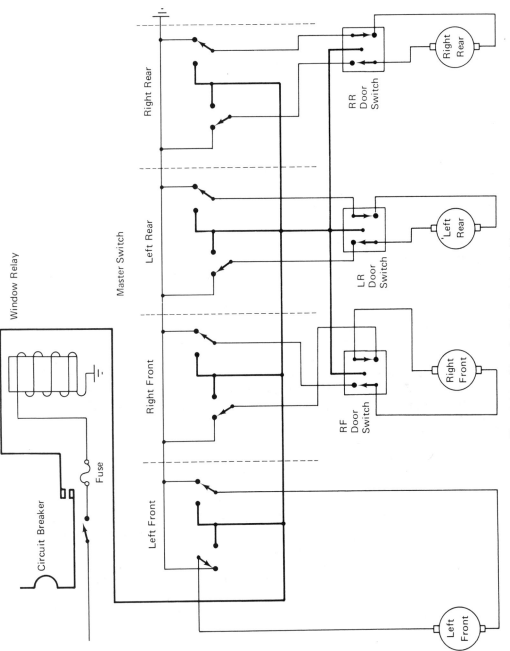

Fig. 12.14.   Chrysler, Ford power windows.

335

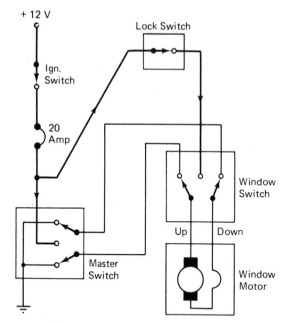

Fig. 12.15. American Motors power window circuit.

drives the unit through a rubber and plastic coupling in the drive unit housing which is bolted to the window regulator.

An individual control switch is provided for each side window. A complete set of control switches on the driver's door enables remote control operation of all side windows. As a safety feature, another control switch allows only the driver to operate the windows.

The ignition switch must be in the on or run position to operate the windows.

General Motors Windows (Fig. 12-16)

Each power window is operated by a rectangular, 12-volt series-wound motor with an internal circuit breaker; the motor is connected to a window regulator by a self-locking rubber coupled gear drive. The wire harness to the door window motor connector is designed with a locking embossment to insure a positive connection. As the motor turns, it drives the window regulator up or down.

The window motors are controlled by a master switch located on the left front door, and by individual switches on each door. The system is protected by a main circuit breaker and by internal circuit breakers in each motor. A relay in the circuit prevents the operation of the power windows until the ignition switch is turned on. The relay is usually located near the fuse block.

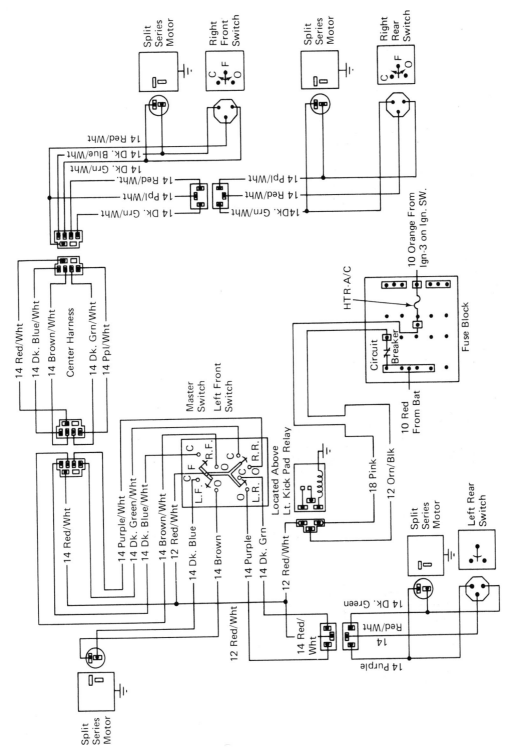

Fig. 12.16(A) Power windows in neutral position.

337

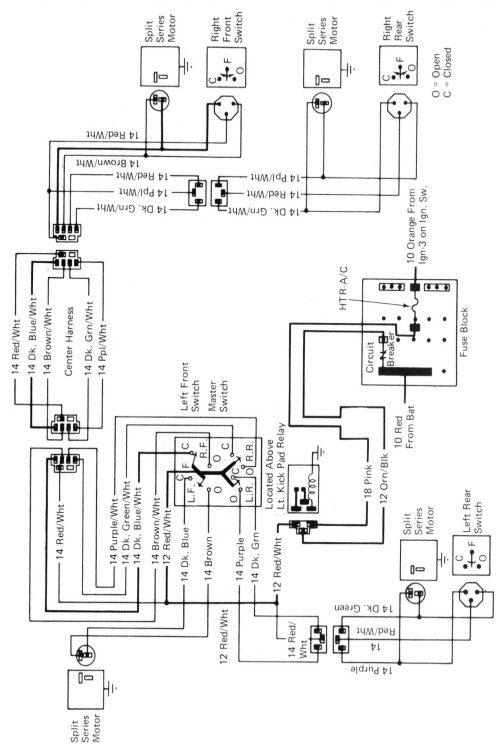

Fig. 12.16.(B)   Right front window circuit. *(Courtesy of General Motors Corp.)*

Some power window circuits incorporate a lock-out switch that enables the driver to control the window operation from the master switch only. The window lock-out switch button should be left in the normal position to permit operation of power windows from all switch locations.

ELECTRICAL TESTING

Before any electrical testing is attempted, the battery should be fully charged and all electrical connections should be clean and tight to insure proper continuity and grounds. With everything connected and the dome lights on, apply switch in the direction of the failure. If the dome light dims, the window is trying to work; this indicates mechanical jamming. If the dome light does not dim, proceed with the following electrical tests.

ELECTRICAL TESTING OF POWER WINDOWS

Ford, Chrysler, and American Motors:

In this power window operation, the master switch provides the only ground for all the power windows. It is very important that the *master switch ground wire* makes good contact with the body.

1. Connect one lead of the test lamp to the ground wire and the other lead to a hot wire. The light should light.
2. If the light does not light, remove the lead from the ground wire and connect it to a good body ground.
3. Disconnect the master switch from the multiple connector.
4. Insert two jumper wires as shown in Fig. 12-17. The window should operate.
5. Different combinations of the two jumper wires can activate each power window. If one window does not operate from the master switch, make sure the window switch for that window has returned to its normal position.

Circuit breaker test:

1. Disconnect hot wire from circuit breaker and connect test light between hot wire and ground.
2. Turn ignition switch on. If the lamp does not light, the hot wire has an open or the ignition switch is bad.

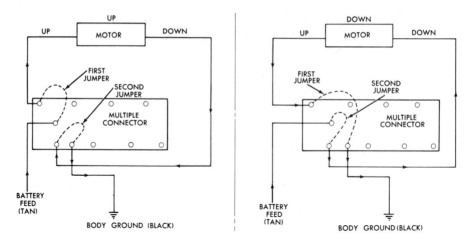

Fig. 12.17.   Ford, Chrysler and AMC testing electrical switch. *(Courtesy of The Chrysler Corporation)*

Relay assembly test:

1. With test light, check relay feed. If the tester does not light, there is an open or short circuit between relay and circuit breaker.
2. Turn ignition on and with test light, check output terminal of relay. If tester does not light, put test light on relay coil feed. If test lamp lights, replace relay.

ELECTRICAL TESTING OF POWER WINDOWS *(continued)*

General Motors

General Motors does not ground their power window motors through the master switch. Power is delivered to a switch. The switch directs the current to the motor. The current goes through the fields and the insulated brush and then to ground through the ground brush.

Checking the window control switch: (Fig. 12-18)

1. Disconnect the switch from the connector.
2. Insert jumper wire (12 gauge) from feed terminal to motor control terminal.
3. If the window operates, the window switch is defective.
4. If the window does not operate, leave wire connected as shown in Fig. 12-18. Disconnect the motor connector from motor.

5. Insert test light in one of the motor connectors. If test light does not light in either motor terminal, there is an open in the wire. Fig. 12-19.

Checking the Feed Circuit (Fig. 12-20)

1. Connect a 12-volt test light to a good ground.
2. Put test light probe in the feed wire terminal.
3. Test light should light.

POWER-OPERATED TAILGATE WINDOW AND TAILGATE

General Motors

The tailgate window is controlled by a gear-box type regulator and a rectangular 12-volt, direct-current, reversible motor with an internal

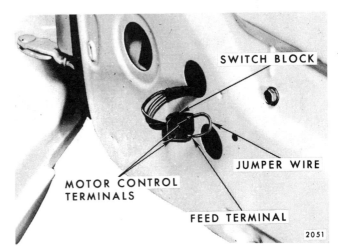

Fig. 12.18. Checking window control switch. *(Courtesy of General Motors Corp.)*

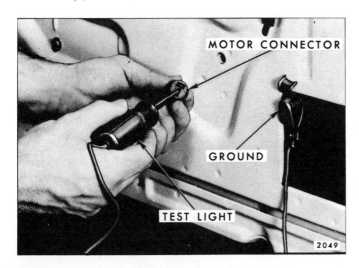

Fig. 12.19. Checking between switch and motor. *(Courtesy of General Motors Corp.)*

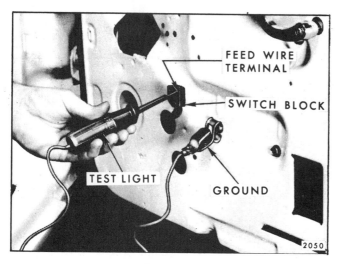

FEED WIRE
TERMINAL

SWITCH BLOCK

TEST LIGHT

GROUND

2050

Fig. 12.20.   Checking feed circuit.

circuit breaker (Fig. 12-21a and b). Another circuit breaker protects the wiring circuit. An ignition relay prevents operation of the tailgate window from the instrument panel switch until the ignition switch is turned on.

The internal tailgate window control switch is mounted on the rear of the right quarter panel adjacent to the tail gate. On styles equipped with a power-operated tailgate, the switch controls both the gate and the glass.

On styles equipped with manually operated tailgate, the switch includes a link to the gate lock lever. Turning the key clockwise will open the tailgate window. After the window is opened about eight inches, the knob can be turned to unlock the tailgate. The window cannot be fully closed until the tailgate is fully closed.

On styles equipped with a power-operated tailgate, the switch includes three detent positions in each of the clockwise and counterclockwise directions. Turning the key clockwise to the first detent position opens the tailgate window. The second detent position opens the tailgate, and the third detent position provides simultaneous opening of the tailgate and tailgate window. Turning the key counterclockwise to the first detent position closes the tailgate window. The second detent position closes the tailgate and the third detent closes both simultaneously.

Chrysler and Ford

The tailgate power window is operated by a 12-volt reversible motor that is controlled by an instrument panel switch or by a key switch located in the tailgate (Figs. 12-22 and 12-23). To operate the power tailgate window from the instrument panel switch, the ignition switch

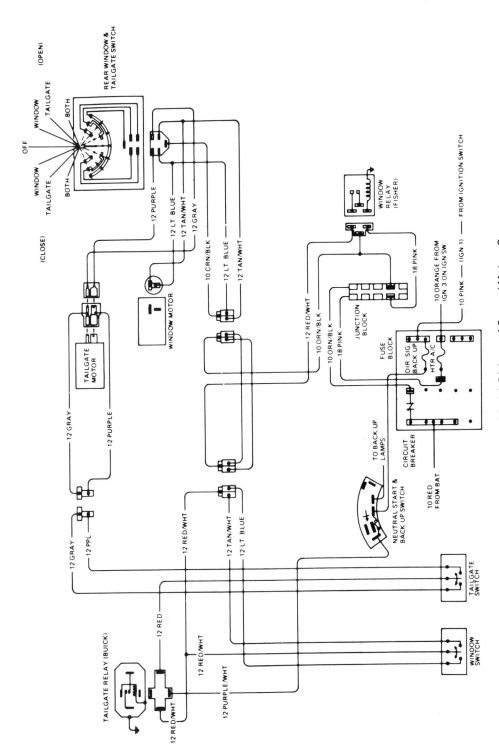

Fig. 12.21(A) *Courtesy of Buick Division of General Motors Corp.*

343

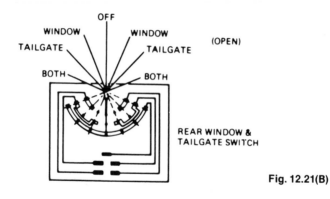

OFF

WINDOW   WINDOW

TAILGATE   TAILGATE

BOTH   BOTH

(OPEN)

REAR WINDOW &
TAILGATE SWITCH

Fig. 12.21(B)

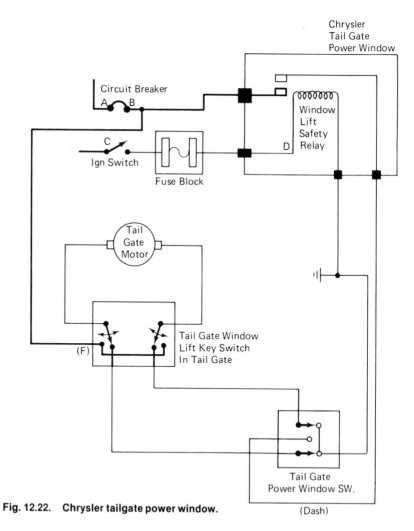

Circuit Breaker

A B

C

Ign Switch

Fuse Block

Chrysler
Tail Gate
Power Window

Window
Lift
Safety
Relay

D

Tail
Gate
Motor

(F)

Tail Gate Window
Lift Key Switch
In Tail Gate

Tail Gate
Power Window SW.

(Dash)

Fig. 12.22. Chrysler tailgate power window.

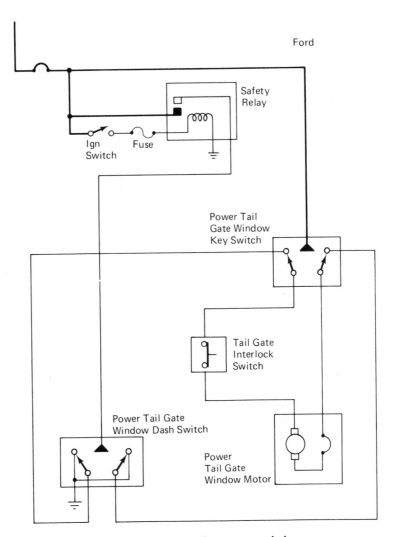

Fig. 12.23.   Ford tailgate power window.

must be in the run position. When the key is in the run position, it
energizes the window lift safety relay, which permits current to flow to
the tailgate power window switch.

The tailgate window lift switch in the tailgate can be operated
any time the key is inserted into the tailgate switch and turned
clockwise or counterclockwise. The circuit is protected by a circuit
breaker. The window lift safety relay is protected by a fuse.

Test Points (Fig. 12–22)

1. Circuit breaker	Points A & B	Battery voltage
2. Ignition switch	Point C	Battery voltage
3. Safety relay	Point D	Key on—Battery voltage
4. Tailgate window switch	Point E	Key on—Battery voltage
5. Tailgate key switch	Point F	Battery voltage

Tailgate Interlock Switch (Fig. 12-24)

Some stationwagons have a tailgate interlock switch that will not allow the tailgate window to be operated unless the tailgate is fully closed. The tailgate interlock switch is generally located in the latch mechanism. The tailgate switch must be bypassed if the tailgate window is to be operated with the tailgate open. This should be done only if the tailgate window needs repairing.

Caution: Keep your hands out of the panel when testing for motor operation.

Fig. 12.24.   *Courtesy of General Motors Corp.*

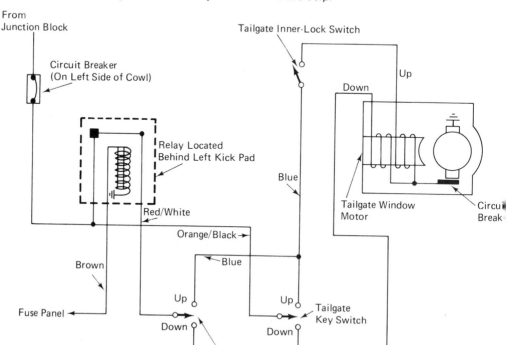

SAFETY RULES

Do not operate motor with your hand inside the door or tailgate panel.

Warning (General Motors): The regulator lift arms are under tension from the counterbalance spring and the weight of the door glass is required to neutralize the spring during motor removal. If door glass has been broken or removed, the sector gear must be securely fastened to the regulator back plate prior to motor removal to prevent serious injury. Drill a 1/8-inch hole through the regulator sector gear and back plate. Do not drill hole closer than 1/2-inch to edge of sector gear or back plate. Install a sheet-metal tapping screw (10-12 x 3/4) in the drilled hole to lock the sector gear in position.

Warning (Chrysler): Whenever it is necessary to remove the motor from the regulator, it is imperative the linkage be clamped in a vise to lock it in place. Failure to do this allows the assist spring to drive the mounting bracket around the lift pivot and could cause serious body injury.

ELECTRIC BACK WINDOW GRID DEFOGGER

The optional back window grid defogger system consists of a tinted glass that has a number of horizontal ceramic silver compound element lines and two vertical bus bars baked into the inside surface during the glaze-forming operation. Braided wire is soldered to the bus bars on each side of the glass. The lead wires are spliced to the braided wire and covered with an extruded plastic sleeve to insulate them from body material.

The system operates on 12 volts with a current draw of 20 amps when glass is at 75°F. Under some conditions, heat from the glass may not be detected by finger touch. The length of time required to remove interior fog from the back glass varies with conditions such as vehicle speed, outside glass temperature, atmospheric pressure, number of passengers, etc.

The system utilizes an instrument-panel-mounted switch with an integral indicator lamp. Once the switch has been activated, the system will operate continuously until the switch or the ignition is turned off. A relay is used in conjunction with the air conditioning system to regulate the blower motor speed when the heated back glass is in operation. On some styles the system will operate for approximately ten minutes and then will be automatically turned off by a timer. When the electrib back window grid defogger is turned on, the blower motor will return to low speed.

Testing Grid Lines

To locate inoperative grid lines, start the engine and turn on the electric grid defogger system. Ground one test lamp lead and lightly touch the other prod to each grid line. Figure 12-25 illustrates the pattern of test lamp brilliance to be expected with a properly functioning grid.

If test lamp shows full brilliance at both ends of the grid lines, check for loose ground wire contact to body metal.

The range zones in Fig. 12-25 may vary slightly from one glass to another; however, the bulb brilliance will decrease proportionally to the increased resistance in the grid line as the prod is moved from the left bus bar to the right.

All grid lines must be tested in at least two places to eliminate the possibility of bridging a break. For best results, touch each grid line a few inches on either side of the glass center line. If an abnormal light reading is apparent on a specific grid line, place the test lamp prod on that grid at the left bus bar and move the prod toward the right bus bar until the light goes out. This will indicate a break in the continuity of the grid line. To repair grid lines, refer to manufacturer's specifications.

The electrical circuit for the electric back window grid defogger is shown in Fig. 12-26.

Fig. 12.25.   *Courtesy of General Motors Corp.*

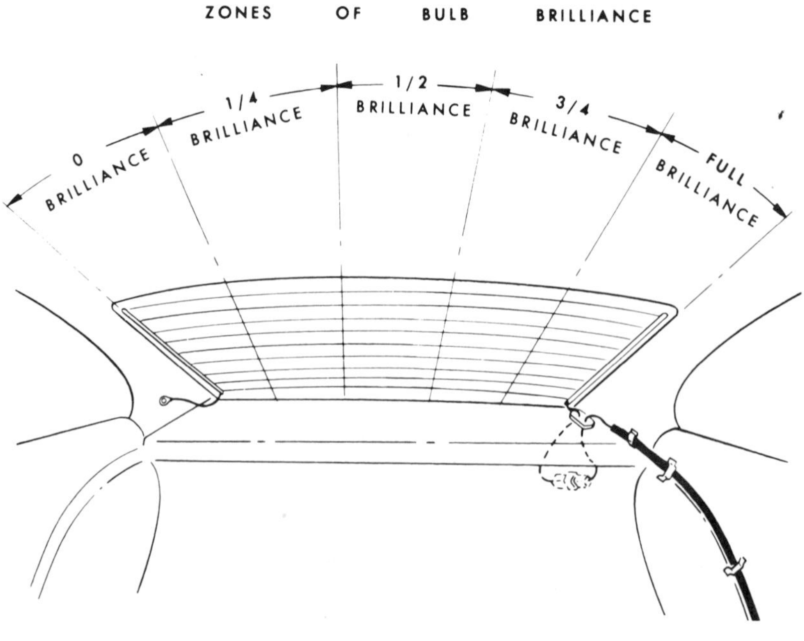

ZONES   OF   BULB   BRILLIANCE

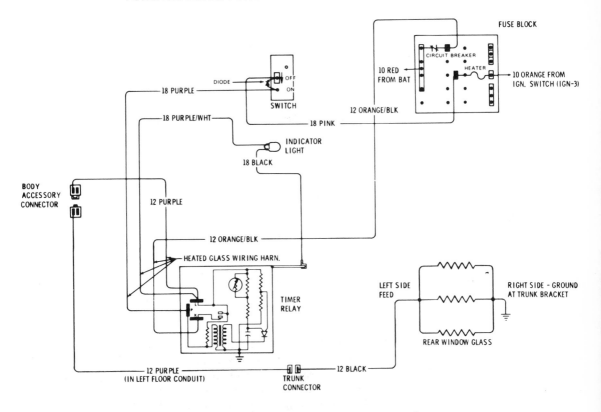

Fig. 12.26. *Courtesy of Buick Division of General Motors Corp.*

Review questions

1. What are the three different power seat options available?

2. What two electrical systems are used to operate the power seats and windows?

3. The four-way and six-way seats on General Motors Cars are operated by a motor and what other unit?

4. How many motors are used to operate the four-way and six-way power seats on Ford, Chrysler, and A.M.C. cars?

5. What two types of motors are used on power seats and windows?

6. For safety reasons, the power windows will not work unless a certain switch is on. What is that switch?

7. What is the purpose of the ignition relay in some power window circuits?

8. What is the purpose of the interlock switch in the tailgate?

13

Electric Windshield Wipers and Washers

Windshield wipers were one of the first safety devices used on automobile vehicles. They've come a long way from the days when they were hand operated to the present electric-motor-driven systems. Electric windshield washers are tied into the wiper system as a standard safety item; they are operated either by a pump attached to the windshield wiper motor or by means of a separate motor-driven pump mounted on the solvent reservoir. Control of the washer system is usually integrated into the windshield wiper switch. A tailgate wiper and washer system is available as a factory option on some station wagon makes and models.

WIPER MOTOR GEAR AND LINKAGE DRIVES

All wiper motors have an attached gear box containing a parking switch in addition to the gear train (Figs. 13-1 and 13-2). The gear train functions to give the wiper motor a torque boost and reduce motor speed. A cam mechanism is incorporated in each gear train to operate the park point switch. The park point switch ties in with the wiper switch on the dash and opens the motor circuit when the wiper blades reach their exact position at the end of the wipe cycle.

The drive linkage arrangement in Fig. 13-3 is typical of most wiper systems. Attached to the motor drive is a crank arm that connects to a drive link and wiper pivot (the left pivot in the illustration). To complete the hook-up, a connecting link couples the

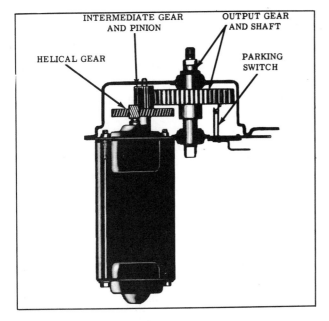

Fig. 13.1. Gear train. *(Courtesy of Buick Division of General Motors Corp.)*

PARK SWITCH CAM LIFT

ON OUTPUT GEAR

Fig. 13.2 *Courtesy of Buick Division of General Motors Corp.*

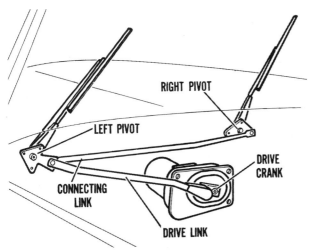

RIGHT PIVOT

LEFT PIVOT

DRIVE CRANK

CONNECTING LINK

DRIVE LINK

Fig. 13.3. Typical wiper drive linkage. *(Courtesy of The Chrysler Corporation)*

left windshield wiper pivot to the pivot at the right side of the car.

On depressed park applications, where the blades park off the glass when the final wipe cycle is completed, the overtravel feature (disappearing act) is incorporated in either the crank arm and drive link or in the motor assembly itself.

Whatever system is used, the idea is to give the drive link to the wiper pivot a longer effective stroke during the park or off cycle.

To mechanically accomplish this, the wiper motor rotation in most cases is reversed. Let's look at an example of a reversing motor where a cam action between the crank arm and drive link provides the extra travel (Fig. 13-4). During normal operation the motor and crank arm rotate in a counterclockwise direction. The cam mechanism on the end of the crank arm is positioned so that the effective crank throw length is 2 5/8 inches.

When the wiper switch is turned off, the wiper motor reverses and rotates itself and the cam in a clockwise direction. Rotating the cam clockwise increases the effective crank throw length to 2 7/8 inches. This 1/4 inch in the crank throw causes the wiper blades to travel several inches further so that they park in the "off glass" or "depressed park" position. The linkage changes to its original length when the motor is turned on.

When the motor reverses for park, the wiper blades will continue to finish their normal wipe cycle.

CHRYSLER WINDSHIELD WIPER SYSTEMS

Three different wiper motors are used on Chrysler Corporation car models. One is a two-speed nonreversing motor, the second is a

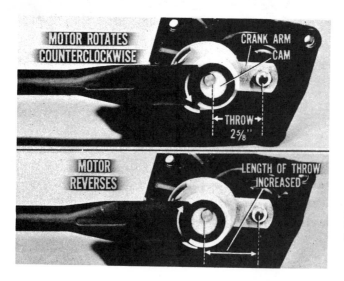

Fig. 13.4. Cam action provides extra travel. *(Courtesy of The Chrysler Corporation)*

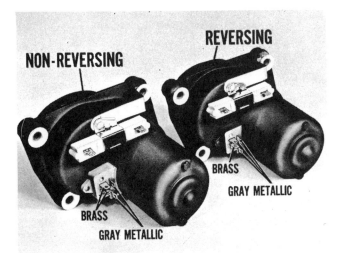

Fig. 13.5. **Chrysler two-speed wiper motors** *(Courtesy of The Chrysler Corporation)*

Fig. 13.6. **Chrysler two-speed motors—on the car installation.**

two-speed reversing motor, and the third is either a three-speed motor or a variable speed motor, depending on the type of switch used to control the speed of the wipers.

Two-Speed Motors

The two-speed nonreversing motor and the two-speed reversing motor are permanent-magnet motors and look alike (Figs. 13-5 and 13-6). They are not, however, interchangeable because there are differences in their internal circuitry which require different wiper switches (Figs. 13-7 and 13-8). In early versions of these two motors,

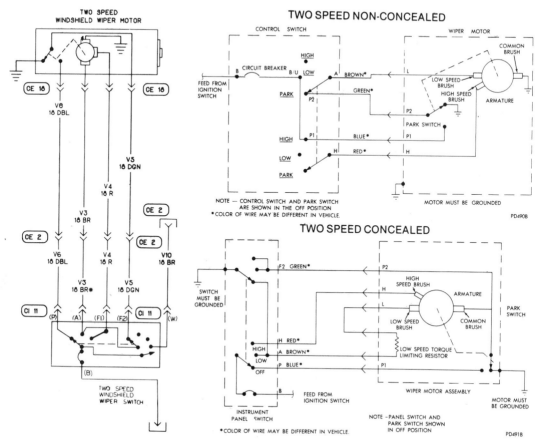

Fig. 13.7. Chrysler two-speed wiper motors wiring schematic (non-concealed wipers). Motor circuit is completed through grounded motor brush. *(Courtesy of The Chrysler Corporation)*

Fig. 13.8. Chrysler two-speed wiper motor wiring schematic (concealed and non-concealed wipers). *(Courtesy of The Chrysler Corporation)*

as shown in Fig. 13-5, the nonreversing motor was identified by two brass terminals and the reversing motor by one brass terminal. As another identification aid, a recent armature design change using fewer turns of wire in the non-reversing motor has eliminated the need of the white ceramic resistor on the outside of the motor. When used on the two-speed motors, the resistor is connected in the low-speed brush circuit to limit the low-speed torque. Without the resistor, excessive low-speed torque would be developed by the motor in the case of frozen blades and the motor could chew up the drive gears.

The reversing motor is used on vehicles with concealed windshield wipers (depressed park).

Three-Speed Motors

The three-speed wiper motor is a wire-wound compound motor (series-shunt); see Figs. 13-9 and 13-10. The motor speeds are controlled by resistance in the shunt field. The high- and medium-speed resistors are located in the instrument panel switch. For low-speed operation, a full 12 volts is applied to the shunt field. On variable-speed motors a rheostat controlled by the switch knob replaces the fixed switch resistors.

The three-speed wiper system has a "depressed park" feature that is accomplished by reversing the motor.

The power feed for Chrysler wiper motor circuits usually comes from a direct tap off the ignition switch. The wiper system and vehicle wiring are protected by a circuit breaker attached to the wiper switch.

Fig. 13.10. Chrysler three-speed wiper motor wiring schematic. *(Courtesy of The Chrysler Corporation)*

Fig. 13.9. Chrysler three-speed wiper motor installation—on the car installation.

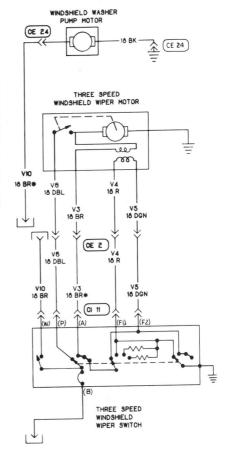

Washer Pump

Figure 13-10 shows the windshield washer pump motor tied into the wiper system at the wiper switch. This is typical for all three wiper systems. When the windshield washer pump motor is switched on, the wiper motor low-speed circuit is activated.

FORD SYSTEMS

Ford Motor Company uses two basic windshield wiper systems, referred to as "non-depressed park" and "depressed park." Both systems use a two-speed permanent-magnet motor, but they vary in complexity of design in both the motor and external circuit. The non-depressed park system is usually used on small cars.

The non-depressed park motor is pictured in Fig. 13-11; and Fig. 13-12 shows a schematic wiring diagram of the system.

Figures 13-13 and 13-14 show the depressed park motor and system wiring schematic. Note that the park switch has a separate terminal connector located at the gear cover end of the housing and the motor brushes have their own terminal connector at the brush end of the housing. "Depressed park" is accomplished by reversing the motor.

Intermittent Wipers

Offered as a factory option for depressed park systems is an intermittent wiper feature. The intermittent operation of the wiper motor is controlled by a variable resistor in the windshield wiper control switch which ties into an electronic pause control known as the governor.

Fig. 13.11. Ford "non-depressed" two speed motor.

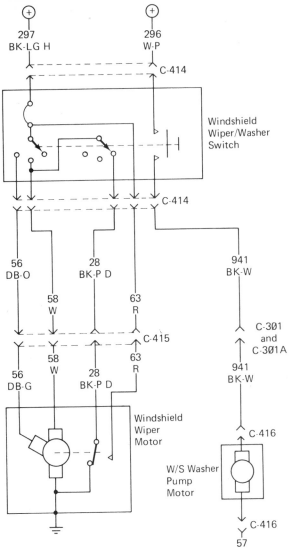

297
BK-LG H

296
W-P

C-414

Windshield
Wiper/Washer
Switch

C-414

56
DB-O

28
BK-P D

941
BK-W

58
W

63
R

C-301
and
C-301A

C-415

941
BK-W

56
DB-G

58
W

28
BK-P D

63
R

Windshield
Wiper
Motor

C-416

W/S Washer
Pump
Motor

C-416

57
BK

Fig. 13.12. Ford "non-depressed park" two-speed wiper motor wiring schematic. *(Courtesy of Ford Motor Company)*

Fig. 13.13. Ford "depressed park" two-speed motor—on the car installation.

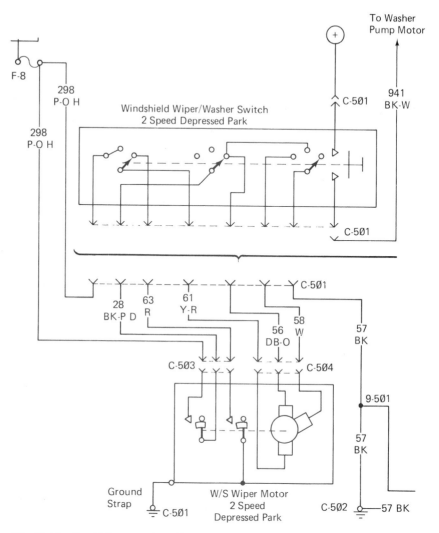

Fig. 13.14. Ford "depressed park" wiper motor wiring schematic. *(Courtesy of Ford Motor Company)*

For intermittent operation, the wiper-washer knob is rotated to the left. The more the knob is rotated, the greater the resistance in the switch and the longer the time interval between wiper blade sweeps. The resistance in the switch controls the amount of current to the electronic pause control, resulting in regulation of the motor operation for the desired time interval. Motor operation is through the low-speed circuit. Early design intermittent wipers used a vacuum-controlled pause system instead of solid state.

For normal motor operation, the wiper-washer knob is rotated to the right for the low- and high-speed position.

Washer Pump

The windshield washer pump motor is controlled by an instrument panel control switch integral with the wiper motor control switch. Refer to Figures 13-12 and 13-14. When the windshield washer pump is switched on, the wiper motor low-speed circuit is activated.

AMERICAN MOTORS SYSTEMS

American Motors vehicles use two-speed permanent-magnet wiper motors, "non-depressed" and "depressed," similar in design to Ford Motor Company motors. The windshield washer system has a motor-driven pump on the solvent bottle reservoir.

GENERAL MOTORS SYSTEMS

General Motors uses two basic wiper motor designs: the rectangular-shaped motor and the round-shaped motor, Figs. 13-15 and 13-16. The rectangular design is a two-speed motor used in a non-depressed park system. The round motor design is used in a two-speed or three-speed depressed park system. Both motors are wire-wound compound

Fig. 13.15.   GM rectangular motor—on the car installation.

Fig. 13.16.   GM round wiper motor—on the car installation.

motors (series-shunt). The motor speeds are controlled by using resistors in the shunt field circuit controlled by the dash switch.

Rectangular Motor

Figure 13-17 illustrates the relationship between the armature and series-shunt field winding in the rectangular motor.

In the low-speed wiper switch position, the shunt and series branches of the circuit are grounded at the switch. With the shunt field at full strength, low speed is maintained (Fig. 13-18). Note that the park points appear to ground the series field and armature circuit.

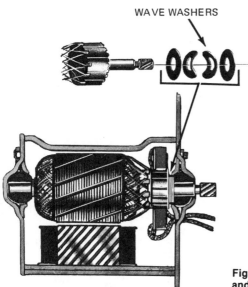

WAVE WASHERS

Fig. 13.17. GM rectangular motor showing armature and field winding.

A   B

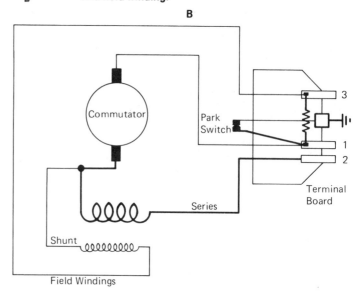

Commutator

Park Switch

3

1

2

Terminal Board

Series

Shunt

Field Windings

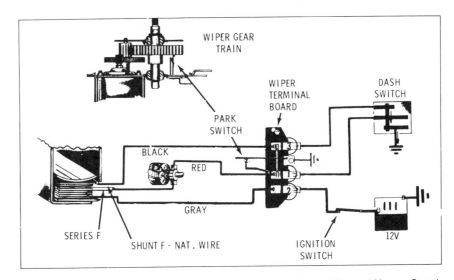

Fig. 13.18. **"Lo" speed circuit.** *(Courtesy of Buick Division of General Motors Corp.)*

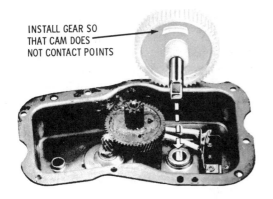

INSTALL GEAR SO
THAT CAM DOES
NOT CONTACT POINTS

Fig. 13.19. *Courtesy of Buick Division of General Motors Corp.*

Fig. 13.20 *Courtesy of Buick Division of General Motors Corp.*

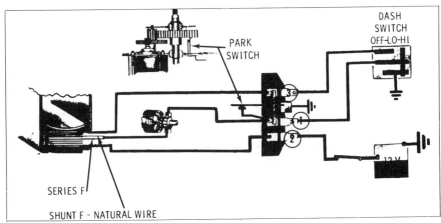

The park points, however, do not offer a steady ground because they are forced open by a cam lift on the output gear during each gear revolution (Fig. 13-19).

For high speed, the shunt field direct ground to the wiper switch is opened. This forces the shunt field circuit to route itself through a 20-ohm resistor across terminals 1 and 3 before it reaches the switch ground (Fig. 13-20). This reduces the shunt field current flow and strength for high-speed operation.

When the car owner first turns the wipers off at the switch and the wiper blades have not reached the park or off position, the park switch points are closed (Fig. 13-21). The wipe cycle will continue until the wiper output gear is turned to a position where its cam opens the park switch.

A circuit fuse is located in the fuse block to protect the wiper circuit and vehicle wiring.

Round Motor

The two-speed round motor circuitry, with some modification, controls the wiper speeds much the same as the rectangular motor circuitry. The wiper dash switch is a grounding switch. For low-speed operation the wiper motor shunt field is grounded through the dash switch for full field strength, and for high speed the shunt field is grounded through a 20-ohm resistor (Figs. 13-22 and 13-23). Notice that the motor ground includes a circuit breaker to prevent overheating of the motor. Otherwise, the circuit is fused at the block to protect the wiper circuit and vehicle wiring. In three-speed versions of the round motor, medium speed is obtained through the use of a special dash switch equipped with a 13-ohm resistor. Thus, the shunt field is connected to ground through the dash switch resistor.

Fig. 13.21. Parking circuit. *(Courtesy of Buick Division of General Motors Corp.)*

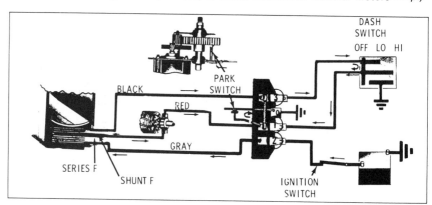

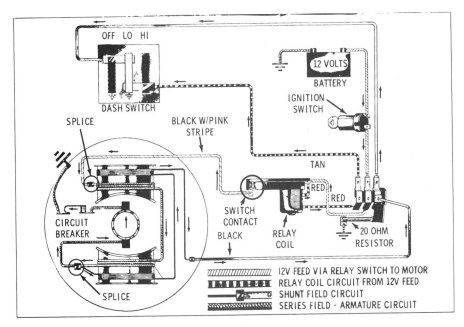

Fig. 13.22.   GM round wiper motor wiring—"lo" speed. *(Courtesy of Buick Division of General Motors Corp.)*

Fig. 13.23.   GM round wiper motor wiring—"Hi" speed. *(Courtesy of Buick Division of General Motors Corp.)*

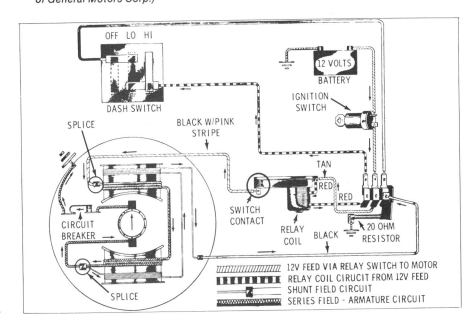

Fig. 13.24.   Relay switch.

Located in the motor gear box is the relay switch assembly, made up of the relay coil, a spring-loaded movable latch arm, and a set of contact points (Fig. 13-24). The movable latch arm is controlled by the relay coil and its spring, and the contact points by the latch arm. When the wiper switch is in the off position, Fig. 13-25, the relay coil is not energized and the wiper gear drive pawl is located in the relay

Fig. 13.25.   GM round wiper motor wiring—"off." *(Courtesy of Buick Division of General Motors Corp.)*

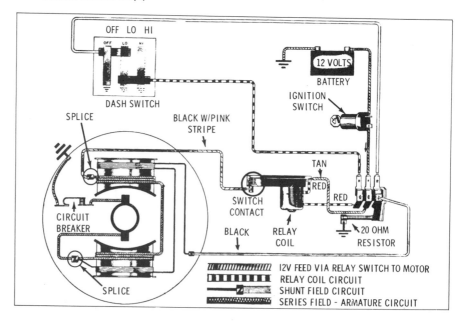

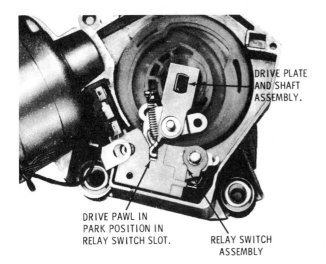

DRIVE PLATE
AND SHAFT
ASSEMBLY.

DRIVE PAWL IN
PARK POSITION IN
RELAY SWITCH SLOT.   RELAY SWITCH
ASSEMBLY

Fig. 13.26. Wiper shut off in park position. *(Courtesy of Buick Division of General Motors Corp.)*

Fig. 13.27. Wiper shut off. Relay points open.

switch slot opening, Fig. 13-26. In this position, the gear drive pawl is pushing against the spring-loaded latch arm of the relay. The latch arm, in turn, pushes against the flexible arm of the movable contact point and holds the switch contacts open (Fig. 13-27). In a more detailed view, Fig. 13-28 shows how the relay latch arm is held away from the relay coil by the spring tension (relay coil de-energized). This positions the latch arm so it can open the switch contacts when it is pushed into place by the gear drive pawl (Fig. 13-26).

When the wiper is turned on at the dash switch, the circuit through the relay switch assembly coil is completed to ground at the dash switch. With the latch arm located directly under the coil, it is magnetically attracted to the coil, (Fig. 13-29). This action trips the latch up from the flexible point arm of the switch and allows the switch contacts to close (Fig. 13-30). With the contacts closed, a 12-volt feed is connected to the wiper motor windings and the wiper motor starts.

Fig. 13.28.

Fig. 13.29.

Fig. 13.30.

When the wiper motor first starts, only the drive gear rotates until a cam built into the gear pulls the drive pawl out of the relay switch slot and locks the output or drive shaft to the gear. This delay action takes approximately 180 degrees of gear rotation (Fig. 13-31). In the normal run position the relay switch latch arm is held in by the magnetism of the relay coil.

Moving the dash switch to the off position opens the relay coil circuit at the dash switch (Fig. 13-32). With the relay coil circuit open, the spring-loaded relay latch arm is free to move out into the path of the gear assembly drive pawl. Since the relay switch points are still closed, the motor continues to rotate until the gear drive pawl engages the relay latch arm. The "park" sequence is shown in Fig. 13-33.

During the engagement process, the drive gear cam action disengages the motor drive shaft, but the gear continues to rotate until the drive pawl moves into the relay switch slot and forces the latch arm to open the switch contacts (Fig. 13-33).

Cam action between the drive gear and drive shaft provides an extended movement of the wiper blades for depressed park. This motor does not need a reversing action.

Pulse Wiper System

The pulse wiper system, introduced as a factory option in 1974, was integrated into the round motor design. The 1974 system (first type) was followed by a 1975 modified pulse wiper system (second type).

Fig. 13.31(A). Drive gear in park position. (B) Drive gear latched onto drive plate and shaft assembly in normal run. *(Courtesy of Buick Division of General Motors Corp.)*

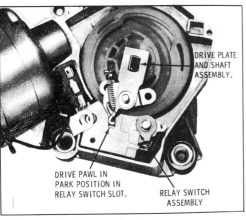

DRIVE PLATE AND SHAFT ASSEMBLY.

DRIVE PAWL IN PARK POSITION IN RELAY SWITCH SLOT.

RELAY SWITCH ASSEMBLY

A

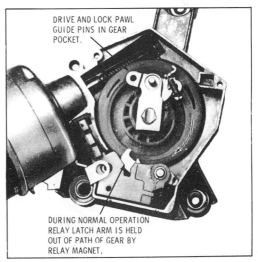

DRIVE AND LOCK PAWL GUIDE PINS IN GEAR POCKET.

DURING NORMAL OPERATION RELAY LATCH ARM IS HELD OUT OF PATH OF GEAR BY RELAY MAGNET.

B

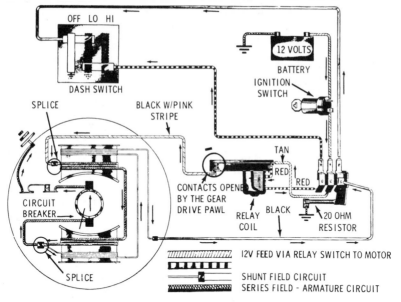

Fig. 13.32 GM round wiper motor wiring—"park." *(Courtesy of the Buick Division of General Motors Corp.)*

Fig. 13.33. *Courtesy of AC-Delco Division of General Motors Corp.*

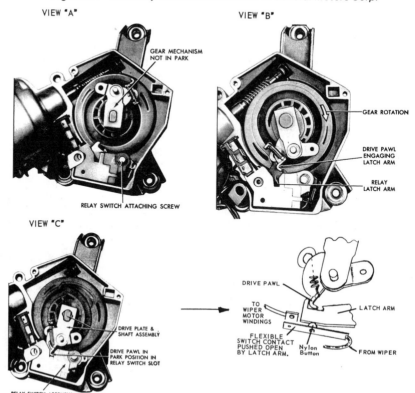

Both pulse systems operate similarly, but their components cannot be interchanged. Therefore, you must properly identify each system before you service or replace any component. The first type has a light gray washer pump cover with three electrical leads coming out of the motor grommet. The second type has a dark gray washer pump cover with two electrical leads coming out of the motor grommet.

The pulse wiper system provides an intermittent wiper feature in addition to the regular motor speeds. The intermittent operation of the wiper motor is controlled by a variable resistor in the windshield wiper control switch which ties into an electronic delay control on the motor.

Movement of the dash lever switch in the "delay" mode changes the resistance in the switch and controls the amount of current to the electronic delay control. This results in regulation of the motor operation for the desired time interval, which can be adjusted between zero and approximately twelve seconds. Motor operation is through the low-speed circuit.

Washer Pump

The conventional jar-mounted washer pump system operated by a permanent-magnet motor is used by G.M. and is similar in operation to those used in other car makes. Unique to G.M. windshield washer systems is the popular use of the pump mechanism attached directly to the wiper motor. A four-lobe nylon cam driven by the motor powers the washer pump (Figs. 13-34 and 13-35). The cam rotates whenever the wiper motor is running. When the pump is attached to

Fig. 13.34.   Washer pump drive—GM rectangular motor. *(Courtesy of Buick Division of General Motors Corp.)*

Fig. 13.35.   Washer pump drive—GM round motor. *(Courtesy of Buick Division of General Motors Corp.)*

FOUR LOBE CAM
(PRESS FIT ON SHAFT)

FOUR
LOBE
CAM

PIN

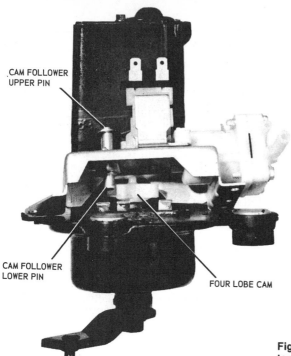

CAM FOLLOWER
UPPER PIN

CAM FOLLOWER
LOWER PIN

FOUR LOBE CAM

Fig. 13.36. Washer pump drive—GM rectangular. *(Courtesy of Buick Division of General Motors Corp.)*

the wiper motor, Figs. 13-36 and 13-37, the four-lobe cam actuates a cam-follower pin that fits through an elongated slot in the base plate.

Since both washer pumps use practically identical pumping mechanisms, we will discuss only the round motor pump to describe the basic action.

The pumping mechanism consists of a spring-loaded piston assembly enclosed in a plastic cylinder. Attached to the piston is an actuator plate that extends out of the cylinder housing and fits on the cam-follower pin (Fig. 13-37). A valve assembly with two exhaust valves and one intake valve attaches to the cylinder housing and controls the washer solution flow.

To simplify the explanation of the pumping action, the washer programming parts are not shown in Figs. 13-38 and 13-39. Also keep

Fig. 13.37. Washer pump drive—GM round wiper motor. *(Courtesy of Buick Division of General Motors Corp.)*

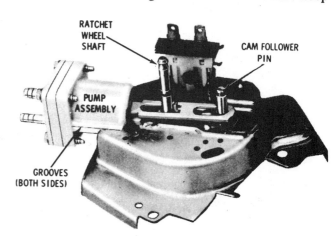

RATCHET
WHEEL
SHAFT

CAM FOLLOWER
PIN

PUMP
ASSEMBLY

GROOVES
(BOTH SIDES)

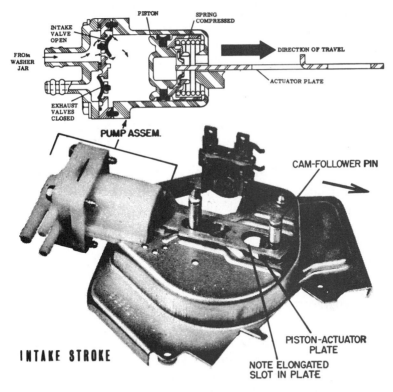

Fig. 13.38. Pump intake valve. *(Courtesy of Buick Division General Motors Corp.)*

Fig. 13.39. Pump exhaust stroke. *(Courtesy of Buick Division of General Motors Corp.)*

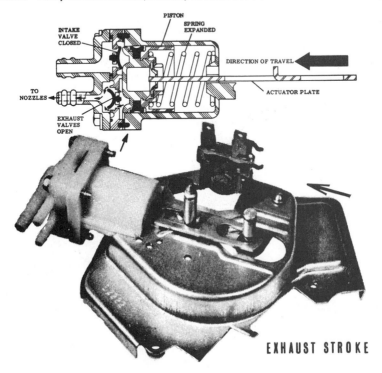

in mind that the cam-follower pin is continuously moving back and forth.

Intake stroke:

When the cam-follower pin moves in the direction indicated in Fig. 13-38, it strokes the actuator plate and piston and also compresses the piston spring. A vacuum is created in the cylinder that causes washer solution to enter the cylinder through the intake valve.

Exhaust:

As the four-lobe drive cam continues to rotate, the cam-follower pin moves in the opposite direction (Fig. 13-39). The compressed piston spring is free to expand and exerts a pressure build-up on the washer solution that forces a discharge past the two exhaust valves.

Programming

Figure 13-40 shows the washer programming section attached to the pump. This is the mechanism that controls the starting and stopping of the pumping action. It consists of a relay, ratchet pawl, ratchet wheel, and ratchet wheel dog.

The only practical way to understand how the system works is to take the cover off the washer and observe the action on the car. Here's a guideline to help you in your observations.

Pump idling:

This means that the wiper motor is working but there is no pumping action. The cam-follower pin should be moving back and forth without the stress of stroking the actuator plate and pump piston. Look at Figure 13-41 and note that the ratchet wheel has blocked the actuator arm on the bottom end of the intake stroke (full right). Also notice that during idling the spring-loaded ratchet pawl strokes with the cam-follower but is locked out of engagement with the ratchet wheel by the relay armature.

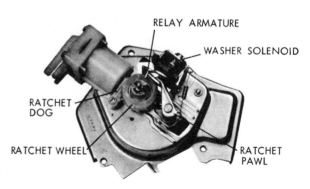

RELAY ARMATURE

WASHER SOLENOID

RATCHET DOG

RATCHET WHEEL

RATCHET PAWL

Fig. 13.40. Pump assembly. *(Courtesy of AC-Delco Division of General Motors Corp.)*

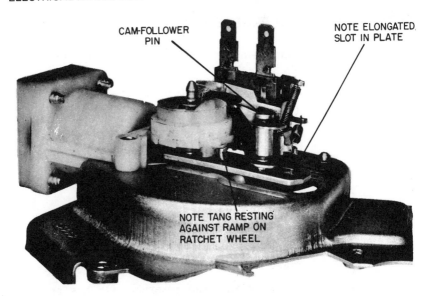

CAM-FOLLOWER PIN

NOTE ELONGATED SLOT IN PLATE

NOTE TANG RESTING AGAINST RAMP ON RATCHET WHEEL

Fig. 13.41. *Courtesy of AC-Delco Division of General Motors Corp.*

Starting the pump:

When the dash switch is actuated for windshield washer operation, the wiper motor is operated at low speed and the washer relay is energized. When the relay is energized, observe that the relay armature is pulled in toward the coil, allowing the ratchet wheel pawl to slip out of the armature lockout and engage the ratchet wheel.

The ratchet wheel pawl can now rotate the ratchet wheel one tooth at a time. Watch the movement of the first tooth. This moves the ratchet wheel ramp off the actuator plate lockout tang and permits the pump to start working.

As the cam-follower moves back and forth, it strokes the piston and the ratchet pawl keeps moving the ratchet wheel.

Stopping the pump:

The ratchet wheel automatically terminates the pumping operation or wash cycle.

When the ratchet wheel approaches the completion of its 360-degree travel, two functions occur at the same time.

1. The relay armature recaptures the ratchet pawl and prevents any further ratchet wheel rotation until the next time the relay coil is energized from the dash switch.
2. The ratchet wheel ramp blocks the piston-actuating plate in the at-rest position (Fig. 13-41).

WINDSHIELD WASHER PROBLEMS AND CHECKS

Windshield washer problems are usually limited to several general areas.

Washers don't work.

Only one side works.

Washers won't stop working.

Washer aim is too low or too high.

By applying some common sense, these problems can be easily checked with the washer pump on the car.

Washers don't work:

This could get complicated; however, you'll find that most of the common causes are easily detected.

Make the following three preliminary checks:

1. Check that the reservoir jar has an adequate supply of washer solvent.
2. Check that the hoses are not damaged and hose connections are tight.
3. Check that there are solid electric connections at the washer pump.

If these items check out, test for a working pump and clogged hoses, nozzles, and jar filter screen:

4. Operate the washer pump. If you hear it working disconnect the system outlet hose and check the discharge as a starting point in determining if there are clogged hoses, nozzles, or jar filter screen.
5. If the pump fails to operate in step 4, make the following motor checks before replacing the pump:

   a. Check for a burned-out fuse.
   b. Check the voltage potential at the motor to test for a faulty voltage switch.
   c. Check the motor ground connection, which may need removal and cleaning.

On G.M. systems where the pumps are attached to the motor, the pump checkout is different. If the three preliminary checks are OK, proceed as follows:

1. Start wiper motor first, then push water button and listen for a "click" as washer relay pulls in. If no click is heard, check

power supply (12 volt) at washer pump wiring connector. No voltage indicates shorted or defective car wiring.

2. If correct voltage reading was obtained in step 1, start wiper first, then connect 12-volt supply to one pump relay coil terminal and ground the other. If washer relay click is heard, an inoperative dash switch is indicated.

3. If washer relay click is not heard in step 2, a faulty washer pump relay coil is indicated.

4. If relay click is heard in step 1, 2, or 3, listen for the soft clicking as the pump ratchet wheel is rotated. If soft clicking is not heard, the pump mechanism is faulty and should be removed from the wiper motor and checked. If soft clicking is heard but no pumping action occurs, replace the valve assembly and recheck pump.

Only one side works:

Obviously, there is a clogged feed line or nozzle.

Washers won't stop working:

This one is easy. Disconnect the wiring from the washer pump and it should turn off, indicating a faulty switch. On G.M. systems a jamming pump piston could cause this problem.

Washer aiming:

Adjust to manufacturer's recommendations by bending the nozzle or moving the bracket assembly (Fig. 13-42).

Fig. 13.42. Washer aiming (V·L Models). *(Courtesy of The Chrysler Corporation)*

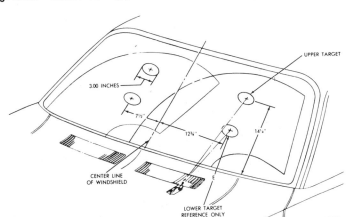

WIPER MOTOR PROBLEMS AND CHECKS

Understanding the circuitry for each position of the wiper switch is a key factor in diagnosing wiper motor circuit problems. You have been exposed to a variety of wiper motor circuits—each one is different, but they have common design characteristics. Each wiper motor has its own specific diagnosis and testing procedure which requires exact details from the manufacturer's service manual. We will not attempt to duplicate this effort, but will approach wiper motor problems and checks with some basic, general advice.

Always try to narrow the trouble down to the switch, the external circuit connections and wiring, a possible bind or hang-up in the linkage, or a defective motor.

A good troubleshooting start can be made by a quick preliminary inspection to check that:

1. body wiring is properly connected to wiper motor and switch terminals.
2. wiper switch-to-dash mounting screws are tight.
3. wiper motor is securely mounted.
4. fuse is not blown.

Try each wiper switch position, including "off," to find out what kind of wiper problem you are dealing with.

All wiper motors can be tested on the car, independently of the car wiring or wiper switch, in all operating positions including "off." Should the motor still fail to operate correctly, disconnect the wiper linkage from the motor, if practical, or manually give the wiper blades a slight assist. If the wiper motor operates, there is a severe bind in the linkage. Failure of the motor to properly operate now means that it must be removed for bench testing and possible repair or replacement.

Wiper-motor armatures can be tested for shorts, opens, and grounds, and wire-wound fields for opens and grounds, in the same manner as the engine starter motor. Figure 13-43 shows use of a test light to check the armature for a ground or open. A growler is used for checking armature shorts.

The wiper motor operation can be fully tested on the bench (Fig. 13-44). If the wiper motor is found to be burned out and nonrepairable, make sure that you make a circuit current draw test with the replacement motor installed and linkage attached. Locate and correct the cause of any excess circuit current.

Repair kits including motor drive gears and park points are generally available through the manufacturer's parts outlets.

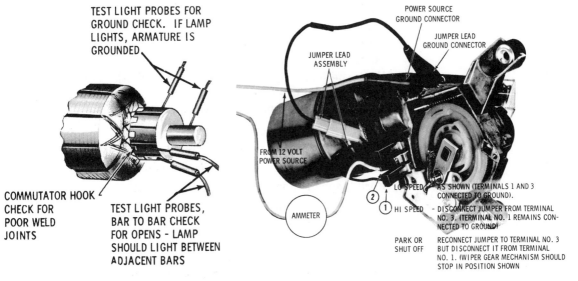

TEST LIGHT PROBES FOR
GROUND CHECK. IF LAMP
LIGHTS, ARMATURE IS
GROUNDED

COMMUTATOR HOOK
CHECK FOR
POOR WELD
JOINTS

TEST LIGHT PROBES,
BAR TO BAR CHECK
FOR OPENS - LAMP
SHOULD LIGHT BETWEEN
ADJACENT BARS

POWER SOURCE
GROUND CONNECTOR

JUMPER LEAD
GROUND CONNECTOR

JUMPER LEAD
ASSEMBLY

FROM 12 VOLT
POWER SOURCE

AMMETER

LO SPEED   AS SHOWN (TERMINALS 1 AND 3
            CONNECTED TO GROUND).

HI SPEED - DISCONNECT JUMPER FROM TERMINAL
            NO. 3. (TERMINAL NO. 1 REMAINS CON-
            NECTED TO GROUND)

PARK OR   RECONNECT JUMPER TO TERMINAL NO. 3
SHUT OFF   BUT DISCONNECT IT FROM TERMINAL
            NO. 1. (WIPER GEAR MECHANISM SHOULD
            STOP IN POSITION SHOWN

Fig. 13.43. Armature testing for ground and open. *(Courtesy of Buick Division of General Motors Corp.)*

Fig. 13.44. Wiper motor and bench testing. *(Courtesy of Buick Division of General Motors Corp.)*

Review questions

1. Briefly describe the types of wiper motors used by Chrysler, Ford, American Motors, and General Motors.

2. What is meant by a "depressed park" and "non-depressed park" system?

3. What terminology is used in describing a series-shunt wire-wound motor?

4. Briefly describe how the motor rotation is reversed in a permanent-magnet motor.

5. Briefly describe how the motor rotation is reversed in a series-shunt wire-wound motor.

6. Briefly describe how the motor speed is changed in a permanent-magnet motor.

7. Briefly describe how the motor speed is changed in a series-shunt wire-wound motor.

8. How can you tell the difference between the shunt field winding and the series field winding in a wire-wound motor?

9. How would an open shunt field affect the wiper motor circuit operation in the low, high, and park positions?

10. How would an internally grounded shunt field affect the

wiper motor circuit operation in the low, high, and park positions?

11. How would an open series field affect the wiper motor operation?

12. With the following motors, how would the loss of a switch ground at the dash affect the wiper motor circuit operation in the low, high, and park positions?

Chrysler 2-speed reversing motor
Chrysler 2-speed nonreversing motor
Chrysler 3-speed "depressed park" motor
Ford 2-speed "non-depressed park" motor
Ford 2-speed "depressed park" motor
G.M. rectangular motor
G.M. round motor

13. How would the loss of a motor ground affect the low, high, and park operation in the circuits listed in problem 12?

14. Briefly discuss the purpose of the relay coil in the G.M. round motor.

15. What closes the relay switch contacts in a G.M. round motor? What opens the relay switch contacts?

16. What is the problem when a series-shunt motor has excessive speed in the high-speed switch position, but low-speed and park operation are normal?

17. What type of wiper circuit problem would be encountered should the park points get burned?

18. What type of weather condition can cause park points to burn? Explain.

19. What are the three visual checks made as a preliminary to troubleshooting a windshield washer system?

20. In troubleshooting a G.M. wiper motor system with attached windshield washer pump:

When the washer button switch is activated, a solid "click" is heard at the wiper motor: What does this tell you?

When the washer button switch is activated, a solid "click" is heard at the wiper motor followed by "soft clicking": What does this tell you?

21. If the wiper motor fails to operate correctly when it is tested independently on the car, what does this tell you?

Appendix

Glossary of Electrical Terms

ALTERNATOR An A.C. generator that produces alternating current which is internally rectified to D.C. current before released.

AMMETER An instrument used to measure the rate of current flow in a circuit.

AMPERAGE The total amount of current (amperes) flowing in a circuit.

AMPERE (*AMP*) A unit of measurement for the flow of electrical current in a circuit.

AMPLIFIER A device used in circuit to increase the voltage of an output signal.

ARC A flow of electricity through the air between two electrodes or contact points that produces a flash and releases a lot of heat.

CANDLEPOWER Unit of light intensity, brightness. One *foot-candle* is the intensity of light on a one square-foot white surface illuminated by an international standard candle placed a distance of one foot from the surface.

CAPACITOR (*CONDENSER*) A device used to store an electrical charge.

CAPACITY The quantity of electricity that can be delivered from a unit, as from a battery in ampere-hours; or output, as from a generator, etc.

CIRCUIT   The path of electron flow from the source through components and connections and back to its source.

CIRCUIT BREAKER   A device, other than a fuse, for interrupting a circuit when the current flow becomes unsafe. Most automotive circuit breakers will reset themselves when the overload is relieved.

CIRCUIT, BYPASS   Another circuit in parallel with the major circuit through which power is diverted.

CIRCUIT, CLOSED   An electrical circuit in which there is no interruption of current flow.

CIRCUIT, GROUND   The noninsulated portion of a complete circuit used as a common potential point. In automotive circuits, the ground is composed of metal parts such as the engine, body sheet metal, etc., and is usually of negative potential.

CIRCUIT, HOT   That portion of a ground circuit not at ground potential. The hot circuit is usually electrically insulated and is connected to the hot side of the battery.

CIRCUIT, OPEN   Any break or lack of contact in an electrical circuit either intentional (switch) or unintentional (bad connection).

CIRCUIT, PARALLEL   A circuit having two or more paths for current flow with common positive and negative tie points.

CIRCUIT, SERIES   An electrical system in which separate parts are connected end to end, using one wire, to form a single path for current to flow.

COMMON POINT   That point farthest from the power source where more than one component receives its power.

COMMUTATOR   A device to provide a current path between the armature coil and the brushes of an electric motor or generator.

CONDENSER (CAPACITOR)   *See* Capacitor.

CONDUCTOR   Any material through which electrons can flow; a path for electrical current flow.

CONTINUITY   The completeness of a circuit. A circuit having continuity is complete in that it has no interruptions.

CURRENT   The flow of electricity in a circuit.

DIODE   A solid-state device that permits current to flow in one direction only. It performs as a one-way check valve.

DIODE, ZENER   A special-type diode that conducts current only when the electrical system line voltage rises above a certain level. It is a voltage-operated, electronic on-off switch.

DIRECT CURRENT (D.C.)   An electrical current which flows in one direction only.

DIRECTION OF CURRENT FLOW   Current flows through a circuit from the positive terminal of the source to the negative terminal (plus to minus, or high potential to low potential).

DIRECTION OF ELECTRON FLOW   Electrons flow from the negative terminal of the source, through the circuit, to the positive terminal.

DRAW (AMPERAGE)   The amount of current required to operate an electrical device.

DROP (VOLTAGE)   The net difference in electrical pressure when measured on both sides of a resistance. The loss of electrical pressure (voltage) which is caused by resistance in a circuit.

ELECTROMAGNET   A coil that produces a magnetic field when current flows through its windings.

ELECTROMOTIVE FORCE   That force or pressure (voltage) which causes current movement in an electrical circuit.

FIELD (MAGNETIC FIELD)   The area in which magnetic lines of force occur.

FILAMENT   A resistance in a light bulb which glows and produces light when a current is forced through it.

FUSE   A device consisting of a piece of wire with a low melting point, inserted in a circuit. It will melt and open the circuit when the system is overloaded.

FUSIBLE LINK   A device to protect the main chassis wiring harness if a short circuit occurs in the unfused part of the wiring. The link is a short piece of copper wire approximately 4 inches long inserted in series with the circuit; it acts as a fuse. The link is four gauges smaller in size than the circuit wiring it is protecting.

GROUND CIRCUIT   *See* Circuit, Ground.

HOT LEAD   A wire, or conductor, in the hot or power circuit. *See* Circuit, Hot.

INSULATOR   A nonconducting substance or body, such as porcelain, glass, or bakelite used for insulating wires in electrical circuits to prevent the leakage of electricity.

KILO   A prefix used in the metric system, and indicating 1,000; e.g., a kilowatt is 1,000 watts.

LEAD   Conductor.

LOAD   An electrical device connected into a circuit to provide a resistance and control the rate of current flow.

MAGNET   Any body with the property of attracting iron or steel.

MAGNETIC FIELD   The area surrounding the poles of a magnet which is affected by its attraction or repulsion forces.

MEGA   A prefix indicating one million.

MICRO   A prefix indicating one-millionth (0.000001).

MILLI   A prefix indicating one-thousandth (0.001).

MOTOR   An electromagnetic device used to convert electrical energy into mechanical energy.

OHM   A unit of measurement of electrical resistance.

OHM'S LAW A law of electricity which states the relationship between voltage, current, and resistance. It takes an electromotive force of one *volt* to force one *ampere* of *current* through one *ohm* of resistance.

Equation—Volts=amperes X ohms (E = I X R)

OPEN   *See* Circuit, Open.

OSCILLATION   A rapid back-and-forth movement.

POTENTIAL   Electrical force measured in volts. Sometimes used interchangeable with voltage.

RELAY   An electromagnetic switching device using low current to open or close a high-current circuit.

RESISTANCE   That property of an electrical circuit which tends to prevent or reduce the flow of current.

RESISTOR   A device installed in an electrical circuit to permit a predetermined current to flow with a given applied voltage.

RHEOSTAT   A device for regulating a current by means of a variable resistance.

SHORT CIRCUIT   An accidental contact between two conductors that bypasses the normal circuit load; an electrical path with little or no resistance. The accidental short could be a copper-to-copper, or copper-to-ground contact.

SHUNT   A conductor joining two points in a circuit so as to form a parallel circuit through which a portion of the current may pass, in order to regulate the amount of current flowing in the main circuit.

SOLENOID A tubular coil containing a movable magnetic core which moves when the coil is energized.

SPLICE   The joining of two or more conductors at a single point by crimping, soldering, brazing, etc.

SUBSTITUTION   Replacing one part suspected of a defect with a like part of known quality.

SWITCH   A device used to open, close, or redirect the current in an electrical circuit.

TERMINAL   A device attached to the end of a wire or cable to make an electrical connection.

THERMISTOR   A special resistor that decreases its resistance with increases in temperature.

TRANSDUCER   A device that changes energy from one form to another. For example, a transducer in a microphone changes sound energy to electrical energy. In automotive air-conditioning controls used in automatic temperature systems, a transducer changes an electrical signal to a vacuum signal, which operates mechanical doors.

TRANSISTOR: A solid-state semiconductor that is a combination current amplifier and switch. An emitter to base milli-amp circuit controls the opening and closing of a high-current emitter to collector circuit. Its action is very similar to that of a solenoid in the starter circuit. A low-current carrying magnetic field circuit closes a high-current carrying switch in the starter circuit.

VOLT   A unit of measurement of electrical pressure.

VOLTAGE   The electrical pressure which causes current flow in a circuit.

VOLTAGE APPLIED   The actual voltage read at a given point in a circuit. It equals the available voltage of the power supply minus the losses in the circuit up to that point.

VOLTAGE AVAILABLE   The voltage delivered by the power supply (battery, alternator, etc.).

VOLTAGE DROP   The voltage lost or "used up" in a circuit by normal loads such as a motor or lamp, or by abnormal loads such as a poor (high-resistance) lead or terminal connection.

VOLTMETER   A device used for reading potential in volts at a particular point in a circuit. It can also be used to test for continuity and resistance.

WATT   The unit for measuring electrical power. One watt is the product of one ampere and one volt (Watts $=$ amps $\times$ volts). Wattage is the horsepower of electricity; 746 watts $=$ 1 horsepower.

METRIC-ENGLISH CONVERSION TABLE

Multiply	by	to get equivalent number of:
	LENGTH	
Inch	25.4	millimetres (mm)
Foot	0.304 8	metres (m)
Yard	0.914 4	metres
Mile	1.609	kilometres (km)
	AREA	
Inch²	645.2	millimetres² (mm²)
	6.45	centimetres² (cm²)
Foot²	0.092 9	metres² (m²)
Yard²	0.836 1	metres²
	VOLUME	
Inch³	16 387.	mm³
	16.387	cm³
	0.016 4	litres (l)
Quart	0.946 4	litres
Gallon	3.785 4	litres
Yard³	0.764 6	metres³ (m³)
	MASS	
Pound	0.453 6	kilograms (kg)
Ton	907.18	kilograms (kg)
Ton	0.907	tonne (t)
	FORCE	
Kilogram	9.807	newtons (N)
Ounce	0.278 0	newtons
Pound	4.448	newtons
	TEMPERATURE	
Degree Fahrenheit	$(t\,°F - 32) \div 1.8$	degree Celsius (C)

Temperature scale:

°F −40 0 32 40 80 98.6 120 160 200 212
°C −40 −20 0 20 37 40 60 80 100

Multiply	by	to get equivalent number of:
	ACCELERATION	
Foot/sec²	0.304 8	metre/sec² (m/s²)
Inch/sec²	0.025 4	metre/sec²
	TORQUE	
Pound-inch	0.112 98	newton-metres (N-m)
Pound-foot	1.355 8	newton-metres
	POWER	
Horsepower	0.746	kilowatts (kW)
	PRESSURE OR STRESS	
Inches of water	0.249 1	kilopascals (kPa)
Pounds/sq. in.	6.895	kilopascals
	ENERGY OR WORK	
BTU	1 055.	joules (J)
Foot-pound	1.355 8	joules
Kilowatt-hour	3 600 000. or 3.6x10⁶	joules (J = one W's)
	LIGHT	
Foot candle	1.076 4	lumens/metre² (lm/m²)
	FUEL PERFORMANCE	
Miles/gal	0.425 1	kilometres/litre (km/l)
Gal/mile	2.352 7	litres/kilometre (l/km)
	VELOCITY	
Miles/hour	1.609 3	kilometres/hr. (km/h)

DECIMAL AND METRIC EQUIVALENTS

Fractions	Decimal In.	Metric MM.	Fractions	Decimal In.	Metric MM.
1/64	.015625	.39688	33/64	.515625	13.09687
1/32	.03125	.79375	17/32	.53125	13.49375
3/64	.046875	1.19062	35/64	.546875	13.89062
1/16	.0625	1.58750	9/16	.5625	14.28750
5/64	.078125	1.98437	37/64	.578125	14.68437
3/32	.09375	2.38125	19/32	.59375	15.08125
7/64	.109375	2.77812	39/64	.609375	15.47812
1/8	.125	3.1750	5/8	.625	15.87500
9/64	.140625	3.57187	41/64	.640625	16.27187
5/32	.15625	3.96875	21/32	.65625	16.66875
11/64	.171875	4.36562	43/64	.671875	17.06562
3/16	.1875	4.76250	11/16	.6875	17.46250
13/64	.203125	5.15937	45/64	.703125	17.85937
7/32	.21875	5.55625	23/32	.71875	18.25625
15/64	.234375	5.95312	47/64	.734375	18.65312
1/4	.250	6.35000	3/4	.750	19.05000
17/64	.265625	6.74687	49/64	.765625	19.44687
9/32	.28125	7.14375	25/32	.78125	19.84375
19/64	.296875	7.54062	51/64	.796875	20.24062
5/16	.3125	7.93750	13/16	.8125	20.63750
21/64	.328125	8.33437	53/64	.828125	21.03437
11/32	.34375	8.73125	27/32	.84375	21.43125
23/64	.359375	9.12812	55/64	.859375	21.82812
3/8	.375	9.52500	7/8	.875	22.22500
25/64	.390625	9.92187	57/64	.890625	22.62187
13/32	.40625	10.31875	29/32	.90625	23.01875
27/64	.421875	10.71562	59/64	.921875	23.41562
7/16	.4375	11.11250	15/16	.9375	23.81250
29/64	.453125	11.50937	61/64	.953125	24.20937
15/32	.46875	11.90625	31/32	.96875	24.60625
31/64	.484375	12.30312	63/64	.984375	25.00312
1/2	.500	12.70000	1	1.00	25.40000

Index